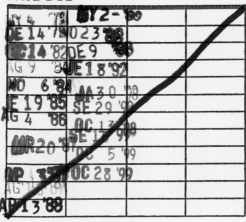

DAN NIMMO

THE
POLITICAL
PERSUADERS

The Techniques of Modern Election Campaigns

A SPECTRUM BOOK

Prentice-Hall, Inc.
Englewood Cliffs, N. J.

C–13-685263-7

P–13-685255-6

Library of Congress Catalog Card Number 79-104850.

Current printing (last number): 10 9 8 7 6 5 4 3 2 1

Prentice-Hall International, Inc. (London)
Prentice-Hall of Australia, Pty. Ltd. (Sydney)
Prentice-Hall of Canada, Ltd. (Toronto)
Prentice-Hall of India Private Limited (New Delhi)
Prentice-Hall of Japan, Inc. (Tokyo)

To Jo

CONTENTS

v

PREFACE

In the last decade students of politics—journalists, political scientists, and practitioners—have expressed an increasing interest in the role played by political campaigns in American elections. There are a number of reasons for this: election campaigns reveal the full range of human ambitions and frailties in stark focus; and, too, we intuitively expect that, since so much time, money, intelligence, and emotional effort is expended on campaigning, it must have an effect on our lives that is worth exploring; finally, the behaviorist movement in the social sciences since World War II has stimulated scholars to examine campaigns as a major dimension of the broader area of inquiry loosely designated political participation.

However, no single contemporary work brings together the results of the many recent studies of individual campaigns and campaigning techniques. This book, although not a summary of all the recorded evidence on political campaigns, does endeavor to organize a substantial number of insights. And it has another equally important purpose—to describe and assess the impact of the rapid changes taking place in the technology of modern political campaigning. In a very real sense it is a prologue to the changes that will affect the elections of the 1970s: changes that portend, among other things, attempts to manipulate an electorate; the growth of professional campaigning into a high-cost, high-risk, and high-reward profit industry; the demise of political parties as effective instruments of campaigning; and a rising demand for a "new politics."

This exploration of modern campaign technology relies on numerous case studies, published and unpublished, of specific presidential, statewide, and local campaigns. References to each appear in the footnotes at appropriate points. The reader will also find data from nationwide and statewide opinion surveys of voting behavior and media exposure and references to published experimental findings concerning the impact of communications on attitude change and perceptual shifts. Some of the findings and generalizations in this book are based on personal interviews conducted in 1967–69 with candidates for public office, party workers, opinion pollsters, campaign managers and consultants, and media specialists involved in recent campaigns in Missouri, Kansas, Colorado, Texas, Georgia, Indiana, and New York. The reader is alerted to the fact that assertions based on these interviews are not cited in the reference notes in order to guarantee the informants' anonymity.

In addition to those who contributed their insights during these interviews, I should also like to acknowledge the following for their assistance. An appointment with the Research Center of the University of Missouri at Columbia afforded both the time for writing and access to the archives of the Public Opinion Survey Unit and the Inter-University Consortium for Political Research. I also extend my gratitude to Roy Pfautch of Civic Service, Inc., for the opportunity to observe the application of modern campaign technology in several campaigns in recent years. I am grateful to Michael W. Mansfield for sharing with me selected findings from his research into the role of public relations in a Texas gubernatorial campaign and to James L. Rose for his descriptions of the problems of vote delivery in local and statewide elections. Finally, I thank Peter Grenquist and Roger Emblen of Prentice-Hall for their interest in the project and Mrs. Janet Hughes for her considerate editorial assistance.

1

CAMPAIGNS AND PERSUASION

One week before Richard M. Nixon's inauguration as the thirty-seventh president of the United States, his defeated Democratic opponent, Hubert H. Humphrey, discussed his own failure in the 1968 election after coming so close his "fingernails could almost touch it." Had the campaign been but a little longer, he conjectured, "surely not more than a week," then, "my own subjective judgment is that we would have gone on to win."

The former vice president's reminiscences of what "might have been" expressed a view shared by many men, both victors and vanquished, who have sought public office—that a candidate's conduct in an election campaign determines his success or failure. As proof they not only cite their own experience, but also point to outstanding examples in American political history. Has not, they insist, the political experience of Richard Nixon demonstrated that campaign conduct can advance or thwart a career? It was in 1952 that Nixon's campaign skills first impressed a national electorate. As the vice-presidential running mate of Dwight Eisenhower, Nixon remained in the background until mid-September. Suddenly he was accused in the press of having accepted an $18,000 "slush fund" from wealthy Californians to relieve his financial burdens as United States senator. Faced with demands that he resign from the Republican ticket, Nixon appeared on nationwide television. He adeptly explained that no money in the fund had gone for his personal use, that his critics had erred in suggesting he had built a personal fortune in politics (he was in debt at the time), and that aside from a cocker spaniel named "Checkers," he had never accepted any political gift. So polished was the performance, and so popularly pleasing the explanation, that any doubts Republicans

1

might have had about Nixon's candidacy were erased. Eisenhower underscored the vote of confidence by greeting his running mate as "my boy."

Nixon was later to write that campaigns contribute to the demise as well as the rise of a politician.[1] Nixon attributed his defeat in the 1960 presidential election to campaign mistakes, particularly the relatively weak showing that he made in the first of a series of televised debates against his Democratic opponent, John F. Kennedy. (Kennedy also claimed that the televised "Great Debate" was a turning point in his successful effort to overtake Nixon's early lead in the various public opinion polls). The defeat in 1960, however, was not the only one Nixon was to attribute to an ineffective campaign; two years later confused campaign priorities, a focus on national rather than state problems, and overconfidence brought about his loss in the race for California's governorship. Most observers thought Nixon had written his obituary as a presidential aspirant in 1962, yet he returned from the political graveyard to capture the presidency six years later— and he and his advisers insisted that the success was due to careful mapping of the campaign trail. His unrelenting efforts on behalf of Republican congressional candidates in 1966, his meticulously planned strategy to rebuild his reputation as a "winner" in the presidential primaries of 1968, and his low-key, media-oriented campaign produced the victory that had eluded him in 1960.

The rise and fall, and subsequent rejuvenation, of Richard Nixon's career is but one of many anecdotes told by politicians to illustrate the importance of campaigning in modern elections. Constantly repeated in political folklore, for example, is the story of how the underdog Harry Truman upset the "sure" winner, Republican Thomas Dewey, by a vigorous, no-holds-barred whistle-stop tour through America. Even if no such stories were told, there would still be abundant proof that politicians believe electoral campaigns to be crucial; the most striking indicator, quite simply, is the increasing amount of money spent on campaigns. It is estimated that at least $140 million was spent on all political campaigns in 1952; this was followed in 1956 by an expenditure of $155 million, $175 million in 1960, $200 million in 1964, and more than $250 million in 1968. The Republicans alone spent $21 million on Nixon's 1968 presidential campaign. Expendi-

---

[1] Richard M. Nixon, *Six Crises* (New York: Pocket Books, Inc., 1962), chap. 6.

tures at other governmental levels are also impressive. Nelson Rockefeller devoted $5 million to his reelection as New York's governor in
1966; candidates in the Texas Democratic primary in 1968 spent over
a million dollars seeking the nomination for governor.

Politicians are willing to spend these extravagant sums because of
their strong belief that electoral campaigns can make or break political careers, parties, and programs. Yet students of politics—particularly political scientists and sociologists—dispute the politicians'
notion that political campaigns make a substantial difference in the
outcome of electoral contests. Relying on evidence gathered by systematic studies of voting behavior, they point out that factors shaping
voting choices are affected only marginally by campaign appeals.[2] The
principal factor consistently related to voting decisions is the party
loyalty of the voter. In the long run, voters identifying themselves as
Democrats usually vote for Democratic candidates and Republicans
for Republicans; even persons who claim no party loyalty—the Independents—more frequently vote for candidates of one party or the
other. And the stronger the voter's party loyalty, the more likely he is
to remain true to his party's candidates. So long as a substantial portion
of the electorate is committed to a party (and studies indicate that
proportion to be four of every five voters), campaigns will have little
effect on voting patterns.

Studies also suggest that most voters make up their minds about
whom to support prior to the campaign. Analyses of the presidential
elections from 1948 to 1968 reveal that approximately one-third of
voters make their decision before the nominating conventions, one-
third decide during the conventions, and the remaining third make
their choice during the campaign. And the more strongly partisan a
person, the more likely he is to decide either before or during the convention rather than during the campaign.

Finally, studies of political candidates suggest that many politicians
deliberately fool themselves into thinking that campaigns make a difference in election outcomes. One analysis designates this tendency
the "congratulation-rationalization effect": winners congratulate them-

---

[2] Bernard R. Berelson, Paul F. Lazarsfeld, and William N. McPhee, *Voting*
(Chicago: The University of Chicago Press, 1954), pp. 132–37; Angus Campbell,
Philip E. Converse, Warren E. Miller, and Donald E. Stokes, *The American
Voter* (New York: John Wiley & Sons, 1960), p. 78; and William H. Flanigan,
Political Behavior of the American Electorate (Boston: Allyn & Bacon, Inc.,
1968), pp. 98–102.

selves by exaggerating the effect of their personal appeals; losers attribute their defeat to forces beyond their control, such as the minority status of their party or overwhelming resources of their opponents, and rationalize that their campaign at least gave them a fighting chance.[3]

For a number of reasons, however, the discrepancy between the politician's and the scholar's assessments of the impact of campaigning is not as large as it initially appears. First, as long as one-third of the electorate is undecided during the campaign, candidates still have a large bloc of uncommitted votes to worry about, a bloc that can be significant in a close election (like the presidential elections of 1960 and 1968). Second, candidates must work to retain their partisan support and, equally important, to stimulate sympathizers to go to the polls rather than stay at home. Third, in an era of mass communications the distinction between "convention" and "campaign" phases is artificial. The nominating convention is frequently staged as an essential feature of the overall campaign. An incumbent president seeking reelection schedules the nominating convention late in the summer, assuming that a long campaign is unnecessary; but a candidate inheriting a divided party may prefer an earlier convention in order to have time to bind up party wounds, build his organization, and raise needed funds. In 1968 the Democratic party held the latest convention in its history (late August); the gathering was marked by division, dissension, and violence so great that Hubert Humphrey was forced to devote much of September to establishing a consensus on his candidacy. The Republicans, on the other hand, had a five-week period between their convention and that of the Democrats to perform the requisite tasks of soothing hurt feelings, planning strategy, and accumulating funds. Fourth, it must be remembered that evidence from voting studies does not apply to primary elections where partisan identification is the same for all voters and where their decisions are delayed because of a general unfamiliarity with the candidates who are running. Nor are the findings based on adequate surveys of voting behavior in state and local elections (including popular referenda). In these elections, far more common than presidential contests, the campaign can be expected to have greater effect. Finally, in evaluating the effects of election campaigns it is a mistake to focus on the short-term impact on

[3] John W. Kingdon, *Candidates for Office* (New York: Random House, Inc., 1966), pp. 22–41.

specific elections. A political campaign can have long-term effects that may not be felt for a number of years—party loyalties may shift, issues are brought to public attention, and candidates are introduced to the electorate. (In some southern states, for example, it is a tradition for a man to seek office once to become known, even in defeat, and a second time for victory.)

The findings of behavioral research, therefore, reveal that political campaigns are less crucial in elections than politicians believe; yet it is a mistake to dismiss campaigns as merely periodic rituals unrelated to voting decisions or as no more relevant to the functioning of the body politic than the appendix to the human organism. This book argues that election campaigns are essential features of democratic politics and that the advent of new technologies adapted to modern political campaigns is working changes in the character of democratic elections. In the pages that follow we will describe the technology of modern political campaigning and draw tentative conclusions about the effectiveness of campaigns and the consequences of campaign technology for the American political system.

 The relationship between campaign technology and voting behavior can be made clearer by outlining the major themes we develop in our analysis and evaluation:

First, we will argue that contemporary political campaigns are not unique but that they possess characteristics similar to those of campaigns conducted in business, academic, charitable, and other fields of endeavor; in short, *modern political campaigns are based on application of the assumptions and techniques of the communication sciences.*

Second, we shall see that *the short-term effects of political campaigns on voter attitudes are greatest upon the persons who are least interested in and committed to democratic electoral processes.*

Third, we will note that political campaigns perform a short-term function which is less apparent than changing voter attitudes, yet equally significant; *campaigns permit voters to adjust their perceptions of political candidates to long-term political prejudices and vice versa;* in this respect campaigns cause people to sort out their preferences, thus deciding which of the opposing camps to align themselves with on election day.

Fourth, we contend that regardless of the immediate short-term responses of the electorate to political appeals, *campaigns are a signifi-*

cant form of symbolic reassurance contributing to the stability of democratic regimes.

Fifth, we will demonstrate that professional campaigners recognize the latent symbolism of campaigns as well as their immediate effects on voting behavior, and have developed a sophisticated technology to tap these short- and long-term responses; *professional expertise increasingly directs all phases of modern political campaigns:* campaign management through the planning and execution of strategy, organization, and finance; campaign research in all its dimensions; and campaign communication, principally through the mass media.

Sixth, we will argue that *political scientists may well underestimate the impact of political campaigning on voting behavior* by noting the absence of widespread changes in voting attitudes while ignoring the consequences of perceptual shifts.

Finally, we will conclude that *the development of modern campaign technology introduces serious problems for the future of our democratic system;* these problems include the high cost of choosing our leaders, the possibility of electoral deception, the absence of meaningful choice, the demise of leadership, and the withering away of election processes in a technological society.

CHARACTERISTICS OF ELECTORAL CAMPAIGNS

CAMPAIGNS AND ELECTIONS

Exhortative appeals have been a traditional feature of American elections for so long that we seldom ask what contributions political campaigns make to democratic government. Indeed, given the frequency of elections at the local, state, and national levels of our political system, many of us grow weary of political harangues, the faces of politicians beaming from billboards, mailboxes overloaded with brightly colored brochures, and preemptions of favorite television programs for yet another "paid political advertisement." Once the election is over we utter our relief only to read in our newspaper that the local school district has scheduled a public vote on a bond issue six weeks hence. Small wonder, then, that many Americans exhibit disdain for campaigns and campaigners.

Wearisome and time-consuming as it may be for both candidates and the electorate, the political campaign is essential to American democracy, most importantly as a method for mobilizing support behind persons competing for the authority to govern. A democracy recruits and selects its leaders through regularized, periodic, open elections. The aim of opposing candidates is to win the election; hence the principal purpose of each candidate's campaign is to achieve victory. Since we take this to be the chief role campaigns play in the political process, our discussion will emphasize the techniques candidates employ in building winning coalitions of community and group leaders, sympathetic followers, and wavering independents.[4]

In addition, we will also consider the implicit function campaigns perform as by-products of efforts to win elections. Among these is a symbolic expression of popular will. Democratic elections not only provide us with a means of choosing our rulers; by voting we acquire the feeling that we as citizens are participating in governing the political system. That feeling is more illusory than real since our voting acts are, at best, only remotely and indirectly linked to the specific policies formulated through presidential, administrative, and legislative bargaining. Yet elections reinforce "the impression of a political system designed to translate individual wants into public policy." Seen from this perspective, campaign communications are symbolic utterances that enlist faith in one candidate, arouse fear of another, create both reassurances and doubts, and provide the illusion of an open debate of issues, personalities, and parties. For the average citizen selectively attending to the campaign provides a way of discovering meaning and order in an otherwise confusing and ambiguous election, thus reaffirming "belief in the fundamental rationality and democratic character of the system" and promoting popular consent to the decisions of leaders chosen to govern.[5]

A second latent function of the election campaign is its ability to provide one of the most frequent settings for the development of political leadership. Current knowledge of political behavior shows that it is scarcely appropriate to think of a "leader" as a person who directs the actions of others because nature has endowed him with superior skills, intelligence, knowledge, strength, or character traits. We now understand that political leadership actually refers to a par-

[4] William J. Gore and Robert L. Peabody, "The Function of the Political Campaign: A Case Study," *Western Political Quarterly*, XI (1958), 55–70.
[5] Murray Edelman, *The Symbolic Uses of Politics* (Urbana: University of Illinois Press, 1964), p. 17.

ticular relationship that exists between a leader and his followers in specific settings. The subtleties of that relationship depend especially on the willingness of followers to support a leader in exchange for certain benefits. To a large degree the leader can influence and coordinate the efforts of others (directing their energies toward electing him if he is a candidate) only if he is able to fulfill their needs. One such need is a yearning for someone to act as the legitimate voice of the political system; to justify their obligations, sacrifices, and deprivations as citizens and to personify their deeply-held aspirations and desires. In sum, leadership "is not to be understood as something an individual does or does not have, at all times and places," but is "always defined by a specific situation and is recognized in the response of followers to individual acts and speeches." [6] The election campaign is one such specific situation, one in which the candidate strives to convey the impression that he is competent to serve, decide, and command. Seldom need this impression be related to specific policy programs; more often the candidate must project the image of one capable of acting in ambiguous situations. In this way he reassures followers by personifying an impersonal government and by symbolizing their desires and fears, aspirations and frustrations.

An emphasis on the symbolic quality of running for office implies that campaigns are built largely on the emotional responses of the electorate. To be sure, we will say a great deal about the symbolic uses of political campaigning in our account. But we should not ignore the fact that campaigns also communicate information about issues and candidates which many voters use for rational decision-making. Several features of American campaigns are poorly suited to this function— unequal access of competing candidates to the communications media, a tendency to ignore policy discussions, the use of unfair personal attacks, high campaign costs, the need for candidates to make "news," and so forth.[7] We shall touch upon a number of these drawbacks at later points. Despite the limitations to open discussion, however, it is clear that an election provides an opportunity for more intimate communication between governors, or potential governors, and governed

[6] Ibid., p. 73.
[7] See Stanley Kelley, Jr., *Political Campaigning* (Washington, D.C.: The Brookings Institution, 1960) and Richard Rose, *Influencing Voters* (New York: St. Martin's Press, 1967) for discussions of the rational model of campaign behavior.

than is normal in the political system. In the process certain problems on the minds of constituents have an opportunity to surface. Some become topics for debate, as did the war in Vietnam and urban rioting in the presidential primaries of 1968; others are ignored, as have been problems of water and air pollution in numerous elections. This, then, is "one of the most important functions of campaigns: the inclusion, exclusion, and crystallization of issues and problems on the agenda of officeholders." [8]

That candidates wage electoral combat to win normally means that they take the electorate much as they find it; that is, they direct much of their attention toward winning votes from the undecided, reinforcing the faith of voters committed to them, and ignoring persons pledged to their opponent's cause. The notion of converting voters to a new belief or doctrine, say from Republican to Democrat, is not common in American campaigns. Yet some attempts at conversion probably occur in all elections, at least to the extent that we can say indoctrination also is a by-product of election campaigns. And in some elections (as in Barry Goldwater's trumpeting of the conservative cause in the presidential contest of 1964) explicit attempts have been made to change prevailing attitudes of the populace.[9]

A PARADIGM OF POLITICAL CAMPAIGNS

In reviewing the support-mobilizing, symbolic, leadership, information-dispensing, and doctrinal functions of political appeals we have spoken of these election activities of candidates as though they bore little similarity to other types of persuasive campaigns waged in American life—advertising, merchandising, public relations, propaganda, and public service appeals. Political campaigns are, in fact, but one form of persuasive communications designed to influence the actions of people. In order to make clear the similarity of a political campaign to campaigns in other fields, let us attempt a definition applicable to all campaigns; we can then isolate the basic concepts useful in studying campaigns, define them in turn, and indicate the relations they

[8] Lewis A. Froman, Jr., "A Realistic Approach to Campaign Strategies and Tactics," in M. Kent Jennings and L. Harmon Zeigler, eds., *The Electoral Process* (Englewood Cliffs, N.J.: Prentice-Hall, Inc., 1966), p. 3.

[9] Karl A. Lamb and Paul A. Smith, *Campaign Decision-Making* (Belmont, Cal.: Wadsworth Publishing Co., 1968); John H. Kessel, *The Goldwater Coalition* (Indianapolis and New York: The Bobbs-Merrill Co., Inc., 1968).

have to one another as well as the assumptions that underlie their use. In short, we will construct a paradigm of political campaigns.

A *campaign* denotes the activities of an individual or group (the *campaigner*) in a particular context (the *campaign setting*) designed to manipulate the behavior of a wider number of people (the *audience*) to his advantage. Specifying these elements indicates that any campaign resembles the basic communication act analyzed extensively by behavioral scientists.[10] That act involves a source communicating in a specific setting to an audience and receiving responses (feedback) in return. In a campaign the source is designated the campaigner; he may be a candidate, a salesman, a preacher, a teacher, an advertising executive, or a television commentator. The setting may be the polity, a used car salesroom, a church, or a classroom. And the audience may be composed of voters, consumers, parishioners, or students.

It should be clear that this definition emphasizes the utilitarian rather than the informational aspects of the campaign, recognizing that information is dispensed not merely for its own sake but to produce some shift in behavior (as, for example, when we are told in television commercials that smoking cigarettes endangers our health, a message intended not merely to make us better-informed but to induce us to avoid smoking).

We can familiarize ourselves further with the major concepts explicit in the definition of campaigning if we examine closely the people, attitudes, and behavior that comprise the campaigners and the electorate, and review the elements of the political campaign setting.

The Campaigners

Who are the people we designate as "campaigners"? What are their attitudes? And in what types of political activities do they engage? Preliminary answers to these questions introduce the kind of information we must consider in light of the technology of modern means of political persuasion.[11] The people most citizens think of as

[10] Bruce H. Westley and Malcolm S. MacLean, Jr., "A Conceptual Model for Communications Research," *Journalism Quarterly*, XXXIV, No. 1 (Winter, 1957), 31–38; Claude E. Shannon and Warren Weaver, *The Mathematical Theory of Communication* (Urbana: University of Illinois Press, 1963); and Paul Watzlawick, Janet Helmick Beavin, and Don D. Jackson, *Pragmatics of Human Communication* (New York: W. W. Norton and Company, Inc., 1967).

[11] John H. Kessel, "A Game Theory Analysis of Campaign Strategy," in Jennings and Zeigler, *The Electoral Process*, pp. 290–305.

campaigners are simply the candidates for political office. But the total complement of campaigners also includes persons who have never sought public office. Here we number followers who work on behalf of office-seekers—the candidate's partisan, volunteer, and mercenary army. Let us consider each in turn, then their attitudes and activities.

    Candidates. A leading student of political participation estimates that less than 1 per cent of the American adult population ever become candidates or serve in a public or party office.[12] With rare exceptions any American citizen is eligible to run for office, but only those who possess a combination of attributes expressed as "availability" become candidates. Availability implies more than just the candidate's desire to run and his capacity to meet specific legal qualifications. Other essential attributes include the candidate's ascribed and achieved characteristics, his personal qualities, his contrived image, and his political resources.[13]

Attractive candidates are those in whom voters see the qualities they desire in public officials; it is important, therefore, that a prospective candidate know both what voters want and what qualities citizens ascribe to him. Voters, for example, want their officials to be honest, intelligent, and educated. To determine what his reputation is among the electorate, a would-be legislator, governor, or president frequently commissions an opinion-polling agency to survey voters and discover what they think of him (an endeavor we shall examine in detail in Chapter 3).

Voters are particularly prone to impute favorable qualities to a political aspirant with a widely-known, respected family name. Hence, the Kennedys, the Roosevelts, and the Rockefellers nationally and the Longs in Louisiana, the Blairs in Missouri, and the Scrantons in Pennsylvania have seemed especially attractive. The electorate's proclivities to act upon the basis of "name recognition" can have startling consequences; for example, in 1954 Democrats in Massachusetts nominated

---

[12] Lester W. Milbrath, *Political Participation* (Chicago: Rand McNally & Co., 1965), p. 19.

[13] For detailed discussions of the attributes necessary for candidacy see David A. Leuthold, *Electioneering in a Democracy* (New York: John Wiley & Sons, Inc., 1968), pp. 23–31; Herbert M. Baus and William B. Ross, *Politics Battle Plan* (New York: The Macmillan Company, 1968), pp. 7–39; David M. Olson, *Legislative Primary Elections in Austin, Texas, 1962* (Austin, Texas: Institute of Public Affairs, The University of Texas, 1963), pp. 8–18; idem, *Nonpartisan Elections: A Case Analysis* (Austin, Texas: Institute of Public Affairs, The University of Texas, 1965), pp. 20–35.

a political unknown, John Kennedy, for state treasurer. The man was not the then junior Senator John F. Kennedy, nor even related to the future president. The advantages of name recognition are more marked in primary than in general elections; in the former voters are frequently faced with a string of candidates about which they have little opportunity to learn anything other than names.[14]

Voters also are interested in a candidate's achievement; whether his experience has prepared him for public office, for example, and whether his record justifies his return to office if he is an incumbent. Few attributes contribute as much to electoral success as incumbency. Voters know that a man seeking reelection to an office possesses requisite experience; incumbency also carries with it the advantages of frequent exposure to the electorate through news coverage, sufficient previous campaign experience that an accurate assessment of successful strategies and tactics is possible, and invaluable contacts with party, group, and governmental leaders. Occasionally, however, a challenger with a celebrated name can overcome his incumbent opponent's advantages. Although politically experienced, Ronald Reagan had never held public office prior to his successful, and professionally-managed, campaign against Governor Pat Brown in California in 1966. And in his first attempt at elective office, Edward M. Kennedy won the Democratic nomination for senator in Massachusetts, defeating the more experienced Attorney General Edward McCormack in the primary and the son of Henry Cabot Lodge, George Cabot Lodge, in the general election.[15]

In addition to what voters think of him and his record of experience, an aspiring candidate must consider his personal qualities before deciding to enter an election. Ambition, motivation, and desire underlie every successful candidacy; without them it is impossible to exude the enthusiasm demanded of a candiate. In 1964, for example, Governor William Scranton of Pennsylvania decided belatedly to contest the frontrunner, Senator Barry Goldwater of Arizona, for the Republican nomination for president. Although his supporters had implored him to enter the race earlier by participating in the primaries, Scranton apparently had little taste for the rigors of a presidential campaign. His last-minute effort to woo delegates (he became a

---

[14] L. J. Kamin, "Ethnic and Party Affiliations of Candidates as Determinants of Voting," *Canadian Journal of Psychology*, XII (1958), 205–13.

[15] Murray B. Levin, *Kennedy Campaigning* (Boston: Beacon Press, 1966).

serious candidate only a month before the nominating convention) was based upon his concern for the fate of the Republican party if it should nominate Goldwater. But his brief, unsuccessful campaign carried the aura of a lost cause, one motivated more by duty than desire. Scranton did, however, possess one of the personal attributes most essential to effective candidacy—the courage to make the contest.[16]

Another indispensable personal quality is what political practitioners call "acumen" and social psychologists refer to as undistorted perception:[17] the capacity to look at political reality without reading one's own biases, dreams, or wishes into it. When caught up in the enthusiasm of his supporters, a candidate can easily misperceive the political situation, overestimating his strengths and underestimating his weaknesses. A candidate who is trailing badly in opinion polls finds it hard to accept any alteration in his campaign tactics, especially as long as newspapers endorse his candidacy, he encounters enthusiastic crowds of supporters at rallies, his aides praise his utterances, and his mail is congratulatory. There is evidence, for example, that a principal reason why Goldwater supporters refused to believe public opinion polls which stressed that Goldwater's presidential candidacy was in trouble was the fact that the candidate's mail suggested an overwhelming victory, however, very few potential voters write letters to candidates and efforts to predict the behavior of the electorate from such a small and biased sample is foolhardly.

Candidates vary in the degree to which they possess the reputation, experience, and personal qualities essential to availability. Yet all serious political pretenders must at least act as though they have the necessary attributes. They must convey the illusion of positive characteristics even in the face of less glamorous realities. This means the candidate must select and emphasize the most appealing of his qualities, publicize them widely and repetitiously, and at the same time play down any limitations. The process of selectively publicizing desirable attributes is what professional campaigners term image projection. Richard Nixon, faced in the 1968 presidential campaign with his reputation as a "loser" (he had been defeated in the presidential elec-

---

[16] Kessel, *The Goldwater Coalition*, pp. 91–119.
[17] Kessel, "A Game Theory Analysis," pp. 298–301; Baus and Ross, *Politics Battle Plan*, pp. 12–16; Theodore H. White, *The Making of the President 1964* (New York: The New American Library, 1965), pp. 174–96.

tion of 1960 and the campaign for governor of California in 1962), diverted attention from his personal background and experience. He appealed instead for "New Leadership" and representation for the "silent Americans," the middle-class, white suburbanites not engaging in mass protests but instead "paying their taxes and obeying the laws." The result was a subtle identification with the elements in society "losing" from increasing crime and violence, the war in Vietnam, and rising inflation. Consequently, some of the rougher edges were removed from the "loser image." Image projection has become a chief concern of campaign specialists and we will consider the process in detail in Chapter 4.

A final attribute of availability which warrants mention is resources. The principal resource, of course, is financial. Few candidates have personal fortunes sufficient to finance massive campaign costs; those who do hesitate to use them for fear that reputations as "well-heeled big spenders" will do them political damage. In 1966, for example, businessman Milton Shapp sought the Democratic nomination for governor of Pennsylvania as a political unknown. Using his personal wealth, Shapp financed a highly sophisticated campaign, spending large sums on television programming, to project the image of a man fighting an oligarchical Democratic machine. He managed to upset the party-supported candidate in the primary, but his Republican opponent triumphed in the general election by emphasizing Shapp's primary expenditures and criticizing the attempt to "buy" the governorship. If large personal expenditures can be detrimental to candidates, the political aspirant must have means of raising funds from outside sources (we shall examine such fund-raising efforts in the following chapter).

Organizers. Finances are not the only resources necessary for availability. A candidate also profits from the endorsement and support of nonfinancial contributors—influential interests, political parties, newspapers, friends, neighbors, and well-wishers. By conferring support these groups become campaigners, binding themselves— sometimes tightly and sometimes tenuously—to the candidate's aspirations. They become a part of the candidate's partisan, volunteer, and mercenary organization.

In general elections the various party organizations—party headquarters, funding agencies, echelons of leadership, and precinct workers—are theoretically at the disposal of the party's various candidates for public office. A presidential campaign, for example, depends largely on the organizational efforts of personnel within the Republican and Democratic national committees. As Democratic national chairman, James Farley managed Franklin Roosevelt's successful campaigns for the presidency in 1932 and 1936. Gubernatorial candidates in many states rely heavily on their respective state party executive committees. As in any elaborate organization, there are divisions of labor resulting in numerous specialized, and often overlapping, tasks assigned to party personnel, a matter for discussion in Chapter 2.

Because any election involves many candidates from a given party, because of factional contests within a party, and because candidates must often seek nominations in primaries without party backing, candidates frequently build personal campaign organizations. Such organizations are usually composed of an inner core of the candidate's close confidants, a large circle of personal followers, and a throng (or only a clique for some candidates) of volunteers. The enthusiasm of a voluntary organization often exceeds that of one based on partisan or monetary incentive. Senator Barry Goldwater was able to build a highly effective volunteer organization in his efforts to win the California Republican primary in 1964; his opponent, Governor Nelson Rockefeller of New York, relied primarily on paid workers who performed their duties in perfunctory fashion at critical moments. Goldwater's managers attributed his victory in that election (which assured his ultimate nomination) to the massive efforts of the volunteers committed to the candidate, his principles, and the general cause of conservatism.[18]

Finally, the list of campaigners also includes the specialists who make a profession of managing election campaigns. These include campaign management firms, campaign consultants, public relations personnel, political pollsters, television directors and producers, fundraisers, mass mailing specialists, speech-writers, and a host of others. These professionals now shape the character of modern political campaigning in America. Candidates, political parties, and pressure groups engage their services. They have become, in effect, mercenaries who specialize in applying the techniques of mass persuasion to popular referenda and primary and general elections. Since this book is largely concerned with their activities and their impact on voting,

[18] Kessel, *The Goldwater Coalition*, p. 87.

we will postpone a detailed discussion of these campaigners to later chapters.

Campaign attitudes. We have premised our discussion on the notion that the purpose of campaigning is to win elections. The desire to win, then, is an attitude shared by most campaigners whether they are candidates or organizers. But there are variations on this basic attitude that deserve to be included in our paradigm.

Winning can take several forms. It may mean simply achieving a narrow, but necessary, plurality for election to office; in a bond election or constitutional referendum a simple, three-fifths, or two-thirds majority may be the goal. In either event the accumulation of a minimum number of votes is what we normally regard as "winning" an election. But a minimum number is not always sufficient. Some candidates desire to win by large margins, creating an impression of great popularity that will discourage challenges to their reelection at a later date. This has long been a major strategem of politicians in primary elections in southern states—to overwhelm all opposing factions, minimizing future opposition and assuring tight control of the party organization. An ambitious politician with his sights on higher office prefers large victory margins to publicize his availability for a governorship, congressional seat, or the presidency.[19] John F. Kennedy, for example, regarded his smashing victory for reelection to the U.S. Senate in 1958 as the first step in obtaining the Democratic nomination for president two years later. Richard Nixon was drawn into his ill-fated race for governor of California by the belief that a solid victory would reestablish his credibility as a presidential contender for 1964 and also provide a political base; his defeat removed his chances for 1964, but he captured the 1968 presidential nomination through sizable victories (largely without opposition) in that year's primaries.

Some campaigners may have goals which are more important than victory in a given election. A campaign is built on publicity, the tactic being to expose the candidate to large audiences. For some the exposure itself is a sufficient goal. Many lawyers, for example, campaign for office to win recognition, thus hoping to advertise their existence and win clients. A study of candidates for state legislative seats in metropolitan Houston, Texas, in 1966 revealed that lawyer-candidates tended to use the communications media with the greatest "advertising potential." They employed mass techniques that "attempt to

[19] Froman, "Campaign Strategies and Tactics," p. 2.

reach an audience larger than could be reached by personal physical presence of the candidate or his workers in the field." Nonlawyers, on the other hand, relied more on direct personal contact with fewer voters—tours of shopping centers, coffees, canvassing, and so forth.[20]

⋁ As we noted earlier, some candidates campaign to stimulate organizing for future campaigns, living to "fight another day," or to promote a cause. George Wallace of Alabama sought the presidency in 1968 with no hope of winning the election, but he did manage to sow the seeds of a third party (the American Independent party) in all fifty states. After the 1964 election, Barry Goldwater was optimistic that his 25,000,000 votes indicated a solid base on which conservatism could build.[21]

Thus, the particular character of an election campaign depends in part on the attitude of campaigners toward its purpose. Also vital to the type of campaign waged are the attitudes of contenders toward the rules of the campaign game. Despite the charges hurled back and forth in elections, it has been asserted that most campaigns are waged with the understanding that demogogic appeals to class warfare, racial conflict, religious antagonisms, and the like are not legitimate.[22] Such insights can lead to more subtle techniques to take advantage of the electorate's emotional sentiments. John F. Kennedy, for example, suspected in 1960 that his Catholicism might win the votes of many Republican Catholics, but would drive off Protestant Democrats. Consequently, he derived a strategy of meeting the "religious issue" head on. Seizing the initiative before a conclave of Baptist ministers early in the campaign, he asserted himself as "the Democratic candidate for president" not the "Catholic candidate." He managed to blunt the fears of some Protestants that his religion would bias his political judgment and won their support without offending Catholics among Republicans or Democrats.

---

[20] Thomas H. Fowler, "The Lawyer as a Legislative Candidate," in Public Affairs Research Center, *Legislative Recruitment in Texas* (Houston, Texas: The University of Houston, 1967), chap. II, pp. 1–9.

[21] For a contrary view see Angus Campbell, "Interpreting the Presidential Victory," in Milton C. Cummings, ed., *The National Election of 1964* (Washington, D.C.: The Brookings Institution, 1966), pp. 256–81. One should also consult Nelson W. Polsby, "Strategic Considerations," in Cummings, *The National Election*, pp. 82–110; Nelson W. Polsby and Aaron B. Wildavsky, *Presidential Elections*, 2nd ed. (New York: Charles Scribner's Sons, 1968).

[22] V. O. Key, Jr., *Public Opinion and American Democracy* (New York: Random House, Inc., 1961).

Research concerned with voters' reactions to violations of campaign ethics has been sparse. The scattered evidence we do have, however, clearly indicates that voters detect violations of campaign norms and react against the violater. A study undertaken after the elections of 1968, based on a systematically selected voting sample, uncovered reasons why a certain Republican congressional candidate had lost in a predominantly Republican district, even though Richard Nixon and the Republican candidate for the senate had won easily. The majority of respondents, both those supporting and those opposing the Republican, had reacted negatively to what they described as his "mudslinging" (particularly the candidate's unsubstantiated charges that his opponent was pro-Communist, wanted to register guns instead of Communists, and wished to finance student rioters on college campuses). Given the negative impact of these attacks, it is probable that the Republican's close loss (the winner had 52 per cent of the vote) can be attributed to an overly aggressive campaign interpreted by voters as beyond the limits of fair campaigning.

Campaign activity. During the course of our later discussion we shall describe how campaigners use various persuasive techniques to solicit money and votes. This behavior is conducted within the more general framework of two major activities familiar to all campaigns— the formulation of strategy and the adjustment of tactics. Campaign strategy refers to the overall plan formulated for the conduct of a campaign. It encompasses such features as decisions about which voters are most likely to be swayed by appeals, issues that should be emphasized, fund-raising, allocation of the candidate's time, decisions regarding campaign management and organization, and selection of points on which the opposition seems most vulnerable.

Any political strategy is planned with three phases of the campaign in mind. The first is the *organizing* phase when campaigners establish organization and communication lines, select issues, and so forth. This is followed by the *adapting* phase, which involves modifications in the original strategy to meet the exigencies of the moment. The *closing* phase usually offers a maximum campaign effort on the part of the candidate, his staff, and organization. Campaigners at the close of the campaign seek maximum exposure to the voters, make last-minute appeals (sometimes revelations about the opposition), and step up door-to-door canvassing. Hence much of campaign strategy concerns problems of timing—when to reserve television time, when to visit a particular constituency, when to raise a particular issue, and so forth.

᾽ Campaign tactics become apparent in the adapting and closing phases of the contest. The range of tactics includes responses to questions at news conferences, debates with opponents, inclusion of appealing symbols in speeches, appearances at rallies, attendance at coffees, and negotiation of disputes between rival factions within the campaign organization. Planning the strategy and executing the tactics of a political campaign have much in common with the approach taken to a serious athletic contest. A football coach prepares for each opponent by devising a game plan based on thorough research of his opponent's capabilities and those of his own team. Throughout the game the coach makes adjustments in his offense and defense— sending in substitutes, calling plays, changing the positions of players. As the end of the contest approaches, the coach exhorts his players to added efforts, hoping for a closing momentum that will put the game out of reach of his opponents, salvage victory, or avert humiliation.

The Electorate

The tone of a political campaign is strongly influenced by the attributes of the electorate, their political attitudes, and their voting behavior.

᾽ *American voters.* Americans generally believe campaigning to be a form of "politics" occurring during fairly specific periods of time. For example, September 1 through the first Tuesday after the first Monday in November in a presidential election year is informally considered to be the time for "the campaign"; campaigns in the various presidential primaries run continuously from the opening of the New Hampshire campaign to the date of the California primaries in early June. The tendency to associate campaigns with definite time spans contributes to the popular misconception that campaign activities are restricted to well-defined periods. Actually one of the most significant of campaign efforts, qualifying potential voters, predates by far any informally designated campaign span.

The potential electorate for political campaigns consists of all U.S. citizens, twenty-one years of age or older (with the exception of four states), who have resided in their respective states for a time period sufficient to meet state requirements. But a candidate is interested in the support of potential voters only if they have become members of the qualified electorate. Most states require by law that citizens register their eligibility to vote in local, state, and national elections, frequently several months in advance of the election. In states where registration closes even before informal campaign periods begin, the first strategic problem of candidates who feel they can profit from a large turnout at the polls is to organize a successful voter registration drive. By way of illustration, the contemporary character of presidential politics dictates that Democrats secure support from large numbers of Negroes in the South, perhaps a sufficient number to permit the party to carry many southern states at precisely the time when southern white Democrats are defecting to the Republican party or to third-party movements. In the spring and summer of 1968, 78 per cent of the white population of voting age in eleven southern states were registered to vote; to offset possible losses among these voters, Democrats conducted Negro voter registration drives, successfully registering 62 per cent of potential Negro voters. Nevertheless, the drive did not save Vice President Hubert Humphrey's candidacy, for southern whites turned to the Republican and American Independent parties. However, underscoring the view that registration drives are critical adjuncts to any campaign—especially for Democratic presidential candidates—is the fact that in the only strategy planning session for John Kennedy's 1964 reelection effort (held on November 12, 1963, ten days before his assassination), the president and his advisers devoted attention to long-range planning for a Negro voter registration effort.[23]

Once political candidates have converted potential voters into a sympathetic qualified electorate through registration campaigns, they must mobilize their supporters to vote on election day; that is, they must define the actual electorate to their advantage. The voter mobilization efforts of Republican forces in the 1964 presidential election are illustrative. Campaign workers used two tactics to mobilize Goldwater partisans. First, they devised a "voter quota program." Using data for each state, county, and congressional district concerning the

[23] Registration figures for southern states may be found in Southern Regional Council, Voter Registration in the South (Atlanta: Voter Education Project, 1968). The Kennedy planning is discussed in White, The Making of the President 1964, p. 42.

sizes of the potential and registered electorates in 1964 and numbers of actual voters in the constituency in previous years, Goldwater's tacticians assigned each precinct a quota of votes that Republicans should deliver for Goldwater if he was to win the state's electoral votes. (The technical details of vote quota programs are described in Chapter 3). The other mobilization plan consisted of a canvassing program. Canvassing, a traditional way of winning voter support, involves house-to-house visitations by workers on behalf of a candidate. In the Goldwater program canvassing was conducted by couples rather than a single person, on the assumption that householders would speak more readily with a male and female together. The couples were recruited from activists in local civic organizations, generally those with some familiarity of suburban neighborhoods. Canvassers were organized into county committees responsible to state canvassing committees; the state committees received directions from national campaign headquarters. Detailed instructions from national headquarters requested canvassers to carry flashlights and never enter the house (it would take too much time) and suggested conversation to be used by couples:

"Good evening, Mr. or Mrs. ————. I'm ————, and this is ————. We are volunteers calling tonight to ask you to vote for Barry Goldwater for president. May we count on your vote?"

"We also want you to vote for the other Republican candidates. May we count on your vote for them?"

"We want you to know that we think enough of your vote and our candidates to come by and ask you to vote for them."

This canvassing program contacted almost 3,400,000 voters in 912 counties of 46 states. In those areas where canvassing was completed, the announced voting intention of householders to canvassers proved an excellent predictor of the percentage of popular votes Goldwater later received.[24]

Political predispositions. Candidates for office activate voters through registration drives and mobilization programs, but to win the election they must assure that a plurality of actual voters cast ballots

---

[24] Kessell, *The Goldwater Coalition*, pp. 162–70.

on their behalf. In this area voting studies suggest that campaigns have only marginal, although measurable, effects. The studies conclude that the impact of campaigns on voting decisions is limited in presidential elections because so many voters (perhaps two-thirds of actual electors) are predisposed to one of the contenders before the campaign. We noted earlier that there are appropriate reservations to this standard explanation of voting behavior (particularly in local and statewide elections), but it does suggest that candidates must consider the political predispositions of the electorate when planning strategy, tactics, and techniques.

A number of voter attitudes are relevant to a candidate's campaigning. In an election between candidates of our major political parties (that is, an election other than the "nonpartisan" or referenda variety), the party identification of voters weighs heavily in their decisions. As Table 1-1 indicates, voting studies conducted since 1952 estimate that approximately three of every four American voters are committed to one of our two major parties; and, three of every ten are probably so thoroughly committed (Strong Democrats or Strong Republicans) that it is unlikely that they shift to the opposition during a campaign. Depending on what the distribution of partisan identification is within his constituency (something discovered by the research described in Chapter 3), the general strategy of a candidate is clear: if his party is in the majority, he must conduct a campaign to reinforce the commitments of the party faithful and assure their turnout; if in the minority, the candidate must campaign to hold his own loyalists while winning votes from independents and potential "switchers" who are weakly identified partisans of the opposition.

Not all elections involve party competition but in those that do, other considerations also enter into voting decisions. Voters react to the issues and candidates in the campaign as well as to parties and campaigners must take these orientations into account.

In any campaign the vast majority ignore all but the most general issues. They may, for example, feel that nuclear superiority over the Soviet Union is desirable, but know little about the subtleties of ending nuclear testing, constructing an anti-ballistic missile system, or securing nuclear nonproliferation treaties. And they often rally behind a slogan symbolizing American success in a given endeavor, such as "An American on the Moon by the End of the Decade," yet care little about the tangible taxing and spending priorities such a program implies.

TABLE 1-1

Party Identification in the United States, 1952–68 (percentage distribution)

"Generally speaking, do you usually think of yourself as a Republican, a Democrat, an Independent, or what? If Republican or Democrat, would you call yourself a strong Republican or Democrat or a not very strong Republican or Democrat? If Independent, do you think of yourself as closer to the Republican or Democratic party?"

IDENTIFICATION	OCT. 1952	SEP. 1953	OCT. 1954	APR. 1956	OCT. 1956	NOV. 1957	OCT. 1958	OCT. 1960	OCT. 1961	MAY 1962	NOV. 1962	MAY 1963	JAN. 1964	MAY 1964	OCT. 1964	MAR. 1965	NOV. 1966	NOV. 1968*
Democrat																		
Strong	22%	22%	22%	19%	21%	21%	23%	21%	26%	25%	23%	22%	23%	24%	26%	25%	18%	20%
Weak	25	23	25	24	23	26	24	25	21	25	23	27	27	22	25	25	27	25
Independent																		
Democrat	10	8	9	6	7	7	7	8	9	7	8	6	9	7	9	9	12	10
Independent	5	4	7	3	9	8	8	8	10	9	8	9	10	10	8	9	7	11
Republican	7	6	6	6	8	6	4	7	5	4	6	5	6	5	6	4		9
Republican																		
Weak	14	15	14	18	14	16	16	13	13	15	16	16	14	17	13	13	15	14
Strong	13	15	13	14	15	10	13	14	11	11	12	12	9	11	11	12	10	10
Apolitical, don't know	4	7	4	10	3	6	5	4	5	4	4	3	2	4	2	3	2	1
Total	100%	100%	100%	100%	100%	100%	100%	100%	100%	100%	100%	100%	100%	100%	100%	100%	100%	100%
Number of cases	1614	1023	1139	1731	1772	1488	1269	3021	1474	1269	1289	1301	1489	1465	1571	2195	1291	1553

Source: Survey Research Center, The University of Michigan. Provided through the facilities of the Inter-University Consortium for Political Research, November, 1968.
* Preliminary results from a hand tally

One might assume that campaigners faced with a widespread indifference to issues would avoid emphasizing issues in their strategic considerations. The opposite, however, is the case; campaigners like to run "on the issues." A candidate can do relatively little about the distribution of partisanship in his constituency, but he can maneuver by articulating issues that strengthen his hand. He has at least partial control over issues. He can often relate specific issues to special interests (union workers, Irish-Americans, or soybean growers, for example) for support; he can orient his campaign to the various elites who can provide financial and organizational support as well as votes. At the same time he enunciates symbolic appeals ("Law and Order" or "Let's get America moving") to please the less informed and uncommitted citizenry. Issue positions are much easier to publicize through newspapers, television, and radio than are appeals to partisans or special groups; journalists dismiss the latter as campaign oratory, but cover the former as "policy statements."

A citizen's attitudes toward parties, issues, and personalities affect his decision as a voter; therefore, competing candidates analyze each so that strategy, tactics, and techniques will reflect electoral realities. Bear in mind, however, that these attitudes are seldom separate in the voter's mind. His views of party color his views of candidates and issues; likewise, predispositions about issues and candidates affect attitudes toward political parties. Frequently a voter may be sympathetic toward a candidate of the opposition and experience a conflict between his party loyalty and his candidate preference. The campaign plays a substantial role in resolving such conflicts, a point we shall return to in our concluding chapter.

Voting behavior. We can summarize the types of eligible voters who are targets in most electoral contests. Table 1-2 classifies voter targets according to two variables—the time at which voting decisions are made and the attention voters pay to the campaign. The result is a four-cell presentation of what the campaigner's major goal should be with respect to each voter type, the goal to be pursued if the purpose of the campaign is to win election.

1. Early deciders who pay close attention to the election campaign must be reinforced in their decision by the favored candidates. Persons most likely to fit this category are strong partisans, voters who are concerned about the election outcome and who at the same time support their party's candidate. The opposition candidate stands little hope of win-

TABLE 1-2

A Typology of Campaign Targets (by time of voting decision and degree of voter interest)

	ATTENTIVE VOTERS	INDIFFERENT VOTERS
EARLY DECIDERS	Reinforce attitudes	Mobilize or immobolize voters
LATE DECIDERS	Change attitudes and mobilize	Motivate turnout

ning votes among this group. Whereas one-third of the electorate might fit this description in a presidential election, relatively fewer voters would enter this cell in primary elections, non-partisan contests, or party referenda.

2. Early deciders who pay little attention to the campaign are not likely to be swayed in their vote decisions by alternative candidates. Candidates favored by such voters must mobilize them for turnout on election day; the opposition, in turn, must avoid antagonistic tactics that might shake these indifferents from their lethargy and stimulate them to vote.

3. Voters who pay close attention to the campaign, yet delay their choice until late in the period, are prime targets for campaigners. Most are probably undergoing an attitude conflict of the type mentioned previously; the goal of the campaigner is to resolve those conflicts in his favor and mobilize these voters to prevent them from withdrawing from any decision.

4. A large proportion of the late deciders in any election are persons so indifferent to politics that, unless stimulated to do so by a critical issue or a captivating personality, they will not vote at all. In partisan elections they shift their support from one party to another with little consistency because they have no firm party loyalty (are Independents). They are critical to campaigners who must (a) motivate them to take a last minute interest in the election and (b) secure their votes.

The Setting

After a grueling campaign, news reporters struggling to explain the outcome, particularly if the underdog has emerged the victor, analyze the winner's campaign strategy; as students of group behavior, social scientists focus instead upon the predisposition of voters. The setting is critical in any election, but analysts rarely consider election results as a function of the campaign setting.[25]

   The pseudo character of campaigns. As reported in the news media and experienced by the average citizen, political campaigns are dramatic events, especially when they involve a confrontation of striking personalities or a clash of strongly-held principles. But much of the excitement is less spontaneous than contrived, less real than illusory. Increasingly, the atmosphere that surrounds a political campaign is manufactured by the contenders, a product of the efforts of professional managers to tailor the setting to their candidate's advantage.

   One perceptive analysis of the changes taking place in contemporary American life argues that Americans rarely have firsthand experience of reality; instead they encounter a secondhand, contrived, and illusionary substitute—the pseudo event. A *pseudo event* is planned to deceive in that it is contrived to appear as spontaneous without being so, it is designed to catch the attention of the news media and be widely reported, it camouflages the actual situation so that the underlying reality is ambiguous and obscure, and it is intended to produce consequences to the advantage of a particular group, interest, or person.[26] An airplane crash, a flood, or the heroic saving of a drowning victim may be regarded as spontaneous, but the opening of a Broadway play or a presidential news conference is a pseudo event. Most campaign events possess a pseudo quality. Examples are numerous: carefully staged rallies; skillfully rehearsed and taped television appearances (with retaping of poorly performed or "unnatural" segments); and questions planted with friendly correspondents at news conferences or at "live" telethons where the candidate responds to citizens' telephone queries. Typical of efforts to contrive events and make news is the "spontaneous" public appearance of a candidate or official. For example, Mayor John Lindsay of New York City, both as campaigner and as public official, made a point of walking the streets of his city's ghettos, often in shirtsleeves,

[25] See, however, V. O. Key, Jr., *The Responsible Electorate* (Cambridge: Harvard University Press, Belknap Press, 1966).

[26] Daniel J. Boorstin, *The Image* (New York: Atheneum Publishers, 1962), pp. 9–12; for an effective attempt to analyze a single campaign as a pseudo event see Levin, *Kennedy Campaigning*, pp. 285–304.

mingling with passers-by, conversing with shopkeepers, and visiting with constituents. These forays into Harlem and other districts did more than familiarize the attractive mayor with the citizenry; they were well-publicized, they detracted from pressing problems in the ghettos, and they yielded the image of a vigorous, courageous, and concerned official. In the same vein when admirers tear items of wearing apparel from their favored candidates—John and Robert Kennedy, Eugene McCarthy, Richard Nixon, Hubert Humphrey and others lost cufflinks, ties, and handkerchiefs—television film leaves the impression of a spontaneous outpouring of friendly hysteria; frequently omitted is any report that "thefts" are sometimes planned by campaign managers well in advance.

The purpose of generating pseudo events in a campaign is obvious— to control the campaign setting by making news flattering to the candidate. The voter senses that the candidate is popular, personable, willing to mingle, and that his campaign has momentum. By winning the battle for friendly exposure the candidate acquires both a rostrum for his appeals and the attention of voters he wishes to reach. And exposure, a congenial rostrum, and audience attention are indispensable in contemporary politics.

To achieve its intended purposes a pseudo event must be believed. It is the function of the campaign specialists to generate that credibility—the public relations personnel, advertising executives, press secretaries, pollsters, and others.

The symbolism of campaigns. The settings of political events contribute significantly to the outcome of the events themselves. Although we pay more attention to the words and actions of politicians than to the surroundings in which they take place, we should bear in mind that settings provide an aura that enhances some interests at the expense of others. A man tried for a crime sits in a courtroom furnished with trappings symbolic of the primacy of the state in making laws, enforcing them, and punishing offenders. That symbolism is lost on neither the accused nor the jury.

Relevant symbols also set the stage for campaign actions and, like the pseudo events described above, the symbolic aspects of the campaign setting are assiduously contrived. Symbols are selected and employed to impress a large audience, evoke a sympathetic response from spectators, identify the candidate with the most cherished traditions, rules, and folk heroes of his party and of America, and convey a sense of relevance, meaning, timeliness, and appropriateness to what the candidate is saying.[27]

There is no lack of examples of efforts to use symbols to condition political responses in a campaign. It was no coincidence that Richard Nixon in his 1968 presidential drive reiterated at suburban shopping centers his appeals for "law and order" and a halt to inflation, or that he selected suburban and predominantly white high schools as the setting for his discussions of the role and responsibility of American youth. The Democratic convention of 1964 also illustrates the uses of contrived symbolism. The Republicans had held their convention earlier and nominated Barry Goldwater; it appeared that the Goldwater appeal would be to a narrow segment of the electorate and not in the traditions of Republicanism. To contrast sharply with the opposition, President Lyndon Johnson and his fellow campaigners sought an all-embracing appeal that could win dissident Republicans yet appear as a continuation of the ideals of John Kennedy. The Democrats exploited these themes in their convention by decorating the hall in Atlantic City with references to the "Great Society" (the consensus theme) and the slogan "Let Us Continue" (the Kennedy-Johnson tradition). So as not to antagonize Republican television viewers, convention managers dispensed with the usual procedure of hanging photographs of former Democratic presidents; only one large photograph of John Kennedy and one of Lyndon Johnson graced the walls of convention hall.

By using appropriate symbols campaigners seek to control the context of the election, to define to their own advantage "what this election is about." This leads to decisions that are prized as much for their symbolic aspects as for their substantive consequences. In October of 1960, for example, John Kennedy placed a call of sympathy and understanding to Mrs. Martin Luther King stressing he would attempt to have her husband removed from jail in Georgia, an incarceration that threatened King's life. That act, once publicized, won both the gratitude and support of Negroes previously opposed to Kennedy's candidacy. And, in late October, 1968, President Lyndon Johnson announced a halt in the bombing of North Vietnam, a measure that liberal Democrats and anti-war demonstrators had been demanding if they were to support vice-president Hubert Humphrey.

[27] Edelman, *The Symbolic Uses*, pp. 95–113.

The action taken both for policy and political reasons, gave a last minute impetus to the Humphrey campaign.

The timing of campaigns. The historical epoch in which a campaign occurs affects the conduct and outcome of the election. The Great Depression of the 1930s became Hoover's depression in the mouths of Democrats in 1932; the cry "don't change horses in the middle of the stream" became the slogan of the appeal to retain Franklin Roosevelt as president in the 1944 campaign during World War II; Eisenhower in 1952 capitalized on dissatisfaction with the Korean War; and in 1968 the Vietnam war conditioned much that occurred in presidential primaries, nominating conventions, and the formal campaign.

The timing of campaign events is also important. Campaigners like to "pace" their candidates as though they were race horses. They hold back their largest expenditures of money to the last vital weeks, hoping to "peak" just prior to the election. There is considerable doubt that "peaking" (the point at which a candidate is likely to receive his maximum number of votes) occurs except in the minds of politicians, but the myth governs the timing of many campaign events.

Any public appearance by a candidate is a performance; as with any actor's performance, timing is important to its success. An error in timing can give the wrong impression to an audience and destroy the impact of the candidate's carefully prepared remarks. Barry Goldwater paid a high price for this piece of information in 1964. Accepting the nomination of the Republican party, Goldwater delivered a speech prepared as a tightly knit, concise, and logical statement of his views. Its theme was that conservative and puritan principles stand as valid prescriptions for the conduct of American government. A half-hearted commitment to these moral truths was intolerable; American social and political life could be purified only by active allegiance to Freedom, Justice, Liberty, and Constitutional Government. But acceptance speeches are not received as lectures from an academic podium. They are punctuated by loud rounds of shouting and applause and audiences in the hall or watching on television lose the internal logic of the remarks. Thus, when Goldwater came to a passage intended to suggest that Aristotle's golden mean was inappropriate to the struggle for high principles, it was interpreted as approval of extremism and an effort to read moderates out of the party: "Extremism in the defense of liberty is no vice! . . . Moderation in the pursuit of

justice is no virtue!" The passage, always quoted out of context, became an albatross around Goldwater's neck in the ensuing weeks.

Any political campaign has a legally prescribed day on which it
must end—election day. Thus any candidate has a limited period
following his nomination to build a coalition for the general election
(the organization appropriate for winning a nomination within a
party is not the same as that needed to win a general election), plan
strategy, raise or borrow money, command maximum exposure, adjust
to unexpected emergencies, take the offensive, and win. The demands
of such time limitations challenge the information-gathering and
decision-making capacities of any campaigner.

The level of campaigns. Political campaigns vary according to
the constituency, or level, involved. It is one thing to seek a state
legislative seat, but quite another to aspire to the presidency. And the
problems of winning a gubernatorial nomination in a large and highly
diversified state like Texas differ considerably from efforts to secure
such a nomination in smaller, more homogeneous states like Rhode
Island. The campaign setting determines many things about the
contest itself—the amount of money spent, the campaign resources
available, the comprehensiveness of organization, and so forth. Moreover, the attitudes of the candidates themselves in planning strategy
are affected by the level of office they seek. Candidates for state
legislative office recognize that their office has relatively low visibility;
as candidates they have conservative estimates of how much interest
voters take in campaigns and how much information voters have.
They believe that partisanship, not issue orientations or candidate
personalities, shape election outcomes. Congressional candidates, on
the other hand, design their campaigns in the belief that voters are
aware of the office, interested in it, informed about it, and that they
will vote on the basis of issues and candidates as well as partisanship.[28]

The technology of campaigns. The current era is one of sophisticated campaign technology which opposing campaigners employ in a
fashion calculated to control campaign settings at all electoral levels.
Specific organizational, informational, and communication techniques
occupy our attention in following chapters. Here it is appropriate to
suggest the major change that has occurred in American campaigning
as a result of technical developments.

[28] Kingdon, *Candidates for Office*, pp. 138–41.

Prior to the days of mass organizations, research, and communication, most campaigns relied upon personal contact between the candidate (or his party followers) and individual voters to acquaint the electorate with salient qualifications, issues, and positions. Individualized personal contacts, while by no means a technique of the past, now share center stage with a new campaign technology that relies on the campaigner's contacting voters in a mass. The candidate still talks with voters, but his words are carried to them through elaborate communication channels (television, radio, rallies, and so forth). This one-way communication offers few opportunities for constituents to voice their views to the candidate; consequently, pollsters are engaged to conduct and interpret surveys and relay their results to the candidate. Also standing between the candidate and his constituents are armies of partisans, volunteers, and mercenaries.

The growing insulation of the candidate from the citizen with the advent of the mediated campaign results from many factors. Viable party organizations that once brought the candidate into personal contact with the faithful have declined; partisanship is now more of a symbol with which people identify than a group with which they work. And the growth in the size and diversity of the potential electorate makes it necessary to reach greater numbers of voters quickly and simultaneously. Finally, the theories of mass persuasion mesh with the techniques of the mass media, survey research, and high-speed computers to provide precisely the means of contacting vast numbers of voters that candidates demand.

The theory underlying contemporary campaigning (in advertising, fund-raising, and selling as well as in politics) is the theory of mass persuasion. We should be aware of its essentials for they underlie the application of the techniques described in the following chapters.[29] The theory assumes that a society consists of a differentiated mass— a mass of individuals who absorb the bulk of their information directly from communications media rather than from one another. Certain tendencies are common to all members of this mass, but for the most part people respond in different ways at different times to different stimuli. Appeals to people to buy a particular product, contribute to a given cause, or support a political candidate must be diversified accordingly.

---

[29] John C. Maloney, "Advertising Research and an Emerging Science of Mass Persuasion," *Journalism Quarterly*, XLI, No. 4 (Autumn, 1964), 517–28.

Diversity in mass responses, it is reasoned, is a product of diversified conditioning; although most behavior is conditioned, differences in conditioning stem from attitudes learned in various surroundings. The purpose of mass persuasion is to either change the diverse attitudes into shared ones or trigger identical responses from dissimilar attitudes. But the theory of mass persuasion regards personal attitudes as fairly fixed tendencies to act in certain ways, yet tendencies that are so vague in content that a given attitude may give rise to conflicting responses, depending on the stimulus that triggers the predisposition and the setting within which that cue occurs. (For example, a voter predisposed to the Republican party can still be convinced to vote for a Democratic candidate if the candidate is sufficiently attractive or if the setting influences the voter to discount his Republicanism.) Given this view of attitudes, their stable quality makes it more practical to contrive stimuli and settings to elicit favorable responses than to attempt attitude-change; this is especially true in the short period of a political campaign.

Furthermore, persuasion specialists recognize that a person's attention is selective; selective attention means that we only pay attention to messages that interest us, reinforce what we believe, and are the most agreeable of those competing for our awareness. The selective attention barrier must be manipulated to produce desired buying habits or votes. One method is to package the stimulus attractively by associating it with universally assuring slogans—"Progress is our most important product" (a General Electric slogan); "Give your fair share" (the United Fund appeal); or, "Forward Together" (the theme of the Nixon inaugural). Another method is to attempt to remove or control the elements of the communication setting that compete with the stimulus. Finally, the most practiced technique is repetition. Repeating a message increases the chances that people will eventually pay attention (hence candidates give the same set speech many times in a campaign); assures that the message will reach the individual in a variety of contexts so that a cogenial setting will eventually prompt a desirable response (a weary housewife may ignore a perfume commercial when badgered by her children, yet pay close attention later in the evening when they have been tucked in bed); and offers the possibility that, if heard frequently enough, the message may modify attitudes as well as elicit positive response (a middle-aged man who feels he has no need for a sports car may, upon endless repetition of a commercial, become so intrigued by the promise of rejuvenation that he accepts the offer to "come in and drive one").

Modern campaign techniques approach the electorate as a differentiated mass which is conditioned to behave in certain ways and has little interest in political affairs.

DESCRIBING CAMPAIGN TECHNOLOGY

The remaining chapters of this book bring together the current knowledge about political campaigns, enabling us to describe the technology of campaigning in contemporary American politics and to assess the impact of candidate appeals on voting behavior. Each of the subsequent chapters focuses on one of the three major components of political campaigns identified in our paradigm. In addition, our organization stresses that the communications sciences have made the persuasive efforts in political campaigns into a highly specialized activity requiring the expertise of specialists in management, research, and media. Chapter 2 examines how modern campaign technology emphasizes the role of the professional campaign manager, virtually to the point that they, not the candidates, are truly today's campaigners. Chapter 3 describes the application of new technology to the task of providing information about the electorate through techniques that have become so widespread that campaigners increasingly think of constituents as "voter profiles." Chapter 4 probes the use of the mass media to arrange the campaign setting and render it more congenial to the projection of a candidate's "image." Finally, Chapter 5 employs data from sample surveys and experimental research to generalize about the impact of recent campaign techniques on voting patterns in American elections. In conclusion, we suggest a few of the most critical problems raised for American democracy by the advent of the new politics of campaign technology.

2

CAMPAIGN MANAGEMENT: FROM CRAFT TO PROFESSION?

Every political campaign has its public and private sides. We see its public aspects in speeches, rallies, and televised appeals. Less visible is the campaign to organize talent, finances, technical expertise, and day-to-day "know-how." In this chapter we will examine the activities aimed at maximizing votes through rational allocations of time, money, and personnel—the private world of campaign management.

MANAGING THE NEW TECHNOLOGY OF POLITICS

A century ago candidates relied on their wits, their friends, and a few trusted allies to mount a campaign for office. Few men specialized in selling political advice. The campaign specialists of that day were primarily party politicians; the most skilled built national reputations for their genius: Mark Hanna's adroit handling of President William McKinley's campaigns at the turn of the century and James Farley's efforts on behalf of Franklin Roosevelt in 1936 earned the praise of politicians and historians alike. Today, however, as aspiring office-seekers approach the elections of the 1970s they turn less to party leaders than to professional campaign managers for political expertise. Once a craft pursued by relatively few public relations experts, campaign management has become a highly diversified industry serving a wide variety of clients.

34

THE EMERGENCE OF AN INDUSTRY

As a fledgling industry campaign management is a direct descendent of the public relations profession that matured in this country after the 1920s. The public relations man's chief task in that era was to devise propaganda programs for American businessmen. As press agents they had the responsibility for countering a rising criticism of business goals and practices; to do this they publicized the positive contributions industry was making to American society. In the process they made increasingly adroit use of the means of mass communication; the result was the burgeoning field of mass advertising: "More than to anything else, public relations as an occupation owes its existence to the growth of the mass media of communication." [1] Conditions in California in the 1930s provided an opportunity for public relations personnel to test their advertising skills in the political arena. A great demand for campaign expertise was produced by the fact that California voters not only had to select party nominees and public officials, but also to decide complex policy matters in numerous referenda. These burdens on the voter stemmed from the success of the Progressive movement in the state, particularly in making it easy to have policy issues placed on the ballot. If voters were to be familiar with candidates and issues, extensive political advertising seemed indispensable. Yet strong party organizations—the traditional agencies for organizing mass appeals in electoral campaigns—were nonexistent in California. State laws restricted the discretion of party officials. In addition the parties were weakened by the heavy influx of migrants to California during the depression. These migrants, generally indifferent to party appeals, possessed no firm party allegiance and had no special group identifications. Instead

[1] Stanley Kelley, Jr., *Professional Public Relations and Political Power* (Baltimore, Md.: The Johns Hopkins Press, 1956), p. 202; for discussions of the origins and growth of political public relations see also the following: James M. Perry, *The New Politics* (New York: Clarkson N. Potter, Inc., 1968), pp. 7–40; Robert J. Pitchell, "The Influence of Professional Campaign Management Firms in Partisan Elections in California," *Western Political Quarterly*, XI, No. 2 (June, 1958), 278–300; Edward L. Bernays, "The Engineering of Consent," *Annals of the American Academy of Political and Social Science*, CCL (March, 1947), 113–20; American Institute for Political Communication, *The New Methodology: A Study of Political Strategy and Tactics* (Washington, D.C.: The Institute for Political Communication, 1967).

of providing the parties with a clientele that could be served and mobilized during an election, they comprised a rootless electorate that was particularly susceptible to mass advertising appeals.

This overworked, nonpartisan, indifferent, rootless, and mobile electorate gave birth to the first professional campaign management firm. In 1933 Clem Whitaker (a reporter, lobbyist, and public relations man) joined with Leone Baxter (the manager of a local Chamber of Commerce) to make a business of political campaigning. Their firm, Campaigns, Inc., was the first to attempt to make money from elections; as such it pioneered in the development of the basic techniques of political merchandising still used today. Between 1933 and 1955 Whitaker and Baxter won seventy of the seventy-five political campaigns they managed.[2]

The initial successes of Campaigns, Inc. quickly spawned imitative management firms. California became, and remains today, the capital of campaign management. Following World War II, however, many of the conditions that had disrupted California politics in the 1930s spread nationwide. Population mobility eroded local ties; party allegiances transferred through the country as Republicans moved southward and Democrats travelled west. Social welfare programs weakened party appeals to the indigent, civil service deprived party politicians of patronage positions in the public service, and the movement of people to the suburbs drained party machines in the central cities of prospective supporters. Legislative redistricting posed new problems for candidates; their constituencies were gradually changed and many discovered that they were unknown among their new constituents. Finally, the sheer growth in the size of the potential electorate made it increasingly difficult for candidates to reach all voters by personal contact. The techniques of mass persuasion made it possible for candidates to adjust to these changes: using mass appeals they could attract party supporters wherever they might be and advertise their name and credentials to new constituents without having to depend on weakened party organizations. To take full advantage of mass persuasion, candidates needed the advice of a

---

[2] In the 1960s competitors to Whitaker and Baxter, working for rival candidates, forced a drop in the batting average of Campaigns, Inc. Some losses were notable, for example, the defeat suffered when the firm was belatedly hired to manage the ill-starred campaign of former child actress Shirley Temple Black for a California congressional seat in 1967. See Rodney G. Minott, *The Sinking of the Lollipop* (San Francisco: Diablo Press, 1968).

skilled group specializing in the new techniques of communication and professional campaigners offered their talents.

By the 1960s campaign management had become a nationwide service industry that reached all electoral levels. Initially Republican candidates took greater advantage of professional management, perhaps because of the traditional Republican ties to business firms and public relations. But professional personnel have served both major parties in presidential elections since 1952; few gubernatorial candidates campaign without professional aid; congressional campaigns also attract the professionals (for example, of twenty candidates for Congress in the bay area of California in 1962, three hired campaign management firms and most of the remainder used the services of professional managers);[3] that state legislative candidates also depend on professional managament is attested to by the fact that as early as 1962 five of the thirteen candidates for the Texas legislature in Austin used public relations firms;[4] the 1967 mayoral elections in Cleveland, Boston, and Jacksonville, Fla., and Atlanta's 1969 mayoral race were but a few of the many local contests involving professional management; finally, popular referenda throughout the nation increasingly are conducted under the direction of management firms.

As the industry has grown it has displayed the branching tendencies common in industrial expansion; individual firms have found it useful to create subsidiary agencies to provide specialized services. Whitaker and Baxter, for example, began the California Feature Service to provide another channel for campaign messages by sending a weekly newssheet to California newspapers. Spencer-Roberts and Associates (the firm that managed Ronald Reagan's successful 1966 campaign for the governorship of California) has a subsidiary specializing in demographic and computer analysis of electoral data (Datamatics, Inc.).

Since professional firms manage campaigns for profit, it is understandable that they charge handsomely for the various services they supply. We can get an idea of the costs involved by looking at a few examples. In the 1962 bay area elections cited above, the firms charged approximately $7,500 as a basic fee plus a 15 per cent com-

---

[3] David A. Leuthold, *Electioneering in a Democracy* (New York: John Wiley & Sons, Inc., 1968), pp. 87–88.

[4] David M. Olson, *Legislative Primary Elections in Austin, Texas, 1962* (Austin, Texas: Institute of Public Affairs, The University of Texas, 1963), p. 31.

mission on advertising (deducted from the amounts paid to the media) and payment of expenses.[5] The professional management of a statewide California campaign has been estimated at $50,000 [6] and the minimum for a full-service statewide campaign for a major office in any state at $25,000.[7] Such fees appear exorbitant, but they may be a relatively small price to pay if they assure that the candidate's total resources will be allocated wisely. To a candidate who spends $1 million being elected governor of California, this $50,000 is a menial but profitable investment.

MANAGERS, AGENCIES, CONSULTANTS, AND SPECIALISTS

Professional campaign management is a diversified industry involving individuals and firms, general personnel and technical specialists.[8] Not all management personnel perform the same functions; indeed, some aspects of the industry are so specialized that a candidate may have to contract for the services of several individuals and agencies in order to obtain the variety of expertise necessary. For example, in waging an unsuccessful campaign for the U.S. senate from Texas in 1966 against Republican incumbent John Tower, former Attorney General Waggoner Carr drew upon the services of a public relations man, an advertising agency, a person with responsibility to build local organizations, a finance chairman, a central office director, a campaign chairman, a pollster, press secretaries, and a staff of speech-writers. Such fragmented contracting is often unavoidable, but a number of firms now supply a full range of services.

Campaign management consists of the activities of both management and consultant personnel. A comprehensive listing of persons employed in all aspects of the industry is impossible. Appendix A provides some representative examples, the types of service they perform, and their campaign experience. To obtain an idea of the variety of

[5] Leuthold, *Electioneering in a Democracy*, p. 88.

[6] Joseph Lewis, *What Makes Reagan Run?* (New York: McGraw-Hill Book Company, 1968), p. 62.

[7] Congressional Quarterly, Inc., "Campaign Management Grows Into National Industry," *Congressional Quarterly*, XXVI, No. 14 (April 5, 1968), 708.

[8] Pitchell, "Influence of Campaign Management Firms," suggests that three types of public relations firms are involved in politics—campaign management firms, advertising firms, and individuals with specialized skills.

professional services available let us examine the major divisions of the industry—management and consultant personnel.

Management Personnel

Management personnel are those individuals and agencies who are directly involved in planning and guiding all features of a campaign. They coordinate the energies of the various speech-writers, pollsters, copywriters, neighborhood organizers, press secretaries, advance men, and local contact. As far as possible, management personnel try to attain an overall view of the campaign, assess elements of strength and weakness, and adjust accordingly. Such management personnel are generally of two types—campaign managers and management firms.

Campaign managers plan and coordinate the overall effort and contract out to specialists such tasks as opinion-surveying, advertising, publicity, or fund-raising. It is the manager's responsibility to relieve the candidate of time-consuming campaign details. The campaign manager usually has a close working relationship with the candidate on both policy matters and the technical features. Normally the manager works for monetary gain, but he may offer his services to the candidate without charge out of friendship or he may build a political career of his own by managing the campaigns of a public figure he admires and respects (as did Robert Finch, Richard Nixon's manager in 1960 and 1962, later lieutenant governor of California and secretary of health, education and welfare).

Management firms are public relations agencies specializing in political campaigning in the manner of the original Whitaker and Baxter enterprise. Generally these are full-service agencies. A candidate contracts for its services and the agency performs the planning, organization, financing, research, advertising, and publicity. If the firm has no facilities for handling a particular service, it subcontracts for specialized items like a direct mail campaign, opinion-polling, doorbell-ringing, or television production. Such agencies as those listed in Appendix A vary in size from small operations (Civic Service, Inc. employed less than a dozen specialists in 1968) to large-scale agencies with 250 members. The larger firms have specialized branches to handle specific activities (Publicom, Inc., for example, has specialists on lobbying, legislation, opinion-polling, and public relations as well as campaign operations; a client can contract for any number of services much as if he were shopping at a variety store.)

In earlier days campaign management was not a full-time occupation because the demand for agency services occurred only in major election years. Many firms, therefore, did noncampaign work for business clients, civic groups, and others. But as the relevance of professional management to election victory grew apparent, the management services were required in "off-year elections" as well as during presidential election years. By working in school elections, bond elections, constitutional referenda, and the like, management firms are gradually making politics a full-time rather than a seasonal occupation.

Consultant Personnel

Consultants and specialists in politics provide services of narrower scope. Relatively few consultants devote their services exclusively to political campaigns.

Campaign consultants provide specialized advice for a fixed fee. If, for example, taxation issues are paramount in a gubernatorial campaign, the candidate or his management team may hire a tax economist to prepare position papers and speeches. Consultants usually have limited authority in the overall campaign. In his 1966 campaign in Texas, Waggoner Carr sought advice on speech-writing and general strategy from Julian Read, a professional campaign manager and partner in a campaign firm, but contracted other firms for specialized activities.

Technical specialists are individuals or firms performing such specific services as canvassing precincts, designing and distributing direct mail, or preparing television documentaries. For example, it is possible to hire a firm in California that will circulate petitions to get a particular proposal on the ballot for a cost of fifty cents per signature. Richard A. Viguerie (see Appendix A) specializes in direct mail campaigns and maintains a mailing list of over 600,000 names. For a fee he can flood a state with mailings on behalf of a candidate or an issue. In one senatorial race in 1968 he distributed six million pieces of mail. He researches the problem, develops a theme, writes copy, prepares art work and layouts, prints the mailer, and distributes it. His efforts constitute but a small proportion of a major political campaign, yet they are a technical service candidates are willing to purchase.

Professional campaigners bring to politics skills learned in public relations, journalism, copywriting, arts, acting, and sundry other crafts. But not every trained person has the qualifications to be a successful campaigner. In selecting a manager, agency, consultant, or specialist the client-candidate looks first for a man of tested political experience, then for persuasive skill. A reputation for success is indispensable in the industry; better-known professionals like Whitaker and Baxter, Baus and Ross, Spencer-Roberts, or Harry Lerner point with pride to their records of 90–100 per cent victories. New agencies, therefore, recruit personnel who have previously been successful in the more specialized endeavors. As an example, Campaign Associates, a recently organized management-consultant firm, draws on the talents of Joseph Miller (a public relations expert), John Kraft and Fran Farrell (each the head of a reputable polling firm), an advertising specialist, and a television filmmaker.

THE TASKS OF CAMPAIGN MANAGEMENT

As members of a diversified service industry campaign professionals perform both grand and trivial tasks on behalf of their clients. Their major contribution to a campaign is rationality in allocating scarce resources—time, money, and talent. A serious candidate desires to maximize his electoral strength through efficient expenditure of each resource. Through careful planning and attention to detail, the professional campaigners structure and control the campaign to the advantage of their client, endeavoring to "edit reality so as to publicize the client's assets and hide his liabilities." [9]

In marketing the candidate's best qualities, contriving the campaign setting, and communicating to the electorate, management and consultant personnel enter all phases of a political contest. For convenience we consider two principal tasks in the remainder of this

[9] Murray B. Levin, *Kennedy Campaigning* (Boston: Beacon Press, 1966), p. 183. A good review of the tasks of campaign management for a local election is Conrad F. Joyner, "Running a Congressional Campaign," in Cornelius P. Cotter, ed., *Practical Politics in the United States* (Boston: Allyn & Bacon, Inc., 1969), pp. 143–72.

chapter—recruiting client-candidates and campaign planning; we postpone until the following chapters two other major functions that professional advisers perform for candidates—conducting comprehensive research programs (Chapter 3) and devising techniques for communicating the campaign message (Chapter 4). The division is convenient but artificial, for these phases overlap; there is no step-by-step procedure in moving from one task to another. The orderly surface of a campaign is a mirage; the reality is more akin to a fire brigade running from conflagration to conflagration, adjusting the overall fire control plan to each new difficulty. We should also note that in entering each of these campaign areas, the professional campaigners compete with party politicians who feel it is their right, not the mercenaries', to make substantive campaign decisions. Strained relations between professionals and politicians limit the degree to which any political campaign can be fully coordinated and controlled.

RECRUITING CANDIDATE-CLIENTS

Professional campaigners must have clients to make money and they must win elections to attract clients. These simple facts imply that campaign technicians must either discover promising, talented men and interest them in running for office or screen the available candidates who seek professional advice, carefully selecting potential winners and avoiding sure losers.

Studies indicate that candidates for public office are motivated to run either by private, internal reasons peculiar to each individual (the self-starters) or by the urging by friends, neighbors, and interested parties (the recruits). Of thirteen candidates in a Texas legislative primary, for example, nine were self-starters and the remainder recruits; similar patterns pertain to mayoral contests, congressional candidacies, other legislative races, and to recruitment into party positions.[10] Management experts have not yet invaded the field of can-

[10] Olson, *Legislative Primary Elections*, p. 16; David M. Olson, *Nonpartisan Elections: A Case Analysis* (Austin, Texas: The Institute of Public Affairs, The University of Texas, 1965), pp. 28–30; Leuthold, *Electioneering in a Democracy*, pp. 15–16; Dan Nimmo, ed., *Legislative Recruitment in Texas* (Houston, Texas: Public Affairs Research Center, University of Houston, 1967), p. 13; Frank J. Sorauf, *Party and Representation* (New York: Atherton Press, 1963), pp. 102–3; Lester Seligman, "Political Recruitment and Party Structure: A Case Study," *American Political Science Review*, LV (1961), 85.

didate recruitment on any large scale, but there are notable exceptions. Roy Day, the man credited with discovering Richard Nixon, was a professional campaigner in California in 1944; among his innovations were the coffee hour between candidates and housewives in their homes, extensive use of bumper stickers, and distribution of pencils with the candidate's name. In 1946, as chairman of the Republican Central Committee for Los Angeles, Day formed the Committee of One Hundred to find a congressional candidate to run against the Democratic incumbent Gerald Voorhis. The committee's appeal for candidates appeared on the front pages of twenty-six newspapers; Nixon responded, appeared before the committee, was selected to make the race, and ultimately became a force in American politics for the next quarter of a century.[11] Although Nixon's recruitment was an exception at the time, we can expect professionals to devote greater efforts to discovering candidates in the future. Even now two campaign specialists—Don M. Muchmore in California and E. John Bucci in Pennsylvania—"pretest" potential candidates through opinion polls months and years before elections to discover which should be promoted for a future contest.[12]

As yet, however, agencies and managers limit their candidate recruitment primarily to screening the aspirants who seek expert advice. The general belief in the industry is that not all persons or all causes can be merchandised effectively. Professionals allege that they seek "men of quality" as salable products and that it is particularly important that the client have his own convictions, style, and version of campaign issues. Because of the importance of television in campaigning, managers are concerned about physical appearance. And the professionals also consider the qualities of the candidate's wife, emphasizing that she too must learn to campaign well—dressing modestly, appearing as "one of the girls," and giving the impression that the candidate's personal life is above reproach. One campaign consultant, pollster Oliver Quayle, advised a client whose philandering had been widely publicized to campaign with his wife at his side, thus appearing as a happily married couple. The candidate did and won election.

[11] William Wingfield, "The Man Who Discovered Nixon," *UUA Now*, CL (December, 1968), 24–25.
[12] Congressional Quarterly, Inc., "Political Pollsters Head for Record Activity in 1968," *Congressional Quarterly*, XXVI, No. 18 (May 3, 1968), 992–1000.

Any major management firm screens prospective clients carefully to protect its reputation for handling credible candidates. In 1965 Ronald Reagan, the California actor-politician, approached the Spencer-Roberts agency to handle his campaign for the governorship in 1966. Several sessions were held at which the agency partners questioned Reagan extensively to assure themselves of two things: first, that Reagan, an attractive personality, was more than merely an actor seeking an entourage; second, that Reagan did not intend to conduct a Goldwater-type campaign, a definite possibility since Reagan was a conservative who had strongly supported Goldwater's views and candidacy in 1964. After several rounds of questions Reagan finally grew exasperated and retorted: "Now goddamit, I want to get some answers from you guys. Are you going to work for me or not?" [13] After reflecting for several days the agency agreed to manage Reagan instead of his primary opponent, former mayor George Christopher of San Francisco, whom they regarded as a probable loser to incumbent Governor Pat Brown.

Although professional managers desire candidates of conviction, they are hesitant to manage a campaign for anyone whose convictions are so potentially unpopular that they could spell defeat. In 1964 the firm of Baus and Ross managed Barry Goldwater's victorious primary campaign over Nelson Rockefeller in the California presidential primary. Immediately after the primary, however, Baus and Ross withdrew from any involvement in the candidate's general election campaign on grounds that they were not willing "to give obeisance to gung-ho Goldwaterism gone rampant." [14]

The professional campaigners also consider a candidate's political party in deciding whether or not to run his campaign. Most managers and agencies will support candidates of only one of the major parties. Spencer-Roberts handles only Republicans, as do Civic Service, Inc. and Robert Walker; other firms specialize in Democratic candidates —Matthew A. Reese and Associates, Read-Poland, or Publicom, Inc. Few agencies undertake campaigns for both parties; Baus and Ross is one such exception, having conducted campaigns for Republicans Richard Nixon and Barry Goldwater and Democrat Edmund "Pat" Brown, former governor of California.

[13] Lewis, *What Makes Reagan Run?*, pp. 107–8.
[14] Herbert M. Baus and William B. Ross, *Politics Battle Plan* (New York: The Macmillan Company, 1968), p. 267.

Most management firms have sufficient staff to handle several candidates in a single campaign year. Any major firm may be involved in a half dozen contests scattered throughout the nation. Some firms, however, will manage only a single campaign at a time and thus consider not only the candidates from which to choose but also the election. F. Clifton White and Associates, for example, will accept only one client at a time to permit a concentration of energies.

Finally, of course, professionals must accept candidates who can pay the necessary fee. Since the fees can range from $25,000 to $50,000 for a statewide campaign, the more dependent potential candidates become on professional expertise the more unlikely it is that persons of modest means will be able to vie for office. In this sense the management business adds but one more item to the rising cost of campaigning that, in the long run, makes it impossible for the office simply to "seek the man."

PLANNING THE CAMPAIGN

Normally initial planning takes place in the mind of a candidate long before he contracts for professional assistance. Rare indeed are cases like that of a neophyte candidate for a position on the court of civil appeals in Texas who simply walked into a management firm and asked what to do (he was told first to get to know the major figures in his district). Even here, however, the budding official had given sufficient thought to the problem to know whose assistance he wanted. Regardless of the candidate's preparations, the finalizing of the campaign strategy, organization, and finance awaits the touch of the professional.

The Campaign Strategy

In developing a campaign strategy the manager and his client have a number of decisions to make—where is the authority for making campaign policy to lie, what basic approach shall be taken, what theme is to be used, what issues emphasized, and how is the campaign to be paced.[15] These decisions depend on the factors discussed in Chapter 1 as elements of any political campaign.

[15] Kelley, *Professional Public Relations*, p. 46.

Strategic considerations. The first "given" faced by professional managers is the type of candidate they are running. Factors of personality, temperament, and experience loom large in campaign planning; the strategy appropriate to one office-seeker may be wasted on another.

Candidates, like all of us, are subject to human frailties. They tire physically, their wrists bruise and chafe from endless rounds of handshaking, they lose their voices and sometimes their tempers. Managers who place too many demands on their candidates find their charges unable to stand up under the pressure. Richard Nixon blamed his 1960 defeat in part on physical fatigue produced by attempting to live up to the overly ambitious promise to appear in all fifty states; in 1968 his managers deliberately ran a low-keyed, slow-paced campaign to avoid similar strains. And in that same 1960 campaign John Kennedy, his voice strained from overuse, consulted public speaking and throat specialists to learn less strenuous vocal techniques.

The psyche as well as the body yields to campaign pressures. Spencer-Roberts was forced to adjust to this tendency with Ronald Reagan in 1966. In the gubernatorial primary Reagan appeared with his opponent at a meeting of Negroes; angered by what he considered his opponent's innuendos about his qualifications and insinuations of bigotry, Reagan left the meeting without speaking to the gathered throng. His advisers urged him to return and meet with the participants privately lest his walkout do his campaign irreparable harm and he did return to soothe hurt feelings. Spencer-Roberts, now recognizing the possibilities of another eruption (especially if Reagan was goaded by his opponents), shielded him from further opportunities to demonstrate bad temper by limiting, in so far as possible, his public appearances to small, intimate groups and conferences. This tactic, combined with Reagan's willingness and capacity to learn from elaborate coaching, concealed his more temperamental side from the electorate.

We saw in Chapter 1 that electoral success frequently depends on the candidate's political experience: experienced candidates stand a better chance than do neophytes (although with certain electorates, as we shall see, too much experience may work against the candidate). Professional advisers must convince voters that their clients possess the requisite experience, often transforming men with no prior public service into governors, congressmen, mayors, or the like. The 1960s had many such campaigns, notably those of Edward M. Kennedy for the U.S. Senate from Massachusetts in 1962 and of Ronald Reagan for governor of California in 1966.

Prior to his first campaign for elective office, Ted Kennedy had been active in his brother's 1960 presidential race. He knew politics and possessed resources essential to success in elective politics—he was young, attractive, and dynamic; he was the brother of the president of the United States; he was a Kennedy; and he was able to finance a sophisticated campaign. But did his limited record of public service qualify him to fill the unexpired portion of John Kennedy's senate term? To deal with the "experience issue" both in the primary campaign against Edward McCormack, the Massachusetts attorney general, and in the general election opposing George Cabot Lodge, Kennedy's advisers followed three strategems: first, they propagated the myth of political expertise by having a brain trust coach Kennedy on all major issues, foreign and domestic, so that the candidate could field questions on any topic; second, they put the best face possible on the thirty-year-old Kennedy's meager record of public service with elaborate brochures hailing such "achievements" as having been a member of the board of trustees of Boston University and chairman of the Massachusetts division of the American Cancer Crusade, having been named one of the ten outstanding men of the year by the Boston Chamber of Commerce, and having been a member of the Massachusetts Bar Association; finally, they made not-too-subtle reference to the fact that Kennedy's contacts with the White House would count more than experience by asserting, "He Can Do More for Massachusetts." Through massive use of television, printed material, personnel, and public appearances Kennedy's managers glossed over the fundamental truth that the candidate's record was not that generally associated with a credible aspirant to the U.S. senate.[16]

Spencer-Roberts faced a similar problem with Ronald Reagan's candidacy in 1966—to demonstrate he was a credible candidate for governor of California. Reagan had no brother in the White House (Reagan's older brother, Neil, was a vice-president with the McCann-Erickson Advertising Agency in Los Angeles, perhaps as great an asset to a politician in this day as any other); potentially more troublesome than his lack of visible political experience was his background as a movie actor in such epics as "Bedtime for Bonzo."

[16] An excellent description of this campaign can be found in Levin, *Kennedy Campaigning*, pp. 98–181.

Yet Reagan had been involved in politics in one fashion or another most of his adult life. The Spencer-Roberts solution was to hire a team of academicians at the Behavior Science Corporation (BASICO) to research all significant California problems, provide a brief of each (its nature, alternative solutions, preferred solutions, and so forth) on a four-by-five-inch card, instruct Reagan on the use of this "information file," and accompany the candidate both to advise him and to demonstrate that Reagan indeed knew "intellectuals." Drawing on his capacity to memorize and to express ideas articulately, Reagan studied his file assiduously; the result was a successful pre-campaign buildup—the "out-of-town-tryout" that established Reagan's credentials as an informed and astute "citizen-politician." In some respects the press was so amazed at Reagan's stock of basic information that he was forgiven ignorance on esoteric topics on grounds that, after all, he was no "politician" anyway.[17] As Samuel Johnson once said of the dog walking on his hind legs, you wonder not that he does it poorly but that he does it at all!

Professional strategists often base their campaign plans on whether they are working for or opposing incumbents. Most clients of management agencies are nonincumbents. Incumbency is usually an asset in election campaigns—incumbents are better-known, have better access to finances, and get free publicity. The strategy for the incumbent is to emphasize his accomplishments for his constituency (if he can), to remind opinion leaders of the debts of support owed him, and not to permit his opponent to define the issues or set the pace of the campaign. Most challengers are forced, first of all, to make themselves known for personal qualities and, second, to seize the campaign initiative. Nelson Rockefeller's 1966 campaign for reelection as governor of New York illustrates the elements involved for unpopular incumbents. Rockefeller began the campaign far behind in opinion polls; his adviser William J. Ronan said, "Indications were that almost anyone could beat him." [18] But Rockefeller saturated the state with television commercials reminding New Yorkers of his record in such areas as highway construction, education, and water pollution (see Chapter 4). His opponent, Frank D. O'Conner, suffering from obscurity, lack of organization, and limited financing, lost

---

[17] Lewis, *What Makes Reagan Run?*, pp. 107–16.
[18] Perry, *The New Politics*, p. 110.

the initative and never appeared a credible alternative. Thus the impossible was accomplished and Rockefeller was reelected.

Campaign strategists also face problems posed by the type of setting—the level of the election and the rules of the game. A popular referendum differs considerably from the election of a candidate. In bond elections, for example, no major personality commands public attention; instead the election involves complex debates about the needs for roads, sewers, or schools and the technicalities of funding. The principal problem is to sell the notion that passage of the issue would be a public benefit when in fact some elements of the community have more to gain or lose than others. The Baus and Ross agency suggests that the general strategy for such elections should be to: (1) convince voters that the bonds are self-liquidating—that whatever is built will eventually pay for itself; (2) win the support of homeowners by demonstrating that the improvements proposed in the issue will increase property values; (3) create the impression that unless the issue passes additional taxes may have to be levied to pay for the projects; and (4) tastefully frighten voters into believing that failure of the issue would be disastrous—that failure to replace bad sewers, for example, would spread disease.[19] One final strategem is to create the illusion that the officials supporting the bond issue have nothing to hide, usually by associating them with a "Citizens Committee" of prestigious backers of community causes.

The obvious difficulty in a primary election is that candidates compete for the support of members of their own party; each candidate, therefore, must conduct himself so that, should he win, he can still call upon defeated elements in his party for support in the general election. The tricky strategic problem is how far to go in attacking primary opponents. A frontrunner may be able to avoid all-out attacks, but a challenger attempting to come from behind must attack the frontrunner without offending his supporters. In a general election, however, the frontrunner may attack his challenger without fear of alienating people in his own party. The challenger, on the other hand, emphasizes his personal qualities and usually mutes partisan appeals in an attempt to win votes from members of his opponent's party. A case in point was the general election strategies in the contest for the

[19] Baus and Ross, *Politics Battle Plan*, p. 67.

governorship of Massachusetts in 1960. Democrat Joseph Ward was the frontrunner by virtue of the fact that the ticket was headed by John F. Kennedy running for president (the assumption was that Kennedy in his home state would sweep Democrats into office at all levels). Ward therefore emphasized partisan appeals; moreover, he attacked his opponent—Republican John Volpe—by conducting a television "trial" in a mock courtroom scene of the case of "The People vs. Political Contractor Volpe." The gist of the "charges" was that Volpe as head of the public works department had rewarded people for aiding his Volpe Construction Company and had awarded contracts preferentially. Volpe, however, did not rise to the bait; in order to play down partisan differences and thus lessen the impact of the Kennedy coattails, Volpe ran a "Vote the Man, Vote Volpe" campaign. Studies of the election results (Volpe won) indicate that voters were repelled by Ward's attack—which they regarded as a violation of the "rules of the campaign game"—and voted for the more nonpolitical of the two candidates.[20]

A high percentage of local elections in the United States are non-partisan. Strategies must obviously be tailored to this kind of setting. In such an election the personal qualities of the candidate figure prominently, as do specific appeals to minority groups—Negroes, Mexican-Americans, Irish, and so forth[21]—or to "target voters." [22] Mention of specific appeals to voting blocs suggests the third element of a campaign which strategists consider in overall planning, the type of electorate. In keeping with the basic theory of mass persuasion outlined in Chapter 1, discrete appeals to groups take precedence over mass appeals; such mass appeals as are emphasized are symbolic, abstract, and vague in content. Generally the industry applies the following rules:

1. If the electorate is divided along party lines, the basic strategy for the majority is to emphasize party appeals and play down personal traits,

[20] Murray B. Levin, *The Compleat Politician* (New York: The Bobbs-Merrill Co., Inc., 1962), pp. 272–90; John W. Kingdon, *Candidates for Office* (New York: Random House, Inc., 1966), pp. 132–33.

[21] See Harry Holloway and David M. Olson, "Electoral Participation by White and Negro in a Southern City," *Midwest Journal of Political Science*, I (February, 1966), 99–122; Murray B. Levin, *The Alienated Voter* (New York: Holt, Rinehart & Winston, Inc., 1960).

[22] Baus and Ross, *Politics Battle Plan*, pp. 134–35.

qualifications, and issues that might split off supporting groups; the candidate of the minority, of course, stresses "the man, not the party" (as did Volpe) and any issue that can bring opposition voters into his camp. (Senator John Tower of Texas, for example, won reelection with the support of liberal Democrats by indicating that he supported a limited minimum wage, public housing, and so forth.)

2. If party lines are not clear-cut and there is little party identification, or if, as in a primary, the appeal is to members of a single party, specialized appeals to voting blocs must be worked into the strategy.

3. If the electorate is generally indifferent to politics, then a commanding personality and sensational issues are the best approach to both "turning on and turning out" voters.

In recent years a new strategy has developed concerning one particular type of electorate, that of alienated voters.[23] The alienated voter has three characteristics. First, he feels powerless to the degree that he believes his vote has no effect on political events; in one nationwide survey of approximately 1,500 adults 21 per cent agreed that "It's no use worrying my head about public affairs; I can't do anything about them anyhow," and 62 per cent felt that "Nothing I ever do seems to have any effect upon what happens in politics." [24] Strategically, the approach to this attitude is for the candidate to charge his opponent with usurping the citizen's power and to identify himself as caring enough to help them regain their lost preeminence in politics. One of Nelson Rockefeller's most clever gambits in the 1964 Oregon presidential primary was to offer the slogan, "He cared enough to come" (he was the only contender who campaigned in the state).[25]

Second, the alienated voter thinks that elections are meaningless, that there is no difference between candidates, or that candidates present no information on which to make a sensible distinction and decision. In the previously cited survey, for example, 61 per cent agreed that, "The people who really 'run' the country do not even get known to the voters," implying that an invisible group of decision-

[23] Levin, *The Compleat Politician*, pp. 149–73.

[24] Herbert McClosky, "Consensus and Ideology in American Politics," *American Political Science Review*, LVIII (June, 1964), 361–82.

[25] Theodore H. White, *The Making of the President 1964* (New York: The New American Library, 1965); Daniel M. Ogden, Jr. and Arthur L. Peterson, *Electing the President: 1968 Edition*, (San Francisco: Chandler Press, 1969).

makers make the election process meaningless. Here the strategy is twofold: to endeavor to distinguish the client's candidacy from his opponent's and to provide the type of information about the campaign that people desire. This very frequently leads to distinctions drawn on the basis of personality or to the facile spouting of trivial data to give an impression of informing (as in the Kennedy and Reagan examples).

Finally, the alienated voter believes that the ethical standards of politics are so low that "politicians" are corrupt and seek only personal gain. Again, in the above-cited survey 54 per cent agreed that "Most politicians are looking out for themselves above all else," 65 per cent agreed that "Many politicians are bought off by some private interest" and 46 per cent agreed that "Most political parties care only about winning elections and nothing more." Such a widely held belief suggests that a record of political experience, incumbency, and party endorsements may be detrimental to a candidate running in a constituency with a high percentage of alienated voters. In this case the strategy should emphasize his "citizen" background ("He Is No Politician") and his efficiency as a businessman, engineer, military man, or whatever. Moreover, the client can benefit by detaching himself from the political party, a fact that makes the campaign management firm even more crucial to his election.

Professional management is admirably suited to the types of campaigns that win the votes of the alienated; it emphasizes personality and style over political experience, captivating issues over substantive ones, and the painless and effortless televised method of obtaining information over the more time-consuming and laborious reading of newspapers, books, and brochures. Studies of Ted Kennedy's success in Massachusetts, John Volpe's victories in the Bay State, George Murphey's and Ronald Reagan's victories in California, and Richard Nixon's campaign success as early as 1952 suggest that the alienated occupy a strategic position in contemporary campaign planning.[26]

Strategic decisions. The type of candidate, setting, and electorate are factors strategists consider in making fundamental decisions prior to the unveiling of the campaign. The most fundamental of these

---

[26] A concise view of how modern campaign techniques utilizing televised appeals relate to the confidence citizens have in officials is in Kurt Lang and Gladys Engel Lang, *Politics and Television* (Chicago: Quadrangle Books, Inc., 1968), pp. 304–10.

decisions is to specify the relations between manager and client; that is, how much authority for running the campaign are the professionals to exercise? No uniform pattern exists. In some instances the professionals merely execute the technical details of policies decided by others. Another approach is that of Spencer-Roberts, who regard themselves as chiefs of staff rather than policy-makers.[27] In general, however, there is a tendency to give the professional ever greater authority for making policy for all phases of the campaign; the candidate may be the "star of the show" but the manager must "run the show." To keep the professionals, the party politicians, and the volunteers happy (as well as the candidate), "the candidate and the manager spend half their time on internal public relations, and half in carrying the battle to the opposition." [28]

Deciding the basic attack is the first order of business. Attack, however, does not mean a frontal assault on the opponent's potentially vulnerable points. To attack means to seize the initiative so as to avoid ever being on the defensive: "To attack is to press on the public issues that are to one's own advantage. To attack is not just to give one's own side of the question but to *define* the political situation." [29] No available research records how many votes a well-devised plan of attack wins, but professional campaigners believe a sound plan to be essential. In 1968, for instance, Hubert Humphrey's managers were astounded on the eve of his nomination to find that no campaign plan existed for the contest against Republican Richard Nixon. Joseph Napolitan, according to one account, frantically constructed one pleading, "Do you know there isn't *any* campaign plan? I have to get this ready by tomorrow?" Unable to formulate a plan so quickly, Humphrey's managers left him on his own for the first ten days of the campaign, hoping to pick up the pieces later.[30]

The Republican strategy for the presidential election of 1952— mapped by Robert Humphreys with the aid of the advertising services of the Kudner Agency and Batten, Barton, Durstine, and Osburn— is a classic example of an attack plan. The attack had two elements: First, it advocated retaining the votes of the twenty million voters

[27] Congressional Quarterly, Inc., "Campaign Management Grows," p. 708.
[28] Baus and Ross, *Politics Battle Plan*, p. 264.
[29] Kelley, *Professional Public Relations*, p. 48.
[30] Theodore H. White, *The Making of the President 1968* (New York: Atheneum Publishers, 1969), pp. 394–95.

who had supported Republicans consistently in the past by appealing to the conservatives who had preferred Senator Robert Taft for the nomination; this was achieved by two symbolic gestures—an early campaign trip through the Midwest, the natural habitat of conservative Republicans, and a meeting between Eisenhower and Taft from which the senator emerged to endorse the general. Second, it sought the normal stay-at-home vote, those who seldom participate in elections unless convincingly urged to vote *against* something (hence this plan introduced many of the elements of a strategy calculated to win the alienated voter). The campaign plan emphasized three items Americans could be against—corruption, Communism, and the Korean War. Revelations of corruption in the Truman administration, the growing fear of internal subversion in the era, and the growing malaise over the Korean stalemate thus became the campaign theme—CRIME, COMMUNISM, AND KOREA—stressed by the "nonpolitical" candidate.[31]

In some campaigns the strategy of attack is best served by subtle withdrawal. Republican congressional candidates in 1964 found this to be the case: those who publicly supported the Republican presidential candidate, Barry Goldwater, had much more difficulty winning election than did those who withheld their support. Among congressmen who had won two years before with less than 60 per cent of the vote, the proportion defeated in 1964 was half again as great among Goldwater supporters (48 per cent) as among those who followed the stratagem of remaining aloof from their party's relatively unpopular candidate (30 per cent).[32]

The second item of decision—the campaign theme and its attendant slogans—is directly related to the first. The purpose of the campaign theme is to simplify complex public issues into brief, clear, recognizable statements to the advantage of the candidate. The theme should run through all rallies, television performances, brochures, billboard ads, publicity releases, and other forms of communicating with the electorate. In 1960, for example, John Kennedy's managers guessed that Americans were dissatisfied with the relative calm and, some believed, complacency of the Eisenhower era. Kennedy offered to "Get America Moving Again," a slogan he adroitly

---

[31] Kelley, *Professional Public Relations*, pp. 151–56.

[32] See Robert A. Schoenberger, "Campaign Strategy and Party Loyalty: The Electoral Relevance of Candidate Decision-Making in the 1964 Congressional Elections," *American Political Science Review*, LXIII (June, 1969), 515–20.

and "spontaneously" worked into his televised debates with his opponent, Richard Nixon. Occasionally a theme can be highlighted by some attention-arresting action on the part of a candidate or his managers (what Whitaker and Baxter call a "gimmick"). Eisenhower capitalized on the "Korea" aspect by stating on the eve of the election that, if victorious, "I will go to Korea"; the implication that the war would end quickly was unavoidable. Sometimes themes and slogans backfire, however. Goldwater's "In Your Heart You Know He's Right" made possible a play on words that reinforced his extremist image rather than his sincere dedication to convictions. The slogan was one of five pretested by the MELPAR Corporation in southwestern states; it was least favorably received yet was preferred by the candidate and, hence, adopted.

Failure to have a campaign theme can be frustrating. In the 1968 presidential election Democrats suffered until October from lack of an organizing theme to win back the diverse elements who were disenchanted with Hubert Humphrey as the party's standard-bearer. Finally Humphrey hit on the theme of "Trust," and appealed to partisans and minorities by asking if they could "trust" their futures to either Richard Nixon or George Wallace. It would be impossible to credit this theme alone with bringing Democrats back to the fold, but it injected vigor into Humphrey's campaign and subsequently his popularity did rise in opinion polls.[33]

Election campaigns are fought not "on the issues" but on the themes. Professional advisers define and assert these themes and provide the candidate with a means of countering the themes of the opposition. Spencer-Roberts, for example, took great care to head off a major Democratic attack on Ronald Reagan in 1966. One Democratic theme hinted that Reagan harbored presidential ambitions and that the statehouse was merely a stopover on his way to the White House. The firm countered by sending Reagan's press secretary to various conservative columnists, urging them to deprive the Democrats of any pretext for raising the issue by avoiding and denying speculation of Reagan's presidential aspirations.[34]

A final preliminary decision for strategists is how best to pace the campaign. Campaign pacing refers both to when the client should announce his candidacy (what the professionals call "surfacing") and

[33] White, *The Making of the President 1968*, pp. 418–19.
[34] Lewis, *What Makes Reagan Run?*, p. 155.

to the timing of various phases of the campaign—when to schedule rallies, when to appear on television, when to devote the maximum money and effort ("peaking"), and so forth. "Surfacing" implies that a covert campaign has taken place for some time before it is announced. The campaign becomes public when the candidate can no longer build support in the inner depths; he "surfaces" to recruit new elements to his coalition. The preferred time to begin covert campaigning is "early"—plan early, organize early, research early, raise funds early, and buy media time early. However, the timing of the announcement of candidacy, the accumulation of momentum, and the closing blitz frequently depend on the personnel and finances available. For this reason it is appropriate to consider the organizational and financial aspects of campaign planning.

The Campaign Organization

No precise estimate of the contribution organization makes is possible, but certainly organizational efforts make a difference. Research indicates that effective precinct organization can add 5 per cent more votes than a party would receive without the mobilizing efforts of precinct workers.[35] In 1967 when Pete McCloskey defeated Shirley Temple Black (both Republicans in a virtually nonpartisan election to fill a vacated California congressional seat), estimates were that McCloskey won the votes of 25,000 Democrats, 60 per cent of whom had been contacted by his precinct organization. A final precinct drive, dubbed "Victory Squad Weekend," was coordinated with a media campaign as workers directed voters to a McCloskey television appearance taking place within hours; data gathered by McCloskey's managers suggests the integrating of the media effort and precinct

[35] Phillips Cutright and Peter H. Rossi, "Grass Roots Politicians and the Vote," *American Sociological Review,* XXIII (April, 1958), 171–79; Daniel Katz and Samuel J. Eldersveld, "The Impact of Local Party Activity upon the Electorate, *Public Opinion Quarterly,* XXV (Spring, 1961), 1–24; Samuel J. Eldersveld, *Political Parties* (Chicago: Rand McNally & Co., 1964), pp. 458–73; Phillips Cutright and Peter H. Rossi, "Party Organization in Primary Elections," *American Journal of Sociology,* LXIV (1958), 262–69; Raymond E. Wolfinger, "The Influence of Precinct Work on Voting Behavior," *Public Opinion Quarterly,* XXVII (Fall, 1963), 387–99; Phillips Cutright, "Measuring the Impact of Local Party Activity on the General Election Vote," *Public Opinion Quarterly,* XXVII (Fall, 1963), 372–86.

organization was especially effective.[36] Generally organization is more important for lesser-known candidates for lower-level offices than for well-known incumbents seeking high positions; the latter rely primarily on popularity and reputations for victory. Yet even presidential campaigns depend on organizational strength to mobilize voters.

Organization is directed at coordinating the efforts of three types of campaign workers—the professional managers (the pros), party workers and politicians (the pols), and volunteer workers at all levels (the vols). The interests of pros, pols, and vols in a campaign frequently run counter to one another; as a result disputes within the candidate's organization erupt, relations become strained, and coordination falters. Added to these problems is the fact that a fourth group, prestigious citizens who take no active part in the campaign, are prized for endorsing the candidate; this involves another level of organization in the form of a "Citizens Committee." The realities of internal divisions make it impossible to provide a neat organization chart describing all campaigns or even that of a single candidate's personnel. But certain functional committees exist in any campaign and we can achieve some idea of the problems confronting campaign organizers by considering each.[37]

The organization of the professionals includes at its head the campaign manager. He may be the single individual hired by the candidate, or, if a management firm is organizing the campaign, he is designated by the firm. His responsibility is to supervise everything necessary for victory—planning and execution of strategy, organization, finance, research, and communication. He assures that the candidate receives the "packaged professional political service" purchased. In so far as the campaign has a political boss, it is the professional manager, who puts together an effective team of agency personnel, consultants, and specialists to market the candidate.

The campaign manager surrounds himself with other professionals —the campaign staff. These include a press secretary for liaison with the entourage of newsmen covering the campaign; in recent years press secretaries have become well-known campaigners, as exemplified by Richard Nixon's Herbert Klein, John Kennedy's Pierre Salinger, and Robert Kennedy's Frank Mankiewicz. Speech-writers on the staff

---

[36] Minott, *Sinking of the Lollipop*, pp. 222–23.
[37] John H. Kessel, *The Goldwater Coalition* (New York: The Bobbs-Merrill Co., Inc., 1968), p. 124.

provide both ideas and style for the candidate's public utterances. Another important part of the staff, to be discussed in the following chapter, consists of the research specialists. And a number of media specialists enter the picture—television producers, directors, advertising men, filmmakers—to assure that the candidate's persuasive techniques will have quality production. For example, the television documentary for Milton Shapp's campaign for governor of Pennsylvania in 1966 (discussed in Chapter 1) was produced by Guggenheim Productions, Inc., a film production company from St. Louis.[38] Finally, the advance men precede the candidate to each city, town, and village in which he appears to arrange travel, schedule speeches and meetings, and brief the candidate on local problems and leaders in order that he may mention them in his public statements, thus providing the illusion of knowledgeableness on local matters. Although advance men are common in presidential contests, Edward Kennedy made one of the first effective uses of their services in a senatorial contest.[39]

The organization of the politicians is most active in general elections to rally the political party behind its nominee (although in some states the party may endorse a candidate even in the primary). The key elements in party organizations are the county and precinct levels. Candidates normally appoint a county campaign manager for each county in the constituency; the county chairman is frequently, but not always, elected county chairman for the party. The chief function of the county campaign manager is to mobilize the voters in the various precincts; for this he draws upon each precinct organization—usually the precinct chairman and his precinct committees. The 1965 campaign of John Lindsay for mayor of New York City provided an example of a very elaborate local organization. Lindsay's manager, Robert Price, decided on a "retail campaign," taking Lindsay—his product—to "storefronts" in each neighborhood of the city several times. Storefronts are local headquarters (sometimes located in abandoned stores, hence the name) where passersby wander in and receive coffee or information and from which workers contact the voters of the neighborhood. Storefront workers discussed local problems with visitors and Lindsay discussed these same matters in his travels to the

[38] Perry, *The New Politics*, pp. 41–69.
[39] Levin, *Kennedy Campaigning*, p. 179.

storefronts. In all 122 precincts storefronts provided the contact points for Lindsay with New Yorkers.[40]

The influence of professonal campaign consultants on party organization extends beyond managerial activities in any single election. It is becoming common practice, particularly for Republicans in the South, to hire consultants to reorganize state and local parties. Robert C. Walker, for example, advised on reorganization of the Harris County (Houston), Texas Republican party. The consultant conducts seminars, recommends lines of authority, and helps recruit into the organization neighborhood civic activists (members of women's clubs, professional groups, parent-teacher associations, and so on) not previously involved in partisan politics. The mobilization of female activists, for example, has been a major factor in the resurgence of southern Republicanism.

The organization of volunteers is based on the realistic assessment that persuasion is most effective when the message is conveyed by someone the voter already knows, trusts, and respects. In an effort to enlist the aid of such opinion leaders, committees are organized of voluntary workers at the grassroots.[41] Senator Eugene McCarthy won 42 per cent of the vote in the 1968 New Hampshire Democratic presidential primary with the aid of an effective voluntary organization of college students. Estimates were that 3,000 students contacted 60,000 New Hampshire homes and, in the process, gave birth to the McCarthy movement while discouraging President Lyndon Johnson from seeking reelection.[42] People serve on voluntary committees less for monetary reasons than to serve a cause, gain prestige, and make personal contacts. In organizing volunteers professional managers recruit persons who are well-known in their neighborhoods; they approach civic guilds, church societies, women's organizations, parent-teacher associations, student clubs, and similar gatherings. These groups provide volunteers with two qualifications—they are already activists and they possess contacts. The major difficulty for campaign managers is to keep the morale of these volunteers sufficiently high so they do not quit working in discouragement at critical junctures.

[40] Perry, *The New Politics*, pp. 172–202.
[41] Elihu Katz and Paul F. Lazarsfeld, *Personal Influence* (New York: The Free Press of Glencoe, Inc., 1955), pp. 137–334.
[42] White, *The Making of the President 1968*, p. 99.

✓   *The organization of the prestigious* is aimed at a particular type of volunteer, the person who is willing to lend his name but not his time to a cause. The elements of this organization include a "general chairman" serving as nominal head of the entire campaign, but actually merely holding an honorific title. A person like singer Andy Williams or comedian Bob Hope has many requests to serve as general chairman. A second element is the general campaign committee, again not so much a working committee as a list of notables sponsoring the campaign. The general campaign committee serves an important symbolic function in popular referenda. The assumption is that if such a stellar group of community citizens favor the cause, it must be worth the average citizen's vote. Finally, there are hosts of special committees in any campaign composed of single interests endorsing the candidate—ethnic, religious, racial, age, professional, veterans', occupational, and party groups. The task of the campaign manager in organizing special interest committees is to obtain support without yielding to impossible or embarrassing demands for future benefits.

The 1964 Democratic campaign for the presidency was an object lesson in the organization of prestigious groups. James Rowe, an experienced campaigner on Lyndon Johnson's behalf, organized groups like Rural Americans for Johnson-Humphrey, which worked with members of rural electrification cooperatives and the Farmers Union in the West to enlist agrarian support; the National Independent Committee for Johnson and Humphrey, a group of wealthy business leaders virtually out of *Who's Who*—traditionally Republican—demonstrating dismay at Goldwater's candidacy by backing Johnson; and Scientists and Engineers for Johnson-Humphrey, an effective group of academicians that made political workers out of Nobel Prize winners.

These, then, are the clusters of organization on which the candidate relies to effectively carry his message to voters. The coordination of the professionals, politicians, volunteers, and prestigious poses difficulties. There are only limited means of achieving it. One technique is to design a detailed plan of action for the campaign, then structure a tightly knit hierarchical organization in which each level of personnel is assigned specific tasks; each level is responsible to that above it for completion of the assigned job; authority for new assignments, precisely scheduled in the comprehensive campaign plan, is lodged in upper echelon groups. Such a neat chain of commands conceivably eliminates problems of coordination. The difficulty is that unforeseen things spring up in a campaign, events overlooked in the master plan; moreover, part of the campaign is devoted to responding to unanticipated actions of the opponent; finally, the frayed nerves of campaigners make it unlikely that subordinates will always heed the orders of superiors. For these reasons, few campaign organizations are hierarchical; most are decentralized, possessing groups with overlapping functions that adjust day-by-day to emergency situations within the overall campaign strategy.[43]

The usual approach to campaign coordination is to create a steering committee of limited size, representing the major groups active on behalf of the candidate. The candidate and the professional manager are key members of the committee and take the initiative in proposing policies. Also represented are party leaders, staff personnel, fund-raisers, and members of the candidate's personal entourage or any confidant considered his alter ego. The committee meets frequently throughout the campaign to plan entry into each new phase, approve of advertising programs, discuss finances, deal with problems as they arise, and serve as "the collective brain for the living campaign." [44] When it cannot meet the campaign manager must, of necessity, have authority to decide on pressing matters.

The Campaign Budget

Aside from the continuing research and communications efforts discussed in subsequent chapters, the preparation of the campaign budget is the principal remaining task of the management mercenaries. The earliest professional campaign firm, Whitaker and Baxter, established a pattern in budget preparation still followed today. The firm insisted on centralized control of campaign expenditures; in exchange for that control it assured the client that the campaign would be run within the amount budgeted. As far as Whitaker and Baxter were concerned, the candidate should see that the necessary money is raised, but refrain from spending it.[45]

In arriving at a mutually satisfactory arrangement between manager

---

[43] For a discussion of these organizational and strategic styles see Karl A. Lamb and Paul A. Smith, *Campaign Decision-Making* (Belmont, Cal.: Wadsworth Publishing Co., 1968).

[44] Baus and Ross, *Politics Battle Plan*, p. 212.

[45] Kelley, *Professional Public Relations*, pp. 46–47.

and client like that demanded by Whitaker and Baxter, it is the responsibility of the professionals to provide the candidate with a realistic estimate of campaign costs. In meeting this obligation the firm supplies three budgets—a minimum budget estimates the cost of a campaign without frills or assurance of victory; a maximum budget provides for using every vote-winning campaign technique, assuming that funds will be available; a third budget adds from 25 to 50 per cent to the maximum for a saturation campaign made possible by sheer opulence of the candidate and his supporters. In deciding whether an expenditure is justified, the Baus and Ross firm offers the following rule: "How many votes will *this* expenditure, *this* program, *this* office, *this* mailing, produce?" [46] If the proposed expenditure offers only marginal gains, it is deleted from an austere budget, retained in a maximum budget, and perhaps increased in the maximum-plus budget on grounds that greater spending transforms marginal gains into sizable ones.

We said in Chapter 1 that too much spending, if it leaves the impression he is "buying" the election, can harm a candidate; for the same reason, even if the candidate can finance all costs out of his personal fortune, it is best that he raise funds from outside sources. For the wealthy and the less affluent, therefore, fund-raising is necessary. In recent years some management and consultant firms have responded to their clients' needs in this area by adding campaign funding to their list of services, thus breaking with the older notion of Whitaker and Baxter that the candidate should fill his own treasury.

The professional campaigners deal with funding in a variety of ways. A small number of the full-service agencies simply pay all campaign expenses and figure them into their total charge to the candidate; in the event he encounters difficulty paying the bill, they aid him (for an additional fee) by organizing "victory" dinners ($10–$1,000 per plate depending on the office and size of the deficit) or "appreciation" dinners (in the event the candidate lost). More commonly, however, the campaign agency works closely with the candidate's finance chairman in organizing fund-raising schemes. The finance chairman occupies a vital niche in the campaign organization; it is his principal task to see that money is available as needed. This,

---

[46] Baus and Ross, *Politics Battle Plan*, p. 108.

of course, means that the finance chairman has much to say about how the money is spent, thus making him a decision-maker of considerable importance.

The Goldwater campaign in 1964 illustrates that a lack of coordination between the finance chairman and professional consultants cripples the overall effort. In the opening weeks of a campaign fund solicitation is difficult because potential supporters are not yet concerned enough to contribute: yet this is a critical period for expenditures since radio and television time must be reserved (and paid for) well in advance of the date actually used. A principal fund-raising technique at this stage, therefore, is to borrow money; then, as funds roll in during later periods, loans can be repaid. In the interim vital blocs of air time for the closing weeks of the campaign are reserved. But in 1964 Goldwater's finance chairman Robert Cordiner (former chairman of the board of General Electric) insisted, with Goldwater's approval, on no deficit spending, that the campaign budget remain in the black. Since the campaign treasury was empty in September and seeking credit was ruled out, television time reserved for the last ten days of the campaign (painstakingly negotiated for by the Leo Burnett Agency, the initial advertising consultant for the campaign) was cancelled. But in late October money reached the Goldwater coffers in huge amounts as the result of ingenious funding methods (see below). When Goldwater's technicians sought to repurchase television time, however, no prime time remained. One commentator observed, "Cordiner ended the campaign with a historic record for a financial chairman: the largest surplus in dollars ever shown by any campaign—and the largest deficit in votes and offices lost too." [47]

Campaigners contend that elections are won or lost through fundraising. Hubert Humphrey and a principal manager, Lawrence O'Brien, argue that the Democrats would have won in 1968 with sufficient funds early in the game. Of the $5 to $6 million raised, most came in the closing weeks—$500,000 in the final week when they could buy no television time in California, a key state. With $10 million, estimated O'Brien, "we could have licked Nixon." [48] If O'Brien is correct, criticism that the presidency is for sale in a meaningless marketplace is not without foundation.

[47] White, *The Making of the President 1964*, p. 379.
[48] White, *The Making of the President 1968*, p. 417.

We must assume on the basis of available evidence that the bulk of campaign financing comes from thousands of large and small contributors. Numerous techniques exist for obtaining campaign funds, including personal solicitations (letters, door-to-door campaigns, phone calls, and so forth) and collective solicitations (dinners, cocktail parties, and similar gatherings). Generally management and consultant personnel emphasize mass solicitations directed at the individual citizen without calling on him in person. Increasingly this means direct-mail and televised appeals. One imaginative direct-mail specialist uses lists of all those people who return cards in response to advertising gimmicks such as, "You may have won $25,000 a year for life; send in your Lucky Number and see! No purchase required to win. . . ." He finds these people particularly susceptible to campaign appeals for funds through direct mail. In 1964 Goldwater's fund-raisers acquired almost one-third of their money by direct-mail appeals to more than 300,000 contributors.

Televised fund-raising drives usually depend on the attractive quality of a well-known celebrity to make the appeal. In 1964 the Goldwater campaign featured nationwide televised appeals by actors Raymond Massey, Ronald Reagan, Clint Walker, and John Wayne. Their success was so overwhelming that in 1968 Richard Nixon's managers relied on the services for both fund-raising and vote appeals of football stars (quarterback Jacky Kemp of the Buffalo Bills), television stars (Jackie Gleason), and others. Humphrey's forces countered with such personages as Gregory Peck. The American Independent party candidate, George Wallace, resurrected a baseball hero of the 1940s, Enos ("Country") Slaughter, for similar televised chores.

Perhaps the most notable impact of these direct-mail and televised efforts to raise funds has been to modify a long-term pattern in American politics. Generally campaign funds come from large contributions of $500 or more. The mass appeals of 1964, however, produced a treasury for Republicans of which only 28 per cent came from such large contributions; both Nixon and Humphrey obtained the support of small contributions in 1968. We can probably anticipate that at all levels smaller contributions will become increasingly important as costs rise and as professional campaigners seek to tap this relatively unexploited source of funds.

A recent study indicates that professional campaigners speak of two types of money to be avoided: "political money," contributed in return for promise of future favors, and "dirty money," contributed by the underworld for protection. Campaigners prefer clean, "nonpolitical" funds (no strings attached).[49] How much tainted money enters national, state, and local campaign coffers is impossible to estimate, but it would be naive to assume its total absence. There is evidence that corporations holding government contracts make sizable campaign contributions.[50] We also know that in several states civil servants contribute to certain campaigns, often buying tickets to political dinners, because of indirect pressures. Such corporate and personal contributions fall in the category of political money; unfortunately we know even less about funds supplied by criminal elements.

DILEMMAS IN CAMPAIGN MANAGEMENT

In this chapter we have limited our discussion to the principal services professional campaign specialists perform for client-candidates; these include recruitment, devising strategy, supplying a campaign organization, budgeting, and fund-raising. We have delayed describing the equally important tasks of research (into issues and voters through documents, polls, and data-processing) and communications (especially the use of media for advertising and publicity). We need not, however, delay our consideration of some of the vexing issues that the growth of campaign persuasion as an industry poses for our democracy.

In its relatively rapid emergence as an industry, political public relations has assumed the trappings, but not the substance, of a profession. We generally think of a profession as a vocation whose practitioners apply theoretical analyses to an undertaking; the performance of these practitioners is evaluated according to standards accepted throughout the profession. In treating the sick a medical doctor employs techniques of diagnosis and remedy derived from theories generated over centuries of inquiry into bodily functions; he is responsible to a code of practice common to all members of the medical profession. But few campaign specialists consciously analyze their clients' problems in theoretical ways; instead they manage campaigns as exercises in trial and error, adjusting their overall campaign plan to the

[49] Levin, *The Compleat Politician*, p. 232.
[50] Alexander Heard, *The Costs of Democracy* (Chapel Hill: University of North Carolina Press, 1960).

exigencies of the moment. Aside from the crude theory of mass persuasion outlined in Chapter 1, campaign technicians have no tested body of knowledge on which to draw. Moreover, unlike the doctor or lawyer, no professional standards guide their conduct. Although aspiring to professional status, campaign management is still a craft without theoretical underpinnings and lacking common guidelines.[51] Despite the effort to organize an American Society of Political Consultants in 1969 to consider questions of professional standards, the fact remains that only as specialists working for a fee do management personnel lay claim to the designation of professional at all.

The lack of evaluative standards raises questions of ethics. One public relations man has defined his trade as "the business of representing to the public in the best possible light the firms, corporations, or associations which employ us." Ethically, "the pursuit of public relations is neutral and, as such, can be applied to either good or evil ends." [52] Eugene Jones, a specialist in producing television documentaries and the *Today* show who prepared Richard Nixon's 1968 commercials viewed the ethical problem this way: "I'm a professional. This is a professional job. I was neutral toward Nixon when I started. Now I happen to be for him. But that's not the point. The point is, for the money, I'd do it for almost anybody." [53] The practice of campaign management suggests several problem areas: First, with the exception of a few firms (such as F. Clifton White and Associates), most management and consultant agencies work for several clients during an election. Can the research work performed for a fee on behalf of Candidate A be sold, again for a fee, to Candidate B running in the same district, state, or county? Or is it proper for a firm publicizing a gubernatorial candidate, yet hired separately to arrange rallies for a presidential candidate, to charge two fees when it brings the presidential contender into the state to endorse the gubernatorial candidate? No guidelines suggest what is ethical here, yet it has happened;[54] and what if one firm handles campaigns for candidates of rival parties, as

[51] Alfred North Whitehead, *Adventures of Ideas* (New York: The New American Library, 1933), pp. 64–65.

[52] Patrick J. Sullivan, "Madison Avenue Mafia?," *America*, CII, No. 23 (March 12, 1960), 704.

[53] Joe McGinniss, *The Selling of the President 1968* (New York: Trident Press, 1969), pp. 117–18.

[54] Congressional Quarterly, Inc., "Campaign Management Grows," p. 710.

did one pollster in the 1966 race for governor of California between Ronald Reagan and Pat Brown; whose interests take priority?

Second, many management and consultant agencies work not only on behalf of candidates, but also as lobbyists on behalf of particular pieces of legislation. Ethical problems abound when an agency, in its capacity of lobbyist, wins the legislative voting support of a congressman the firm helped elect when acting in its role of campaign manager. One campaign manager in a southwestern state has been instrumental in helping elect a number of state legislators. Between elections he organizes campaigns for specific legislation, directing his propaganda at the legislators in their home districts before the legislative session begins. In his dual role he has had remarkable success converting legislators to support unpopular causes.

Finally, there are ethical problems associated with the growing influence management and consultant specialists have in making campaign policy. There are signs that in the dynamic relationship between the client-candidate and his manager, the tail wags the dog, and leaves a marked imprint on the political process in the wagging. In advising on the restructuring of state and local parties, the campaign technicians reorganize to fit parties to the management conception of what an election is all about. The party assumes a new "image," but not one necessarily appropriate for its traditional supporters who find themselves replaced in party councils by new recruits. When clients are candidates rather than party committees, the impact on the political system may be even greater. In screening potential candidates the mercenaries have given a new definition to the notion of "availability"; the marketable candidate is selected on the basis of his brand name, his capacity to trigger an emotional response from the electorate, his skill in using mass media, and his ability to "project." Analysis of social problems and issues yields to parroting of themes; televised debates between contenders produce meaningless confrontations rather than rational discussion. Negotiations with party politicians assume the form of "out-of-town tryouts"; primary elections are approached as "presale" campaigns; and general elections emerge as the "Giant Sweepstakes." [55] In the end the candidate owes his election not to party but to his personal organization of paid

[55] For the impact of professional public relations on the political system see Kelley, *Professional Public Relations*, pp. 210–35.

and voluntary workers; once elected he responds not to party programs, but to the interests also represented by the professionals.

In summarizing these ethical issues it should be emphasized that the problem goes beyond the fact that professionally managed candidates can defeat candidates who have no professional advice. The point is that we are approaching the time when all candidates and all proposals in all elections at all levels will be professionally managed. As that time approaches the campaign management industry assumes an institutional character as central to the functioning of American democracy as political parties, elections, the journalistic estate, legislatures, executives, bureaucracies, or the courts. As a coequal in transactions with these traditional centers of democratic government, campaign management will modify their every operation just as those institutions will leave their mark on this emerging profession. It is for this reason that students of politics in the future must not only describe the detailed activities of campaign professionals, but must begin examining the broader impact of the new technology of political persuasion.

3

CAMPAIGN RESEARCH: PROFILING THE ELECTORATE

The management aspects of modern political technology discussed in Chapter 2 differ more in style than in substance from the "old politics" of an earlier era. After all, "old-style" machine politicians also recruited candidates, devised strategy, forged organizations, and raised campaign funds. In the procedures for acquiring accurate information about interests, issues, and voters on which to base campaign plans, however, a difference in kind rather than in degree exists between the old and the new politics. Whereas party politicians once formulated strategies on the basis of the guesses, hunches, and insights of ward heelers, contemporary campaigners turn to behavioral scientists for valid data on public issues and voters' attitudes. By offering systematic inquiry instead of intuition, educated estimates instead of haphazard guesses, research consultants play an increasingly significant role in democratic elections.

RESEARCHING POLITICAL INTERESTS AND ISSUES

The professional approach to campaign research has its greatest impact in the gathering of reliable information about voters' opinions. Before considering the techniques involved in opinion-polling, however, we look at a less publicized area of political research: namely, the efforts of candidates to learn which political interest groups they can depend on for organizational and financial support and which election issues will be most significant.

The prospects for victory of either a candidate or a referendum issue depend ultimately on the sentiments of voters. But campaign managers survey this and other factors before even deciding to enter the contest. For organizational purposes, professional campaigners have borrowed and improved upon a technique from the earlier political era. Successful candidates have always maintained lists of persons they have met through party organizations who could be counted on for help in a campaign. Paid research consultants also compile lists of potential opinion leaders. But instead of relying only on the candidate's personal knowledge, they comb the membership rolls of civic clubs and voluntary organizations and watch closely the subscriber lists of liberal or conservative publications, opinion journals, and political tracts. The result of this surveillance is an impressive roll of potential volunteers with each name recorded on computer tape for quick retrieval—cross-referenced by political viewpoint, campaign experience, hours of availability, and even whether a baby-sitter is needed for a volunteer who is a housewife. On short notice the research consultant supplies the campaigner with a ready-made organization, a job that can easily take up to six weeks for candidates without professional service. Files of potential financial backers are also maintained so that the aspiring politician can estimate his chances for adequate funding and not jump blindly into the electoral fray with little prospect of support.

With the advent of professional campaigning, research into the availability of men and money has become a continuous operation, less likely to wax and wane with the electoral season than in previous eras. The same is true of research into political issues. The public usually respects the candidate who is well-informed on the issues; in any campaign a candidate must at least present the illusion of being well-informed. Consequently, candidates study campaign issues extensively and place a premium on having a coterie of experts on specialized areas. It is the function of these advisors, the candidate's brain trust, to coach him in the use of his "campaign bible." [1]

The campaign bible prepared by the candidate's research consultants presents pertinent facts, arguments, interpretations, and conclusions in three areas. First, it summarizes all issues relevant to the campaign on which the candidate might wish to speak or about which he might be interrogated by reporters, constituents, or even his op-

[1] Herbert M. Baus and William B. Ross, *Politics Battle Plan* (New York: The Macmillan Company, 1968), pp. 184–88.

ponent in debate. We noted earlier that Ronald Reagan's successful campaign for the governorship of California in 1966 was based in part on his skill in using the campaign bible provided by the Behavior Science Corporation (BASICO). That compilation consisted of seven volumes of four-by-eight-inch fact cards, a series of discussion statements, and a volume spelling out Reagan's arguments for a "Creative Society." The Reagan bible was not unique. In 1964 Goldwater's researchers provided him with a volume of concise facts and arguments covering twenty-two issues in the California primary. And in 1960 John F. Kennedy owed much of his success in his first televised debate with Richard Nixon to a fifteen-page mini-bible which surveyed all the issues which were expected to be raised in the confrontation; Kennedy studied these topics, discussed them with his advisers, and entered the debate with his homework done. In 1968 Nixon also employed briefing books; prior to the New Hampshire presidential primary, for example, his staff prepared a fifty-page monograph on that state's politics.[2]

Second, the campaign bible profiles individuals, particularly the important people in a given constituency who are supporting the candidate or his opponent. In 1964, for example, Republican candidates hoped to link President Lyndon Johnson with political wrongdoing by making an issue of the Bobby Baker case. Baker had been secretary to the senate Democratic majority when Lyndon Johnson was majority leader and ultimately resigned because of investigations into charges that he had used his influence to aid government contractors. Richard Nixon urged that Johnson be implicated in the apparent scandal. However, Nelson Rockefeller's researchers found that Baker's case probably implicated as many Republican senators as Democrats. Rockefeller informed Nixon, Goldwater, George Romney, and William Scranton of the preliminary findings[3] and the Baker case did not become a major campaign issue.

Finally, the campaign bible provides details on local issues and problems so the candidate can brief himself for each campaign stop. Thus the voters of Podunk are impressed by the candidate's under-

[2] Theodore H. White, *The Making of the President 1960* (New York: Atheneum Publishers, 1961), pp. 283–84. For Nixon's use of briefing books in 1968 see Theodore H. White, *The Making of the President 1968* (New York: Atheneum Publishers, 1969), p. 6.

[3] Theodore H. White, *The Making of the President 1964* (New York: The New American Library, 1965), p. 184.

standing of, and sympathy with, their concerns. We observed in the preceding chapter that Edward Kennedy's advisers went to great pains to provide their candidate with predigested data on local problems in Massachusetts in 1961.

In preparing the campaign bible researchers rely on a number of sources. The incumbent candidate seeking reelection has an advantage. If he is a legislator, for example, he has probably served on committees dealing specifically with problems which are likely to become campaign issues; he has access to the services of a legislative research service (such as the Legislative Reference Service of the Library of Congress). An incumbent executive official usually runs on his record and certainly has the necessary facts underlying the formulation of decisions he had made. Incumbents often assign government-employed administrative assistants to the task of background research, thus avoiding the expense of a professional consultant.

Nonincumbents have fewer direct sources of information and must work harder at their research. This is one reason why they are more likely to employ research consultants and a partial explanation of why professional campaigners are more frequently employed by political novices. However a few information sources within the party are available without fee. Candidates for Congress obtain some data from their party congressional or senate campaign committee (each of which employs a professional research service). This source usually provides the candidate with information about his opponent's voting record, but is less helpful in researching local issues and problems.[4] The two major parties also hold "candidate training schools" on a nationwide or regional basis. These schools, usually under the direction of professional campaign managers, instruct candidates on how to write speeches, interpret opinion polls, put together effective precinct organizations, make pleasing television appearances, and so forth. Another party-based service for candidates provides information retrieval. The Republican National Committee, for example, codes and categorizes newspaper clippings; if a candidate requests current information on a topic, the computerized retrieval system (labeled Recordak) supplies it without delay.

Party-sponsored research is limited, however, and of little aid to

[4] David A. Leuthold, *Electioneering in a Democracy* (New York: John Wiley & Sons, Inc., 1968), pp. 55–59.

candidates for lower offices, for nonpartisan offices, or in party primaries. Professional researchers at BASICO, PUBLICOM, and similar services fill this void. They maintain newspaper clipping services, pore over legislative statutes, study executive and judicial decisions, survey opinion leaders, analyze voting records, probe public sentiments, and prepare position papers. Avant-garde agencies employ the sophisticated techniques of the behavioral sciences, including computer simulation (to be discussed later in connection with polling) and content analysis. The latter is a technique for analyzing a party platform, a candidate's speech, or any similar document by quantifying its explicit and implicit themes, the intensity of attitudes expressed in the document, and the types of symbols characteristically used to arouse fear, build support, and play upon the voter's emotions. When properly employed, content analysis can provide a candidate with information about an opponent's style, thought patterns, aims, and even predict his future actions.[5]

But sophisticated computerized research techniques do not totally replace older and more exotic methods. Political espionage is also a stock-in-trade of some research consultants. One public relations and research specialist, not having lost a race in a state or local campaign since 1956, attributes part of his success to his ability to "guess" his opponent's plans. The guesses are informed by such "research" as placing an informant on the opponent's staff, bugging devices for electronic eavesdropping, adroit questioning at cocktail parties, and periodic visitations to the opponet's printer to sneak advance looks at upcoming campaign broadsides. Thus research consultants occasionally even offer the skills of television's private detectives.

RESEARCHING CONSTITUENTS

"To run or not to run, and if running, how to win." Like Hamlet, every aspiring politician has dilemmas. Accurate information about his constituents is essential to rational allocations of scarce resources— time, personnel, and money. To acquire usable information, professional researchers employ three basic techniques—interpreting informal sources, analyzing recorded data, and surveying public opinion.

[5] Note, for example, uses of the technique in Philip J. Stone, *The General Inquirer: A Computer Approach to Content Analysis* (Cambridge, Mass.: The M.I.T. Press, 1967).

INFORMAL SOURCES OF VOTER SENTIMENT

A recent study of candidates for public office in Wisconsin in 1964 revealed that 52 per cent of the politicians were uncertain about their campaign's outcome; uncertainty prevailed even among half of the candidates who were sure to win by more than 55 per cent of the vote. One reason for the pervasiveness of uncertainty is that candidates use unreliable means of prediction. Although 18 per cent conducted opinion polls and almost 90 per cent reviewed past election statistics, informal sources of information were much more prevalent—the word of party people, statements from campaign volunteers, personal contacts, the reaction of the press, and the warmth of the reception at various appearances.[6] Other studies have indicated that candidates often rely on their own intuition or their mail to decide whether to run and how to campaign.[7]

Although widely used, these informal sources possess a major defect —they invariably lead the candidate to overestimate his popularity, often leading him to run when he should not or to employ faulty campaign tactics. Party workers and volunteers permit their enthusiasm to get the better of them; since they favor the candidate, they easily believe that everyone they talk to does also. They are often right, because the people they are most likely to talk with are the candidate's sympathizers to begin with! Party workers, eager to please their leader, tell him how well they are doing on his behalf but gloss over failures. The candidate's public contacts are suspect simply because so many people shake his hand, buoying his optimism, but never vote for him.

Candidates interpret the warmth of their receptions at public appearances as a sign of impending victory. They overlook the facts that the people most likely to come to rallies are supporters, that the rallies themselves are carefully staged, and that in some instances "enthusiastic" supporters are actually paid to provide television audiences with a view of cheering throngs. Astute candidates discount warmth of reception as an indicator of popularity. John Kennedy's managers

---

[6] John W. Kingdon, *Candidates for Office* (New York: Random House, Inc., 1966), pp. 86–101.

[7] See Murray B. Levin, *The Compleat Politician* (Indianapolis: The Bobbs-Merrill Co., Inc., 1962), pp. 186–87; Leuthold, *Electioneering in a Democracy*, pp. 49–51.

in 1960 hired a political scientist to analyze crowd reaction and advise how the themes and symbols used in speeches were accepted. As expected, crowds responded best when Kennedy attacked unpopular Republican figures, such as defeated presidential candidate Thomas Dewey. The general analysis concluded, however, that Kennedy could not draw as much optimism from the size and warmth of his receptions as journalists had been suggesting.[8]

The problem with measuring popularity on the basis of a candidate's mail is twofold. First, letter writers are more highly motivated, better-educated, and usually in a higher status and a more financially rewarding occupation than the average American. The opinions expressed in letters are those of a small minority, not a cross section of all constituents. Second, a candidate's supporters are more likely to write him than are his detractors, so the candidate most often sees congratulatory mail. This can help him estimate the types of persons who are likely to work on his behalf and the intensity of their concern,[9] but there is a danger here too: the candidate may obtain a warped view of his constituents' opinions and of his chances for success. The sources of public opinion used by Goldwater's strategists in 1964 included such mail as letters from constituents and letters to newspaper editors. Since only 15 per cent of the nation's population reports having written to public officials and only 3 per cent can recall having written letters to newspapers, it was a mistake to take these letters too seriously. Moreover, the opinions of letter writers in 1964, unlike political opinion generally, were pro-Goldwater and anti-federal government, and tended toward conservative views. To the extent that the opinions of letter writers influenced Goldwater's strategy, his campaign was waged on the basis of highly biased information.[10]

This should not suggest that informal information sources have no value. Taken with qualifications, each can give a hint of the prospects for victory. It stands to reason that, to the extent such informal sources are useful, the incumbent has an advantage over the nonincumbent. He has had experience in working with party leaders and volunteers, he has made many public appearances and can better

[8] Bernard Hennessy, *Public Opinion* (Belmont, Cal.: Wadsworth Publishing Co., 1965), p. 36.

[9] Leuthold, *Electioneering in a Democracy*, p. 49.

[10] Phillip E. Converse, Aage R. Clausen, and Warren E. Miller, "Electoral Myth and Reality: The 1964 Election," *American Political Science Review*, LIX (June, 1965), 321–36.

gauge their success, and he is in a position to receive mail from his constituents. The nonincumbent does not rely on informal sources as naturally; he turns instead (as do an increasing number of incumbents as well) to more formalized ways of acquiring information about voters.

RECORDED DATA ABOUT VOTING BEHAVIOR

Politicians have always used statistics about past elections to evaluate their chances for success in current campaigns. Early procedures were informal, amounting to little more than an effort to determine whether a given constituency traditionally supported Republicans or Democrats. Wiser politicians noted the ethnic composition of a district and generalized that the Irish voted Democratic, the Germans voted Republican, and so forth. These useful, though sometimes crude, estimates were made possible because counties, municipalities, and the federal government have for decades recorded turnout rates, candidate totals, registration rolls, and census breakdowns for voting precincts. It was only natural that professional researchers, armed with computers, statistical techniques, and impressive jargon, should invade damp courthouse basements and dusty libraries of official records. Today these consultants, assisted by the helpful but rarely necessary mystique of computers, package relatively simple analyses of relevant data for marketing to clients as "sophisticated intelligence." Let us examine the contents of a few of these packages.

Identifying Stable Vote Patterns

One rule of election campaigning is, "Go hunting where the ducks are." The aim is to concentrate on areas where one is likely to win votes; a Republican, it is argued, can expect little return from heavily Democratic precincts. This strategy requires that a candidate know his strong and weak regions before scheduling his campaign activities. One of the most systematic efforts to obtain and use such information occurred in Michigan in the 1960s as political amateur George Romney became three-term governor of the state.

Romney's director of research during this period was political scientist Walter D. DeVries. Working with pollster Fred Currier of the Market Opinion Research Company, DeVries relied on election-return analysis to identify "ticket-splitters"—voters who split away from their traditional party loyalties when casting ballots for president or governor. Romney's researchers were especially interested in Democrats who had voted for Republican presidential or gubernatorial candidates. The percentage of ticket-splitters in each precinct was easily computed: if, for example, a Republican candidate for a minor state office received 35 per cent of the precinct vote, but the Republican gubernatorial candidate received 40 per cent, the 5 per cent difference was attributed to ticket-splitting. (The technique relies on the difference in votes received for party candidates at various levels. Since the net percentage difference conceals ticket-splitting taking place in opposite directions—Democrats to Republican and Republican to Democrat—it may understate the amount of ticket-splitting in a precinct.) The statewide analysis concluded that ticket-splitting was as low as zero in rural counties, but increased to as much as 10 per cent in suburban areas, particularly those outside Detroit. The next step was obvious; namely, to concentrate the campaign in areas with a high incidence of ticket-splitting.

DeVries perfected a technique to assure effective allocation of campaign resources—particularly the candidate's time—in 1964. He computed the percentage each county contributed to the statewide turn-out in the most relevant preceding election and the percentage it contributed to Romney's total vote. The candidate's schedule then devoted optimum time to those counties and precincts with substantial potential votes. For example, in a high-turnout, high-Romney-support county, the candidate would make door-to-door tours of precincts where ticket-splitting had occurred in previous elections; but in a traditionally Democratic county the candidate might spend a short time boosting the morale of Republican workers rather than calling on voters.[11]

The DeVries approach is straightforward and without pretense. It was specially developed by a technician for a single candidate and his team rather than as a general device to sell to clients. Datamatics, Inc., the research and data-processng arm of the Spencer-Roberts management firm, offers a similar service. The system—the Precinct Index Priority System, or PIPS—uses a computer, but does little that the candidate's staff could not do with pencil and paper. Basically, the

[11] James M. Perry, The New Politics (New York: Clarkson N. Potter, Inc., 1968), pp. 87, 99–100, 158.

procedure ranks census tracts (small geographic districts containing several city blocks within metropolitan areas) on the basis of the votes each tract can provide to a given cause. The criteria for ranking include registration rates, past election turnout, and votes for previous candidates. The character of each census area can be determined from sociodemographic data. A candidate can use the ranking to assign volunteers, mail letters, or conduct telephone campaigns in high priority areas.

Estimating Turnout Needs

Elections turn on the types and numbers of people who vote; a candidate may have an overwhelming majority in his district, but unless his sympathizers go to the polls they do him no good. Goldwater's managers in 1964 tried to compensate for the greater number of Democrats than Republicans in the country by achieving higher turnout rates among Goldwater supporters. For this purpose they developed a precinct quota program (used in conjunction with the voter canvass described in Chapter 1).

The idea behind the quota program was to assign to each state, county, and congressional district in the nation a number of votes that had to be cast for Goldwater if he was to win. More than one hundred volunteers worked for twelve days to compile the following data on 3,700 electoral units: registration figures, the number of registered and unregistered nonvoters, the size of the potential electorate, and the votes cast in the presidential, gubernatorial, and congressional elections of 1956, 1958, 1960, and 1962. Vote quotas were assigned on the basis of this data, the knowledge that the electorate size had expanded by 10 per cent since 1962, and an estimate of Republican strength in the state. This estimate was based upon an evaluation of twenty-five factors, including such matters as Goldwater's popularity, the strength of Republican organizations, the friendliness of the press, and expected support from Negroes, senior citizens, and other groups. Each factor was rated on a scale running from zero to four. These ratings could be used to estimate whether Goldwater would do better or worse in the state than previous candidates; vote quotas were adjusted to account for these differences.

The national quota was 40,155,000 votes, or 53.0 per cent of the total votes cast; each state quota was large enough to assure that

Republicans would carry the state. Each state was encouraged to reach its quota by "hunting where the ducks were"—to increasing the Republican vote in areas which had previously cast heavy Republican majorities.[12] Unfortunately for Goldwater's strategists, the plan overlooked the fact that many Republicans would vote for Johnson-Humphrey on November 2.

Identifying Demographic Correlates of Voting

One limitation in analyzing past election statistics for a given precinct, district, or constituency is that it is impossible to characterize individual voters. The researcher cannot say why an individual voted for Richard Nixon, Hubert Humphrey, or George Wallace in 1968 by studying aggregate voting records. What he can do, however, is to categorize geographical areas in terms of the social and demographic characteristics of their residents. By matching these group characteristics with the area's voting patterns he can then make such assertions as, "Predominantly middle-class, suburban districts gave Nixon heavy majorities" or "Rural townships were Wallace's principal areas of strength."

The Datamatics Corporation has borrowed a technique developed by social scientists for identifying the social characteristics of metropolitan areas and converted it into a salable commodity. The technique relies on information collected in the decennial surveys of the United States Bureau of the Census (available to any citizen from the Government Printing Office). The data, grouped by census tracts and states, details for example, the percentage of tract residents with various levels of education who live in single-family or multiple-family dwellings, who have Spanish surnames, who have foreign-born parents, who work in the central area of the city rather that the suburbs, who are members of the labor force, and so forth. The data is broken down by sex, age, and race. By employing a method used for many years in the social sciences—the Shevky-Bell technique—one can group tracted areas according to three indices: (1) a social ranking, based on various occupational and educational levels; (2) an urbanization ranking, based on type of housing, proportion of women in the labor force, and fertility rates; and (3) an ethnic rating, based on the proportion

---

[12] John H. Kessel, *The Goldwater Coalition* (Indianapolis: The Bobbs-Merrill Co., Inc., 1968), pp. 162–66.

of Negroes, foreign-born, and other minorities in the area. These rankings are combined and displayed on a map to indicate at a glance the composition of the city as a whole and of each electoral district.

Datamatics performs this analysis of census data and labels the product, "Social-Area Analysis." Using multicolored maps and plastic overlays, these research consultants provide clients with a systematic description of their constituencies. Since the average candidate-client is a political novice, these descriptions appear sophisticated and mysteriously complex, and therefore must be worth the price. Were more candidates better informed about techniques of social science research, they might be chagrined to learn that they could obtain the same service with a relatively small expenditure for volumes of census data, the fundamental "cookbook," [13] maps, colored pencils, and a few untrained clerks.

Checking Residence and Registration

A piece of information that is relatively hard to acquire in any election is an accurate listing of the registration status and residence of each member of the electorate. Americans change residences with high frequency and official records of their eligibility fail to keep up with the movement. The candidate relying on outdated registration rolls often finds that the voters he had hoped to contact have moved to a different neighborhood, perhaps out of his constituency, while new residents determine his fate. In many counties election and registration records are poorly kept or so tightly guarded by a dominant political party that a minority candidate has no chance to use them. One of their first campaign tasks for many candidates is the accumulation of accurate voter listings.

Winthrop Rockefeller set out as a Republican in 1964 to win the governorship of Arkansas, a traditionally one-party, Democratic state. His defeat in 1964 taught him that to win in 1966 he would need an accurate listing of Arkansas voters. He moved in two directions. First, he hired a firm which specialized in tabulating mailing lists from telephone books; that firm listed the name, address, and tele-

[13] The technique, including the label, is borrowed from Eshref Shevky and Wendell Bell, *Social Area Analysis: Theory, Illustrative Application and Computational Procedures* (Stanford, Cal.: Stanford University Press, 1955).

phone number of every person in every telephone book in Arkansas. To determine age, registration status, political inclination, current residence, and other relevant political information about these people, Rockefeller volunteers conducted a door-to-door canvass and a telephone survey in the thirty most populous areas of Arkansas. This effort was particularly successful in Little Rock, where 90 per cent of the homes were surveyed.

To assure efficient use of this information, the Rockefeller forces moved on a second front. All relevant data about each person was coded on a punch card for computer processing. The computer was programmed to prepare specialized lists of potential voters—all medical doctors, all high school teachers, all insurance salesmen in Pulaski County, or recent migrants to Arkansas from a particular state—who might have a particular interest in supporting Rockefeller. These persons were contacted by what appeared to be personal letters from the candidate (but were actually prepared by the computer) and urged to register (registration rose by 60,000 in mid-1966), campaign, and vote.

For his reelection in 1968 Rockefeller expanded his data-gathering and processing operation to include more than 200,000 names (with 65,000 in specialized categories and another 50,000 who could be identified for campaign work), each of whom could be contacted quickly by computer-prepared letters.[14] Few politicians have made such a massive effort to use recorded political data.

Projecting Elections

Before closing our discussion of researching recorded election data we digress to mention a technique which is not yet employed by candidates, but which has figured prominently in recent American elections—computer-based election forecasts. Although now employed primarily by television networks to win a large audience, these projections could be combined with simulation procedures to evaluate the impact of proposed strategies far in advance of the election.

Computerized forecasts of election outcomes date back to 1952; widely publicized use was first developed in the 1960s. In 1962 pollster Louis Harris (who had worked for John Kennedy in 1960)

[14] Perry, *The New Politics*, pp. 142–48.

signed a six-year contract with the Columbia Broadcasting System to develop an election forecasting technique. The system—Vote Profile Analysis—was first introduced in 1962, but made its biggest impact in 1964. During the same period the National Broadcasting Company was developing its Electronic Vote Analysis with the aid of consultants Richard Scammon, former director of the U.S. Census Bureau, Dr. John W. Tukey, a mathematician, and Charles E. Young, of the University of California. The American Broadcasting Company relied on a system developed with the aid of Dr. Jack Moshman and pollster Oliver Quayle.

Each system predicts the outcome of an election on the basis of early returns from a relatively small number of the nation's more than 175,000 voting precincts. Precincts in each state are selected which accurately reflect the characteristics of voters throughout that state. If, for example, 15 per cent of the state's voters are suburbanites, this proportion will be reflected in the makeup of the system's representative precincts. Precincts are also selected on the basis of voting patterns in previous elections—what candidate of what party carried the precinct in previous elections and by how much? In 1964 both the CBS and NBC systems selected approximately 2,000 "key" or "tag" precincts and placed reporters in each with direct telephone lines to central computing facilities to permit rapid reporting of early returns.

The projection, or predicting, procedure is basically the same in all the systems. Before the election critical data for each selected precinct is gathered, coded, and stored in the computer for high-speed processing: sociodemographic characteristics of the precinct's voters, turnout rates in past key elections, winning margins for the majority candidate in previous elections, voter turnout estimates for the current election, past voting proclivities of special groups within the precinct, comparisons of vote percentages received by candidates in the precinct with their statewide and nationwide percentages, and so forth. The computer takes the early returns from selected precincts and matches the vote margins of the leading candidate with the vote margins of the candidate in other precincts within the state having similar social and political characteristics and the margins of candidates who carried the state in previous elections. On the basis of repeated comparisons a pattern emerges indicating the range of votes each candidate is likely to acquire from all precincts and the statistical probability that a given candidate will win the election.[15]

The record of these forecasting efforts has been mixed. In the California Republican primary of 1964, both public opinion polls and official returns indicated a Rockefeller victory. Yet CBS at 7:22 P.M. PDT with 2 per cent of the vote actually counted and thirty-eight minutes remaining before poll closing in northern California accurately predicted a Goldwater victory. And in the 1964 presidential election NBC predicted a Johnson victory at 6:48 P.M. EST, again with only 2 per cent of the total vote counted (the polls in western states were to remain open for more than two hours). But there have been fiascoes as well: the networks called the wrong winner in the Maryland and Georgia gubernatorial races in 1966. No network was willing to go out on a limb in the tight 1968 presidential contest.

The rapid rise of election forecasting has raised concern among candidates who feel that election projections discourage voters from going to the polls or encourage them to join the projected winner's bandwagon. Pierre Salinger argued that his defeat by George Murphy in the 1964 California senatorial race had come about in part because many Democrats did not vote once they heard Johnson was an easy victor in the presidential election; Goldwater's forces, on the other hand, believed that their supporters had stayed away from the polls when they heard Johnson was to win. Studies were undertaken in 1964 to assess the impact of election projection. Their findings must be interpreted with caution since: (1) the 1964 presidential election was a landslide victory and not a close race and (2) some of the studies were hastily designed and executed. The findings indicate that televised election projections as a single factor probably accounted for few vote shifts. One study indicated that 97 per cent of California voters surveyed voted as they had intended before election day; of the remaining 3 per cent, only one-fifth had even been exposed to reported projections.[16] In a nationwide sample of more than 1,500 adults, fourteen switched their votes from previous intentions, but only 3 of

---

[15] See James Coleman, Ernest Heau, Robert Peabody, and Leo Rigsby, "Computers and Election Analysis: *The New York Times* Project," *The Public Opinion Quarterly*, XXVIII (Fall, 1964), 418–46.

[16] Harold Mendelsohn, "Election-day Broadcasts and Terminal Voting Decisions," *The Public Opinion Quarterly*, XXX (Summer, 1966), 212–25.

them had heard the forecasts (two of the three shifted to Gold-water).[17] A third study (based on interviews in the bay area of California) indicated that the eagerness of voters may have been affected by televised forecasts, but vote switches were minimal. Such forecasts, the authors point out, are but one source of election information available to the voter, including polls, news commentaries, and voters' perceptions,[18] any one of which may produce changes in intentions. Finally, there is a suggestion in this research that the voters most likely to be influenced by such projections are those who are most susceptible to all forms of campaign persuasion—those who are uninformed and indifferent about the election, of low political motivation, and who delay their voting decision and then grasp any piece of last-minute information that helps them out of their dilemma.[19]

This digression into the uses of election projection suggests that recorded data has been analyzed (with computer processing) in ways not yet employed by political candidates. There is no reason why the techniques of election projection could not be combined with those of opinion polling to give any campaigner a day-by-day prediction of his election chances and an assessment of his strategy, tactics, and techniques. We will get some idea of these possibilities after first examining the uses of political polling.

OPINION POLLING AND ESTIMATING VOTING DECISIONS

The most widely employed technique of campaign research is the opinion poll. It has become such a central feature of political persuasion that it deserves our detailed consideration. In the remainder of this chapter we shall discuss the extent, purposes, and procedures of political polling in American elections.

[17] Robert P. Knight, "Voters, Computers and TV Forecasts," Freedom of Information Center Publication No. 169 (Columbia, Mo.: School of Journalism, University of Missouri, October, 1966), pp. 7–8.

[18] Kurt Lang and Gladys Engel Lang, Voting and Nonvoting (Waltham, Mass.: Blaisdell Publishing Co., 1968), pp. 56–65.

[19] Douglas A. Fuchs, "Election-day Radio-Television and Western Voting," Public Opinion Quarterly, XXX (Summer, 1966), 226–36; idem, "Election Day Newscasts and Their Effects on Western Vote Turnout," Journalism Quarterly, XLII (Winter, 1965), 22–28; and Douglas A. Fuchs and Jules Becker, "A Brief Report on the Time of Day When People Vote," Public Opinion Quarterly, XXXII (Fall, 1968), 437–40.

The Pervasiveness of Political Polling

It is rare that a candidate for a major statewide, congressional, or national office does not employ the services of a private political pollster in his primary and general election campaigns. A study of twenty-four governors who had faced significant opposition in the 1966 elections revealed that all of the thirteen governors who responded had used polling in their campaigns; eleven had employed private pollsters and two had used polls undertaken by party workers.[20] Pollster Louis Harris estimated that two-thirds of the senatorial candidates in 1962 used polls;[21] by 1966 another estimate placed the use at 85 per cent of winning senatorial candidates and more than half of elected congressmen.[22] Harris himself was instrumental in opening presidential campaigns to private polling; in the 1960 Kennedy campaign he polled more Americans (23,000 Wisconsin voters alone) than ever before surveyed in our history.[23]

Although opinion surveys are widely used in American politics today, the use of scientific surveying techniques is less than four decades old. "Straw votes," the precursors of contemporary polls, date back 150 years.[24] These devices include the "Tele-Vote" polls conducted by television stations that ask viewers to phone their opinions on certain questions. Another variation was the "chicken feed" poll of 1948, conducted by a Kansas miller who offered his customers feed in bags illustrated with either a donkey or an elephant. The Blevins Pop Corn Poll sells theater patrons popcorn in boxes decorated with the pictures of presidential candidates. Although Blevins came within 3.3 per cent of Kennedy's winning margin in 1960, such accuracy is unusual for haphazard polling procedures.

[20] Robert King and Martin Schnitzer, "Contemporary Use of Private Political Polling," *Public Opinion Quarterly*, XXXII (Fall, 1968), 432.

[21] Louis Harris, "Polls and Politics in the United States," *Public Opinion Quarterly*, XXVII (Spring, 1963), 3.

[22] King and Schnitzer, "Private Political Polling," pp. 433–34.

[23] White, *The Making of the President 1960*, pp. 51, 93.

[24] Bernard C. Hennessy and Erna R. Hennessy, "The Prediction of Close Elections: Comments on Some 1960 Polls," *Public Opinion Quarterly*, XXV (Fall, 1961), 405–10; Charles W. Roll, Jr., "Straws in the Wind: The Record of the Daily News Poll," *Public Opinion Quarterly*, XXXII (Summer, 1968), 251–60; Claude E. Robinson, *Straw Votes: A Study of Political Predicting* (New York: Columbia University Press, 1932).

Although Franklin Roosevelt contracted for opinion surveys on an informal basis, the first major use of a paid privately conducted poll on behalf of a candidate occurred in 1946; the Elmo Roper organization polled the Twenty-first Congressional District of New York for Jacob K. Javits' first campaign for public office.[25] (George Gallup had conducted a political survey in 1932 without pay on behalf of his mother-in-law, who was running for secretary of state in Iowa.) From these modest beginnings developed a flourishing industry (more than 200 firms conducted polls in 1968) offering specialized services tailored to the needs of each candidate-client.

Appendix B lists the major private, public, and academic political pollsters in the United States in the late 1960s and early 1970s. Private political pollsters include the professional campaign consultants described in Chapter 2; they conduct opinion surveys on behalf of a candidate for a fee and their findings become the confidential property of their client. Public pollsters undertake continuous surveys of opinion and sell their findings in article form to newspapers and other publications. Academic pollsters are usually social scientists at major universities who conduct studies on behalf of scholar-clients; their findings appear in scholarly books and academic journals. A few of the organizations in each category conduct nationwide surveys (the Gallup Poll is the leading example among public surveys). Most, however, limit themselves to regional or statewide projects (the California Poll, the Texas Poll, or Mid-South Opinion Surveys are examples).[26]

Quite naturally our concern here is with the private polls commissioned by campaigners for use as confidential intelligence reports rather than with public or academic studies. Any annual *Directory of Market Research Agencies and Management Consultants* lists more than a hundred firms in the business of conducting political polls for private clients. The quality of their work varies considerably. Most of these firms are primarily engaged in marketing research and undertake political polls only in election years. As a result the nuances of probing political attitudes often escape them, particularly if the firm assigns its apprentices to political accounts. In some instances a candidate

[25] Jacob K. Javits, "How I Used a Poll in Campaigning for Congress," *Public Opinion Quarterly*, XI (Summer, 1947), 222–26.
[26] Congressional Quarterly, Inc., "Political Pollsters Head for Record Activity in 1968," *Congressional Quarterly*, XXVI (May 3, 1968), 992.

pays the price of a major poll only to find that his "survey" consists of questions added as "trailers" to a marketing study. Or he may be equally disconcerted to find that he is one of several dozen candidates, of both parties, being served by a single private polling firm. Unfortunately, most politicians are not knowledgeable about polling techniques and are easily deceived into purchasing substandard opinion surveys. There are, however, private political pollsters who are painstaking in their service to clients and who take a greater interest in their political than their commercial accounts. They not only provide the poll, but also attempt to educate the client so that he can define clearly what he wants to know and with what degree of accuracy so that he can translate the results into decisive action. These firms provide the client with a written proposal, prepared in consultation with sampling statisticians in complicated cases, which outlines what the pollster intends to do, how, and at what cost.

Private polls are expensive. The increasing use of polls has undoubtedly been a major factor contributing to today's exorbitant campaign costs. In 1968 approximately $6 million was paid to private polling organizations for their professional services at all campaign levels. In 1964 the Republican National Committee spent $165,000 on polls during the months between the national nominating conventions and the elections; Goldwater's supporters spent $135,000 before his nomination. At an average cost of $10 per interview, an in-depth national survey alone costs from $15,000 to $25,000; a survey of a congressional district averages $10,000; a representative cross-section survey of a state such as Texas costs $15,000; and four surveys in the Cleveland mayoral race in 1967 cost a total of $12,000. It is unlikely that these costs will decrease. Campaign consultant and manager Joseph Napolitan estimated that by 1972 Democrats should be prepared to spend $250,000 for a year-long survey of voter attitudes. The Republicans, with the financial support of the American Medical Political Action Committee, began after the elections of 1968 to conduct continuous surveys in selected congressional districts as a part of the preparations to deliver Richard Nixon a Republican Congress in 1970. A conservative estimate is that total costs over the two-year period will reach $400,000.

Polling costs are so high that some politicians cannot use polls. Candidates for lesser political offices—school boards, state legislative seats, or small town mayor's posts—simply cannot afford costly polls;

a single poll would consume most of their campaign budget. Of sixty-one candidates for all levels of offices in Wisconsin in 1964, 74 per cent made no use of polls, mostly candidates for non-statewide offices.[27] But prohibitive costs are not the only deterrent to maximum use of polling. Some politicians place little faith in poll results and use them "only as yardsticks" or for the "prestige of having a pollster's name associated with mine." One candidate for statewide office in Texas used polls merely to "juice up my campaign workers" by offering evidence that their efforts were paying off. Richard Nixon has been quoted by one reporter as believing in the usefulness of polls that reveal popular opinions on issues, but discounting polls that merely test the popularity of alternative candidates.[28] Professional campaign managers are also cautious in their evaluation of private polls. A few will permit poll results to define issues, as in the 1965 mayoral race in Houston, Texas; polls indicated that citizens were worried about water rates and challenger Louis Welch made that concern into a winning issue. Other managers are reluctant to place so much confidence in polls and use them only as crude barometers of vague public sentiments.

The value of a confidential poll to a candidate-client depends in part on the additional services the pollster provides with the survey findings. Many firms simply supply statistical tables with little or no interpretation. A few refuse to report the poll findings if they contain bad news for the candidate; a smaller number engage in the questionable practice of "hedging" unfavorable poll results. The more experienced and reputable firms, however, provide truthful accounts of findings, then go on to interpret those findings and recommend courses of action to their candidate-clients. This, of course, places the pollster in the role of adviser as well as technician, a situation one management team has likened to "a doctor selling medicine he prescribes." [29]

Pollsters are divided over whether they should advise candidates as well as inquire for them. Louis Harris, once a leading private pollster who has since limited his activities to public polling, feels that opinion specialists are admirably prepared to give campaign advice: "I've polled in more than 200 races. Most politicians face less than a dozen

[27] Kingdon, *Candidates for Office*, p. 91.
[28] White, *The Making of the President 1968*, p. 169.
[29] Baus and Ross, *Politics Battle Plan*, p. 194.

races in their lifetimes. I feel as if I have 200 years of political experience." Oliver Quayle, who polls for a hundred candidates in an average election year, says, "I've been in more than 1,000 elections. All candidates expect our counsel, so we give it." But, observes Mervin D. Field of the Field Research Corporation, the "hybrid occupation" of "researcher–campaign manager" inevitably causes problems. The researcher may risk coloring his findings by using inexpensive techniques, in an effort to maintain the confidence of financial backers and bolster the spirits of the candidate and his workers.[30] Regardless of the arguments, the fact is that private pollsters play an ever larger role in mapping campaign strategy and tactics. Since he is paying such a high price for their services, it behooves the candidate to learn more about pollsters' methods. And since their potential leaders depend increasingly on poll results, it behooves citizens as well to become more knowledgeable about these methods.

The Informational Content of Private Political Polls

Professional pollsters provide information for planning, conducting, and evaluating campaign strategies through three basic types of polls—precampaign polls, surveys during the campaign, and postelection polls.

Precampaign polls. It is becoming customary for politicians to take opinion soundings long before their campaigns surface. From these confidential polls professional campaigners derive clues regarding the chances for electoral success. Many politicians will not decide whether to make a race until they have polled voters to see if they can win. Throughout 1967 President Lyndon Johnson retained the services of professional pollsters to assess his chances for reelection. At the time published Gallup and Harris surveys indicated that any Republican would defeat the president. In November Johnson's advisers circulated a private poll showing the president leading all contenders in a "bellwether" area. The man responsible for the poll, Archibald M. Crossley, reported that his findings had been distorted and that, in fact, the area was a traditionally Democratic New Hampshire county. Few of the president's confidential polls contradicted

[30] Knight, "Voters, Computers and TV Forecasts," p. 1; "Polling and the Political Process: Remarks by Mervin D. Field and Remarks by Oliver A. Quayle III," *Public Opinion Quarterly*, XXXI, (Fall, 1967), 438–40.

the published surveys indicating little chance for his reelection. In contemplating a challenge to President Johnson and Senator Eugene McCarthy for the 1968 Democratic presidential nomination, Robert F. Kennedy took opinion soundings into account. Reportedly his decision was influenced in part by a poll taken on behalf of Jesse Unruh, Speaker of the California legislative assembly, by the John Kraft organization; that poll indicated that in a California primary Kennedy might expect 46 per cent support against 21 per cent for Johnson and 13 per cent for McCarthy. The findings, revealed on March 2, helped persuade Kennedy to declare his candidacy on March 16.[31]

Hints about the images of candidates constitute a second type of information gained from precampaign polls. A reliable poll can tell party leaders what type of person makes the best candidate in a particular constituency. Some pollsters specialize in providing this information. Don Muchmore, of Opinion Research of California, and John Bucci of Pennsylvania, for example, conduct "preselection" polls in nonelection years far in advance of campaigns to discover a party's strongest nominee. Once a candidate has decided to run, polls are especially helpful in informing managers what the public considers as his good and bad points. The congressional campaign in the Seventh Congressional District of Texas in 1966 is an example. The area in Houston, Texas had traditionally sent Democrats to Congress, but the specific district was newly created containing Republicans and conservative Democrats. A Republican businessman, George Bush, challenged Democrat Frank Briscoe, the county's well-known district attorney. Pollster John Kraft conducted precampaign polls for Bush that revealed the Republican was not well-known among voters, was not regarded as "warm" or "sincere," had little support among Negroes, and trailed Briscoe badly in overall popularity; voters regarded Briscoe as an effective district attorney, but cold and aloof. The pollster recommended that Bush become better known, appear moderate enough to receive Negro votes, and endeavor to project warmth and dynamism. This produced a theme, "Vote for

[31] The impact of opinion polls on the strategies of the early leading contenders for the Democratic presidential nomination in 1968 is discussed in Norman C. Miller, "Opinion Surveys Play an Ever Widening Role in Political Campaigns," *Wall Street Journal*, March 8, 1968, p. 1; Jules Witcover, *85 Days: The Last Campaign of Robert F. Kennedy* (New York: G. P. Putnam's Sons, 1969); David Halberstam, *The Unfinished Odyssey of Robert Kennedy* (New York: Random House, Inc., 1969).

Bush and Watch the Action," designed to build name recognition and a new image. On billboards Bush was pictured peering intently into the future, jacket slung over his shoulder, eager to serve. His television spots combined action with warmth; again pictured with jacket over his shoulder, Bush paced briskly on a sidewalk in a middle-class suburb, encountered a covey of small children, one of which he swept into his arms. By comparison Briscoe's campaign appeared stilted and as cool as the polls suggested voters viewed him. The "activity plus warmth" campaign aided a Republican victory.

Precampaign polls also reveal the issue and ideological orientations of voters, permitting candidates to plan their campaigns accordingly. Again we turn to Texas for an example, the senatorial race in 1966. Republican incumbent John Tower employed the services of the John F. Kraft polling organization. The first poll was conducted in the summer of 1965, sixteen months prior to the election, when the Democrats as yet had no candidate (the Democratic primary was not scheduled until May, 1966). The poll estimated Tower's chances against three possible challengers—Governor John Connally ("not a very hopeful situation" for Tower), Congressman James Wright ("unknown to the voters of Texas"), and Attorney General Waggoner Carr ("shows enough strength to make the assessments realistic"). (Tower's opponent in 1966 was Carr.) The precampaign poll revealed that Tower was well-known, but controversial because of his conservative ideology, his pro-Goldwater position in 1964, and various issue stands. On ideological matters the poll revealed that Texans classified themselves as one-third conservative, one-third moderate, one-tenth liberal, and the remainder "not sure." The recommendation, therefore, was for Tower to moderate his stands, take over the middle-of-the-road, and force any opponent to the left. Older Texans worried about welfare; Tower had voted against the Medicare bill providing medical aid to the elderly through Social Security and explained that he was for a better solution to the elderly's medical problems than Medicare. The poll revealed that race should not be made an issue for any stand would offend more voters than it could please. For these and other issues Tower was provided with Texans' views, advised to be moderate, and always to appear to understand the problems. In the course of the campaign he did emerge as the "moderate" candidate to the extent that he not only held his basic conservative Republican support, but also won votes from sizable numbers of Texas liberal Democrats. He was the victor in an election that Texas politicians said, after the debacle of 1964, no Republican could win.

Finally, precampaign polls indicate not only popular opinions on issues, but reveal what groups hold those opinions. On the basis of Kraft's 1965 poll in Texas, Senator Tower was urged to appeal to women by emphasizing issues of education and living costs, to appeal to middle-income groups by adding job security as an issue, to retain his support of upper-income groups by emphasizing "government interference" and taxation issues, and not to arouse labor unions by discussing "right to work" issues. In 1961 Edward Kennedy's polls revealed his strength among Irish and Italo-Americans, the upper middle class, and those of low income, the less-educated, and women; but they revealed a lack of support among suburban Democrats, Jews, the well-educated, civil libertarians, and academicians—all of whom were worried about his youth and inexperience. Thus as we noted in the last chapter, his managers contrived a campaign to demonstrate his knowledge and experience in managing political affairs.[32]

Campaign polls. The precampaign polls provide confidential intelligence that is useful in planning strategic appeals on the basis of style, issues, ideology, and group interests. As the campaign progresses polls measure the impact of these strategies and suggest areas where adjustments are in order. Two types of polls are conducted during the campaign. The first consists of a series of three or four "one-shot" surveys in which each poll interviews a different sample of voters. A "panel" survey, on the other hand, involves interviewing a single sample of voters at three or four separate times during the campaign.

We can obtain some idea of the uses of these campaign polls by noting specific examples. When he decided to seek the Republican nomination for president in 1968, George Romney entered the New Hampshire primary. During that campaign his private pollster, Fred Currier of Market Opinion Research, conducted surveys in the state. Each confirmed a sad fact that Romney was running far behind Richard Nixon. Romney withdrew from the contest a week before the election. Thus just as precampaign polls may dictate whether a candidate runs or not, a campaign poll can determine whether he stays in the race.

[32] Murray B. Levin, *Kennedy Campaigning* (Boston: Beacon Press, 1966), pp. 150–51.

Candidates also adjust their strategies on the basis of campaign surveys. In 1966, for example, Representative Henry Helstoski (a New Jersey Democrat) opened his campaign by asserting that bombing of North Vietnam should be halted. His pollster, Joseph Napolitan, discovered that 70 per cent of Helstoski's constituents opposed the candidate's view. Helstoski stopped speaking on the issue and ultimately won a narrow victory.

Senator John Tower in 1966 discovered from campaign polls that his precampaign strategy was effective. His appeal to key groups was paying off. In the precampaign poll 30 per cent of women said they would vote for Tower over Waggoner Carr, but by October of the election year 45 per cent of women favored Tower; similarly, a panel survey indicated that Tower picked up support from Negroes, Mexican-Americans, older voters, and both middle- and lower-income groups. Hence Tower made no adjustments in his approach to issues or groups because of what was revealed in the polls. He did, however, mobilize voters on election day because of suggestions in the polls that he could win only with a maximum turnout.

An extensive study of the use of polls in Senator Edward W. Brooke's successful 1966 campaign in Massachusetts suggests that the first election by popular vote of a Negro to the U.S. Senate is partly attributable to strategic adjustments suggested by opinion surveys. Brooke's managers hired the Opinion Research Corporation to conduct seven statewide surveys. These included precampaign polls in 1965 and mid-1966, a three-wave panel survey during the campaign, and a last-minute telephone survey. Studies in September, 1965, revealed a 67 to 21 per cent lead (the remainder were undecided) for Brooke over his opponent, former Democratic Governor Endicott Peabody. In May, 1966 that lead held at 66 to 23, but fell to 59 to 29 in August and 50 to 37 in September. The surveys attributed the decline in Brooke's popularity to the racial issue. Brooke had taken no strong stand throughout the time when there were racial conflicts in America's big cities, the "Black Power" movement was being advanced, and there was much publicized talk of racial strife. Among voters classified as "least prejudiced" Brooke's silence did not seem to hurt him, but among "most prejudiced" and "less prejudiced" voters his support dropped sharply. In October Brooke spoke on the racial issue in all televised appearances. He stood against violence as a means of gaining civil rights, against the Black Power movement, and against white racists. He took a moderate position between extremes. By mid-October the decline of support among "most prejudiced" groups ended and was reversed among the "less prejudiced." Brooke's popularity climbed to a 57 to 31 ratio; he defeated Peabody by a 61 to 39 per cent margin.[33]

Postelection polls. The polls most frequently used by candidates are conducted during the campaign; precampaign polls are used less often. Even more rare is the postelection poll. Losers seldom have much enthusiasm for discovering their mistakes, winners feel no necessity for proving they were the "better" candidates to begin with, and neither losers nor winners have sufficient funds to employ pollsters to evaluate their efforts. Yet postelection surveys are becoming crucial tools in American politics as politicians realize that any campaign really begins the day following the preceding election.

In 1964 the Opinion Research Corporation conducted a postelection survey on behalf of the Goldwater campaign organization. The survey was part of a broader panel study that began with a "base" study following the Republican National Convention in July. Subsequent interviews were held with the same panel throughout the campaign with a postelection interview terminating the study. The series revealed that although Goldwater became better known through the campaign (72 per cent of respondents knew something about him after the election where only 51 per cent had knowledge of him in July) and his favorable qualities became more salient to voters, he was unable to change many votes through his personality, issue stands, or television appearances. The fact that he became better known to the panel of respondents is itself not too indicative of a successful campaign since the reinterviewing procedure itself acquainted sampled voters with the candidate.[34]

Following the 1968 elections the Republican party contracted for several postelection surveys in selected "marginal" congressional districts in which the party candidate had lost to the Democrat by less than 5 per cent of the popular vote. The purpose was to determine the reasons for the Republican loss and provide recommendations for

[33] John F. Becker and Eugene E. Heaton, Jr., "The Election of Senator Edward W. Brooke," *Public Opinion Quarterly*, XXXI (Fall, 1967), 346–58.

[34] Thomas W. Benham, "Polling for a Presidential Candidate: Some Observations on the 1964 Campaign," *Public Opinion Quarterly*, XXIX (Summer, 1965), 185–99.

getting a head start on winning those seats in 1970. Private polling firms in the Midwest like Central Surveys and Civic Service conducted studies in selected districts. A typical survey revealed that the Republican candidate had offended voters by "mudslinging," had been unimpressive on television, had appeared too "homey," and had failed to identify either with the Republican presidential or senatorial candidate (both had carried the state). The pollsters advised that a candidate for 1970 be groomed early and be introduced to voters gradually rather than suddenly; that periodic research on issues and on the incumbent should begin immediately (there were rumors of personal problems in the incumbent's family); and that a front committee (Citizens for Better Government) should carry the attack to the incumbent so as not to taint the Republican candidate. Such postelection surveys were supported from an $8 million fund set aside by Republicans for the 1970 congressional elections. That fund is made possible by $10 and $25 sustaining memberships in the party. In 1969 the Democrats, having never before relied on such fund-raising schemes, announced a similar program to pay for surveys to be conducted on behalf of party candidates.

The Art and Science of Political Polling

To serve as a reliable basis for planning and executing campaign strategy a professionally conducted poll must provide an accurate reflection of constituency opinions. In the brief history of the polling industry, the procedures of opinion-surveying have been refined until its most cautious practitioners describe polling as an art and the most confident researchers label it a science. To possess a full grasp of the strengths and limitations of the product client-candidates purchase at such a high price, we need to examine these procedures.

The sample. The first step in a properly conducted political survey is to select a group of individuals for interviewing whose opinions accurately reflect those of all adults of voting age in a given constituency. The sample need not be large, but it must be representative.

The average citizen who is only casually acquainted with political polling is reluctant to accept the notion that pollsters can derive an accurate approximation of what an electorate thinks by talking to 1,500 adults (frequently the maximum size sample used by private firms). Yet pollsters do precisely this. Governor George Romney withdrew from the New Hampshire presidential primary after his pollsters delivered pessimistic forecasts based upon surveys from 700–800 potential voters. Certainly there are possibilities of inaccuracies in small samples. But the refinement of polling procedures is such that, if the sample is properly drawn, it is possible to reduce the range of sampling errors so that in ninety-nine cases out of a hundred the results of a survey of 1,000 properly selected adults will be within 4 per cent of accuracy. For example, let us assume that in a nationwide survey of 1,000 adults 40 per cent of respondents say they approve of the way the president is handling his job. The chances are ninety-nine out of a hundred that somewhere between 36 and 44 per cent of American adults hold this opinion. If our sample size had been 4,000, our range of error would have been 2 per cent, permitting us to estimate that 38–42 percent so evaluate the president's performance. Had our sample consisted of 17,000 adults, the error range would be 1 per cent. But there is a point at which it ceases to be profitable to reduce sampling error by increasing sample size. Sample precision increases with the square root of the number of persons interviewed; to cut sample error in half, the size of the sample must be increased four times, or the square of the error. At a minimum cost of $10 per interview, a 1 per cent error range would be a $170,000 luxury; at those prices both pollster and client are willing to tolerate a 4 per cent error in a survey costing $10,000. Another important point is that the size of the population under survey has little bearing on the size of the sample required for a given degree of precision. If we seek a 5 per cent error, we are wise to use a sample of 700 respondents whether we are trying to represent the opinions of 200 million Americans or 650,000 North Dakotans. The general rule is "the size of the population has little bearing on sample size whenever the sample size is less than 5 per cent of the population." [35]

Although *"no major poll in the history of this country ever went wrong because too few persons were reached,"* [36] many have gone wrong because of the way those persons were selected. Political pollsters employ two principal sampling procedures—probability and

---

[35] On problems of sample size, consult Charles H. Backstrom and Gerald D. Hursh, *Survey Research* (Evanston, Ill.: Northwestern University Press, 1963), pp. 28–33.

[36] George Gallup and Saul Forbes Rae, *The Pulse of Democracy* (New York: Simon and Schuster, Inc., 1940), p. 68. Italics in original.

nonprobability sampling. A probability sample is not designed to select people to be interviewed on the basis of their individual characteristics, but instead gives every person an equal chance to be selected, thus ensuring that every segment of the population will be proportionately represented. The ideal technique would be to list every adult of voting age in the constituency, then draw the necessary number of names of interviewees at random. Two conditions make this unfeasible: comprehensive and up-to-date lists of voting age adults are impossible to obtain; and to assure accuracy, once names were selected interviewers would have to traipse all over the constituency in search of the selected respondents, a considerable chore if the aim is to find 1,500 individuals in the whole of the United States, or even in Arkansas. Pollsters have adjusted to these limitations and devised a modified random sampling technique referred to as "cluster" or "pinpoint" sampling. Instead of selecting individuals at random, geographical areas of a constituency—counties, precincts, city blocks, or housing units—are chosen at random in a series of steps (first a requisite number of counties is selected, then precincts within those counties, then city blocks and rural areas, and finally households). Since lists of areas are easier to compile than lists of voters and since interviewers are directed to specific areas to select respondents, the major limitations of random sampling are avoided. The added convenience carries a cost, however, for in order to achieve a given level of tolerable sampling error, the number of individuals interviewed should normally be half again as large as necessary had the sample been selected by simple random procedures.[37] If a simple random sample of 1,000 respondents could be expected to yield an error range of 4 per cent, 1,500 persons should be included in a cluster sample to assure that the range is no larger. Interviewers, under specific instructions, select the individual to be questioned. For example, if there are two adults living in the housing unit, one of whom is a male, the interviewer may be instructed to question only the woman; if there are four or more adults, two males, instructions may read to interview the youngest woman. These instructions are designed to assure that random procedures are maintained at each level of sample selection as far as possible; otherwise the interviewer might select the first person who came to the door, increasing the likelihood that women, for example, would

[37] Backstrom and Hursh, *Survey Research*, p. 32.

be overrepresented in the sample since they tend to be home frequently during the day.

Nonprobability samples, of which the quota sample is the most common, select people on the basis of specific characteristics or even convenience. One crude method is to decide what characteristics should be represented, then assign interviewers the task of finding people with those characteristics. If, for example, 12 per cent of the population is Irish, then 120 of 1,000 sampled should be Irish; each interviewer is assigned a quota and instructed to find such respondents. With nonprobability procedures ordinary tests of statistical accuracy are not applicable. The selection of the sample depends not on chance but on the interviewer; the procedures are less random than haphazard. Since it is impossible to estimate the degree of sampling bias, a candidate should be reluctant to place much confidence in a quota survey. Although most pollsters have abandoned nonprobability sampling (it was one factor leading pollsters to predict Thomas E. Dewey's election over Harry S. Truman as president in 1948), there are still several private consultants using modified quota methods. Some, for example, select shopping centers as places for conducting interviews (each center being chosen to represent a particular neighborhood's income, ethnic, educational, and other relevant characteristics) and question passersby. Others mail out questionnaires to citizens' homes and residences and analyze the completed and returned responses (thus overrepresenting those highly motivated and educated citizens who are most likely to return their answers). A frequently used approach is to conduct telephone interviews (thus taking the chance of biasing responses since telephone service—despite what A. T. & T. argues—is still far from universal and since some persons will say things over the telephone they will not say face-to-face). Therefore, although nonprobability samples have largely been discredited, many private pollsters continue to use them because they are less expensive, can be generated at a moment's notice, and may be useful in limited situations.[38]

The questionnaire. In spite of efforts to minimize errors through

[38] On cluster and quota sampling procedures consult Leonard W. Doob, *Public Opinion and Propaganda* (New York: Holt, Rinehart and Winston, Inc., 1948), pp. 100–103; Morris H. Hansen and Philip M. Hauser, "Area Sampling: Some Principles of Sample Design," *Public Opinion Quarterly*, IX (Summer, 1945), 183–93; Clarence Schettler, *Public Opinion in American Society* (New York: Harper & Row, Publishers, 1960), pp. 472–74.

careful sampling techniques, an opinion survey can still produce invalid data unless the correct questions are asked. A question put to an interviewee is a stimulus to which he responds. Irrelevant stimuli are likely to produce irrelevant responses. Just as they have endeavored to refine their sampling procedures to reduce sampling errors, so pollsters have attempted to refine their questionnaires to reduce irrelevant, inaccurate, and invalid responses. As a result, a sophisticated questionnaire usually contains the following sorts of questions.[39]

A questionnaire seeks certain "cover sheet" or *validation* data. Questions appear on the cover of the interview booklet pertaining to area of residence, age, sex, race, and other social data about the respondent, which provide a check on the sample. If the pollster finds he has too many women, too many elderly, too many elderly women, or other respondent types in comparison to the constituency's sociodemographic composition, he will interpret his findings accordingly.

There are also *filter* questions designed to reveal if the respondent has given any thought to the election, its candidates, and issues. For example, "Have you read or heard anything about this year's city elections?" The purpose of these questions is to check the respondent's awareness of politics, thus providing a clue as to the relevance of his responses to more substantive questions at later points.

Information questions are introduced. An affirmative answer to a filter question does not prove that the interviewee actually knows much about the elections at hand. Hence he may be asked a two-part question to determine how much he really knows about the campaign: "Do you happen to know the names of the candidates in the mayor's race?" and, if he supplies them, "What do you think some of the major issues are between these candidates?"

Information questions lead easily into *open-ended* questions which give the respondent the opportunity to express himself freely about the candidates, major problems, issues, and so forth. A typical question might be, "What do you think are the most important problems facing our city today?" Usually respondents consistently cite the same qualities, issues, or problems, facilitating the tabulation and interpretation of responses. But in precampaign polls the situation may be so ill-defined in the respondent's mind that such questions elicit rambling answers that are difficult to analyze.

[39] George Gallup, A *Guide to Public Opinion Polls* (Princeton, N. J.: Princeton University Press, 1944).

There are usually several *closed-end* questions that force the respondent to make a selection from certain specified alternatives. For example, "Do you usually think of yourself as a Republican, a Democrat, or what?" If the subject being investigated is complex, a sequence of increasingly specific questions may be required to obtain the desired data. If for example, the respondent describes himself as "Independent" it might be desirable to inquire, "As an Independent, which of the two major parties do you normally favor?"

Explanation questions of both open-end and closed-end varieties try to probe the reasons why the respondent wants to vote for John Doe, is a Democrat, or favors higher taxes to pay for city schools. The key word in these questions is "why."

Finally, *intensity* questions attempt to determine how strongly a person holds a particular opinion or feels about campaign subjects. Each pollster has a favored type of question for this purpose. Fred Currier of Market Opinion Research, for example, uses the semantic differential, a technique that asks respondents to rate candidates or policies on a nine-point scale according to abstract qualities: hot-cold, fast-slow, candid-evasive, handsome-ugly, and so forth. The result is a profile of the respondent's perceptions. Using this technique Currier discovered that Michigan voters in 1966 preferred a "moderate" for the U.S. Senate and advised the Republican candidate, Robert Griffin, to de-emphasize his conservatism, move to the center, and contrast himself with the favorite, liberal Democrat G. Mennen Williams. Griffin did and won. And, using the semantic differential for Richard Nixon in 1968, researcher John Maddox found that Americans perceived Nixon as lacking in personal warmth, a trait they deemed important in the ideal president. Nixon was not made warmer, but his managers closed the "personality gap" by designing television commercials making him appear so. Paul Keyes, a writer for the popular *Laugh-In*, was hired to give Nixon's presentations a "sense of humor." [40] Pollster Oliver Quayle uses a different technique; he asks respondents which political candidates they can most easily visualize watching selected television shows—"The Lawrence Welk Show" (programmed for older viewers), "Peyton Place" (a soap opera), and others. Roy Pfautch of Civic

---

[40] An account of the Griffin campaign can be found in Perry, *The New Politics*, pp. 84–99; the use of the semantic differential in the Nixon campaign is described in Joe McGinniss, *The Selling of the President 1968* (New York: Trident Press, 1969), pp. 79–81.

Service, Inc., hands respondents a chart with colored squares keyed to a "best-worst" scale and asks them to rate candidates. The variety in techniques is sometimes imaginative, sometimes of limited value, but geared to the peculiar interests of the pollster.

The overall questionnaire is a tightly drawn document containing a sequence of questions, logical transitions, specific questions, and interviewer instructions. Reputable firms refine their questionnaires over many campaigns, pretesting each innovation before using it for a client.[41]

The interview. An opinion survey is no more reliable than the interviewers. A pollster can centrally control the design of a sample, the construction of the questionnaire, and the framing of instructions to interviewers, but rarely can he control the interview itself. Although interviewing techniques can be taught in training sessions, good interviewing depends ultimately on each interrogator's ability to make a congenial initial contact, establish and maintain rapport, and create a mood that does not bias the respondent. In short, he must play the role of interviewer, forgetting his own views and prejudices. He must be able to phrase questions objectively, not encourage or discourage the respondent by his mannerisms, and probe in a delicate fashion.[42]

The interviewer must be persistent in order to overcome problems in the field. One is the task of finding the respondent at home. An average of 3–14 per cent of prospective respondents are not found at home in surveys.[43] The "not-at-homes" are especially numerous in large cities. Some pollsters employ callbacks to contact inaccessible respondents. Failure to interview them can mean a biased survey, since research indicates these "not-at-homes" differ in many respects from persons more easily contacted.[44] George Gallup, however, does not use callbacks, but instead weighs more heavily those found at home

[41] Eleanor E. Maccoby and Robert R. Hold, "How Surveys are 'Made'," *Journal of Social Issues,* II (May, 1946), 45–57.

[42] J. Allen Williams, Jr., "Interviewer Role Performance: A Further Note on Bias in the Information Interview," *Public Opinion Quarterly,* XXXII (Summer, 1968), 287–94.

[43] Frederick F. Stephan and Philip J. McCarthy, *Sampling Opinion* (New York: John Wiley & Sons, Inc., 1963); H. Lawrence Ross, "The Inaccessible Respondent: A Note on Privacy in City and Country," *Public Opinion Quarterly,* XXVII (Summer, 1963), 269–75.

[44] Ernest R. Hilgard and Stanley L. Payne, "Those Not At Home: Riddle for Pollsters," *Public Opinion Quarterly,* VIII (Summer, 1944), 254–61.

at a given time who report they are not ordinarily at home at that time. In the 1968 presidential election a September Gallup poll indicated Richard Nixon had the support of 44 per cent of interviewees; a Harris poll taken at the same period indicated 39 per cent favoring Nixon. Aside from the differences attributable to sampling error in these polls, inability to reach respondents contributed to the discrepancy. Encountering inaccessible respondents in Negro ghettos, Harris utilized callbacks and found many of these "not-at-homes" favorable to Hubert Humphrey; Gallup, not using callbacks, did not detect the same Humphrey support among ghetto dwellers until later.

People may simply refuse to be interviewed, even if at home. Gallup encounters around 8 per cent refusals; the Harris poll in 1968 failed to reach 10–15 per cent of its sampled people either because they were not at home or because they refused to be interviewed. The problem was especially troublesome among apartment dwellers in city areas in 1968. No satisfactory way has been discovered to deal with these refusals. Also bothersome is the reluctant interviewee: he agrees to the interview, then evades questions. One study discovered that 20 per cent of respondents found questions objectionable; of these 13 per cent refused to answer, but 5 per cent responded reluctantly, probably with less than valid expressions.[45] To adjust to reluctant respondents, pollsters have adopted the use of the secret ballot technique when asking people how they would vote in a particular contest. The respondent marks a ballot and places it in a box carried by the interviewer, thus avoiding a public declaration of preferences.

The interpretation. All the possible sources of error—in selecting the sample, in framing questions, in finding and interviewing respondents—pose problems in interpreting the final data. There are other considerations as well, principally what to do about nonvoters, undecideds, and meaningless views.

In any survey many potential voters will be interviewed who do not show up at the polls on election day. Yet campaign managers are interested only in how voters feel. The competent pollster, therefore, sifts out the nonvoting respondents. The principal technique is to incorporate filter questions into the interview concerning the respondent's political interest and previous participation in politics: Has he voted in recent elections? Has he followed the current campaign? Is

[45] Elizabeth H. Hartmann et al., "Public Reaction to Public Opinion Surveying," *Public Opinion Quarterly*, XXXII (Summer, 1968), 295–98.

he familiar with the candidates? Is he registered to vote? Does he know his polling place? Will he be in town on election day? Does he plan to vote? On the basis of responses, scales of participation can be constructed which rank interviewees by the likelihood of their voting, eliminating the least likely from the analysis.[46]

From 5 to 10 per cent of people sampled are usually undecided in their candidate preferences, views on issues, or perceptions of the campaign. An accurate appraisal of constituent's opinions must be adjusted to this indecision. According to Gallup, using closed-end questions and secret ballot techniques usually reduces the number of undecideds who have reached a decision but are reluctant to commit themselves from 15 to 4 per cent. A second approach is to infer the commitments of undecided respondents from their answers to other questions in the interview. Many pollsters argue that the party iden-tification of an American is so strong that it can be taken as an indi-cator of how undecideds will vote. Unfortunately many undecided voters claim no partisan preference. A third technique, usually risky, divides undecideds among the candidates in the same percentages ex-hibited by decided respondents. The risk lies in the fact that many undecideds have little political motivation or knowledge, are disinter-ested in the campaign and indifferent to the candidates, and make last-minute decisions on the basis of a candidate's style or a sensational issue. A disproportionate number of undecideds may vote for one can-didate, if they vote, rather than dividing as the decided do.

Another problem of interpretation stems from the pollsters' recog-nition that any opinion expressed in an interview is a response both to the question asked (the stimulus object) and to the situation (the interview, the campaign, and the entire political environment). A respondent may have been influenced prior to the interview by a con-versation with a friend and be reacting to that rather than to the choices posed by the interviewer. Asked the same questions a day later, he may have "changed his mind." But what has happened is that on one day he expresses an attitude toward a situation (his rela-tions with a friend) and the following day toward an object within that situation (the interviewer's question).[47] Moreover, if a man has

[46] Robert P. Knight, "Polls, Sampling and the Voter," *Freedom of Information Center Publication* No. 168 (Columbia, Mo.: School of Journalism, University of Missouri, September, 1966), p. 11.

[47] Milton Rokeach, "Attitude Change and Behavioral Change," *Public Opinion Quarterly*, XXX (Winter, 1966–67), 529–50.

not thought about a campaign, the interview may force an unreliable opinion. The interview is a contrived situation in which the respondent plays an unfamiliar role. He expresses a single opinion when, in fact, he may have a variety. Since he has no responsibility for acting on his opinion, the respondent's expression may be considerably less meaningful than a vote cast on election day.[48] Yet it is on the basis of such potentially meaningless expressions that campaigners risk their futures when using poll data to support their decisions.

Because of the difficulties in interpreting survey data, some managers use polls as guides to the images their candidates should present rather than as indicators of what voters think about issues. Professional campaigners, both managers and polling consultants, reason that voters have a vague idea of the qualities they want in a president, governor, mayor, legislator, or other official. But it is unreasonable to expect voters to express informed opinions on issues. And while voters may have abstract concerns about what is right and wrong in government, they should not be asked to suggest specific solutions. John Volpe's managers in the 1960 Massachusetts gubernatorial election knew from polls that voters did not want a stereotyped Massachusetts politician as governor—loud, aggressive, and slick. They advised Volpe to be a soft-spoken, relaxed candidate. With style being more important than content to alienated voters (see Chapter 2), Volpe's pollsters suggested a winning style.[49]

Opinions about candidates in one context can differ sharply from those expressed in another. In 1968 Nelson Rockefeller entered the campaign for the Republican presidential nomination too late to run in party primaries. He hoped to prove, however, that he and not Richard Nixon would be the stronger candidate against any Democrat, thus detracting from Nixon's primary victories. As subsequent polls appeared, Rockefeller emerged the stronger candidate in each "trial heat" against possible Democratic contenders. Then, on July 21, a Gallup poll publicized a marked reversal: Nixon led Hubert Humphrey 40 to 38 and Eugene McCarthy 41 to 36. Rockefeller was even with Humphrey, 36 to 36, and led McCarthy only 36 to 35. Although a Harris poll two days later showed Rockefeller ahead of both Democrats 40 to 34 and Nixon trailing both, the damage had been done.

---

[48] Leo Bogart, "No Opinion, Don't Know, and Maybe No Answer," *Public Opinion Quarterly*, XXXI (Fall, 1967), 331–45.
[49] Levin, *The Compleat Politician*, pp. 202–3.

Coming on the eve of the Republican convention, the Gallup poll stunned Rockefeller. Why the difference in polls? Remembering the 4–5 per cent possible sampling error, the Rockefeller range against Humphrey in the Gallup poll was from 40 to 32 and in the Harris poll from 44 to 36. In both polls the Rockefeller percentages overlapped in the 40 to 36 range, suggesting that the polls did not in fact differ in their estimates of Rockefeller's strength. Even had a marked difference existed, the Harris poll was taken one week later than Gallup's. By the time of the Harris poll it seemed apparent that Nixon had a commanding lead in convention delegates. In short, the situation had changed; it is conceivable that some Rockefeller backers surveyed by Gallup responded to the changed situation by accepting Nixon as their likely candidate.

Astute campaign managers interpret opinion polls with an eye to the context within which the surveys were taken. In 1968 public polls in September gave Richard Nixon a substantial margin over Hubert Humphrey. One of Humphrey's campaign technicians, Joseph Napolitan, believed that the polls revealed Humphrey's lack of media exposure rather than a greater popular preference for Nixon. But Napolitan could raise no money for a media campaign since potential contributors, reading the published polls, gave Humphrey no chance for victory. There is, thus, a vicious cycle in modern campaign techniques: media exposure affects poll results, poll results affect fund-raising, fund-raising affects media exposure. Only in mid-October did Napolitan break the cycle and raise funds for his media campaign which superficially seemed to give Humphrey a boost in the polls.[50]

Computer Simulation as a Technique in Campaign Research

In 1960 political researchers combined survey and computer technology in a successful simulation of the presidential election. The project was undertaken by The Simulmatics Corporation, a group of social scientists and politically oriented businessmen under the sponsorship of the Democratic party.[51]

---

[50] White, *The Making of the President 1968*, pp. 396–97.

[51] The project is described in detail in Ithiel de Sola Pool, Robert P. Abelson, and Samuel Popkin, *Candidates, Issues and Strategies* (Cambridge, Mass.: The M.I.T. Press, 1964).

A computer simulation uses the memory and manipulative capacities of a computer to imitate the processes of a system; in this instance a computer was programmed to manipulate data about American voting behavior in order to predict how voters would behave. In order to conduct this simulation researchers required a problem, relevant data, and a notion of how voters reach decisions.

The basic problem was to predict if voters would select John F. Kennedy or Richard Nixon, a problem complicated by the fact that presidential elections are decided not by popular vote, but by electoral votes. Since a state's electoral votes go to the candidate winning a plurality of that state's popular votes, the simulation had to predict the popular division in each state (the continental 48 states were ultimately used). Since voters react to different stimuli during a campaign, an adequate simulation had to predict electoral outcome for each set of circumstances. Specifically The Simulmatics Corporation was asked to assess the outcome if Kennedy's Catholicism became an issue, if foreign policy was stressed, or if civil rights was important, for example.

The data for the simulation consisted of voters' responses to sixty-five national surveys in each presidential and congressional election year from 1952 through 1960. The Williamstown Public Opinion Research Center, an archive for surveys conducted by Elmo Roper and other pollsters, furnished the data. These polls accumulated data for more than 100,000 persons. Simulmatics researchers reduced this total to 480 "voter-types." Each type consisted of all voters possessing a particular set of socioeconomic characteristics. One voter type, for example, was composed of eastern voters, residing in metropolitan areas, white, of lower-income, Catholic, female Democrats. Another was rural southerners, upper-income, white, Protestant, male Independents. For each of 52 "issue clusters" (attitudes toward the United Nations, federal aid to education, the Democratic party, or the Republican party, for example) the number of each voter type that had been asked poll questions on the issue was computed as well as the percentage of that voter type pro, anti, and undecided on the issue. Since each of 48 states was simulated, an estimate of the proportion of each state's electorate in 1960 matching each of the 480 voter-types was made on the basis of census and other available data.

The notion (or model) of how voters reach decisions was borrowed from attitude-change theory in psychology, which holds that people endeavor to hold consistent attitudes toward related objects. If, for example, a Democrat has a friend and he discovers that friend is a Republican, the Democrat may relieve the inconsistency in his attitudes by becoming less intense as a Democrat, by thinking less highly of his friend, by misperceiving the situation by holding that his friend calls himself a Republican, but actually thinks like a Democrat, or by avoiding any discussion of politics in his friend's presence.

Applied to the simulation data on the issue of Kennedy's Catholicism, for instance, the reasoning went as follows: A Protestant Republican would experience no imbalance between his religious and political convictions; indeed, Kennedy's Catholicism might reinforce the Protestant Republican's decision to vote for Nixon. A Catholic Republican, however, would be torn between his partisan and religious inclinations. On the basis of examining previous voting studies, but still arbitrarily, researchers estimated that one-third of Catholic Republican voter-types who had voted Republican in the 1958 elections might resolve the imbalance by voting Democrat in 1960. Catholic Democrats and Independents would experience no imbalance, or cross-pressure; indeed, it was estimated that many who had crossed to support Republicans would come back to the Democratic column. The most cross-pressured type would be Protestant Democrats and Independents. The simulators estimated that anti-Catholic Democrats and Independents (as indicated by survey data) would vote for Nixon. The predicted behavior of each of these voter-types was adjusted to compensate for varying turnout. The simulation predicted an index of Kennedy strength for each state. A perfect correlation between that index and the Kennedy vote in the election would have been 1.00. If we compare the actual correlation (.82) with the correlation between what opinion polls predicted for each state and the Kennedy vote (.53), there is an indication of the effectiveness of the simulation.

The Simulmatics Corporation delivered several reports to the Democrats before the start of the active campaign in 1960. It is impossible to know how much impact these reports had on Kennedy's strategists. Kennedy may have decided to face the religious issue squarely, take a firm stand on civil rights, and stress foreign policy without the counsel of the Simulmatics reports. The personnel involved in the simulation suggest they helped "bolster by evidence one set of alternatives."

Since 1960 campaign simulation has gained new advocates as a tool

for providing accurate estimates for strategic decisions. The Simulmatics Corporation ran a simulation in 1964, but campaign decisions
were not based on it and in 1968 the Corporation was not active. The
Merrill/Wirthlin firm completed a simulation model for elections in
the Rocky Mountain area in 1968, but the partnership dissolved. The
possibilities of simulation of community referenda have also been ex-
plored.[52]

PROBLEMS IN PROFILING DEMOCRACY

Professional research consultants are indispensable to modern political
campaigns. Candidates now depend on reputable firms for precise
campaign intelligence. And since it has become a matter of status for
each campaign to have its research director and pollster-in-residence,
even firms that are not so reputable are assured of handsome profits
in election years. But reputable or not, professional researchers pose
problems in democratic campaigning that deserve our attention.

One set of problems has to do with the unpublicized limitations of
efforts to profile the mind of the electorate. Criticisms of polling often
focus on sizes of samples or the question, "How come no one has ever
asked for my opinions?" Yet there are other limitations. Polls, for example, have become important tools in prenomination campaigns,
with candidates entering or withdrawing on the basis of what the polls
suggest. Poll findings in primaries are particularly hard to interpret,
however, for a number of persons are disinterested in, and don't know
about, candidates in primaries. The environment surrounding a primary campaign is poorly defined. The voter is asked, "If the election
were held TODAY. . . ." But the election is not held until many to-
morrows and many situations hence. In primaries no partisan loyalties
serve as stable attitudes. The attitude-toward-object expressed TODAY
may be nothing more than an attitude-toward-situation differing
markedly from the attitudes toward that object (candidate) expressed
in a later campaign setting. "The answers one gets from a respondent
depend upon which of his many roles he is playing and which of his
many moods he is indulging at the precise moment the questions are
asked." [53] The candidate favored by a woman in her role as mother

[52] Robert P. Abelson and Alex Bernstein, "A Computer Simulation of Community Referendum Controversies," *Public Opinion Quarterly*, XXVII (Spring,
1963), 93–122.
[53] Reo M. Christenson and Robert O. McWilliams, *Voice of the People* (New
York: McGraw-Hill Book Company, 1967), p. 534.

chasing children from the room in January may not be the same as that favored by the same woman in her role of taxpayer in April, Californian in June, Baptist in September, or Democrat in November. To survey opinions is to describe the responses given under certain circumstances, but "it is to ignore or discount *possibilities* and the response to changed perspectives that political acts themselves might create it if the actors were less bemused by popularity polls." [54]

Another set of problems concerns the ethics of the polling industry. A private pollster describes, in confidence, how the electorate perceives a candidate under particular circumstances. But polls can be used as tools of propaganda as well as information; the art of pollsmanship parallels the art of polling. Granted that leaking polls is the exception rather than the rule (Louis Harris had only 11 of his five hundred and fourteen private polls revealed in six years),[55] the exceptions are always timed for maximum publicity purposes. To leak a confidential poll is to create a pseudo event (see Chapter 1), to create a news story about a candidate where otherwise none would appear. A major pollster in Texas, for example, was paid by a Republican to publicize his qualification by conducting a survey to determine which of two Republicans would run the better race against an incumbent Democratic senator. The client had entered several elections, won some, and was well known; the other Republican had only recently migrated to the state. Naturally, the better known candidate was mentioned by respondents as the proper opponent for the Democrat.

Too often a rival candidate produces his own confidential survey indicating that he leads. With widespread ignorance of such subtleties as sampling error, questionnaire construction, situationally-confined interviewing, and survey interpretation, the electorate becomes confused, bored, and not a little cynical. We are not merely repeating the "bandwagon" argument, that polls showing a candidate ahead incline voters to join in his support. The evidence on bandwagon effects is mixed and neither supports nor refutes the possibility.[56] We

[54] Murray Edelman, *The Symbolic Uses of Politics* (Urbana, Ill.: The University of Illinois Press, 1964), p. 119.

[55] Harris, "Polls and Politics in the United States," p. 7.

[56] See, for example, Bernard Berelson et al., *Voting* (Chicago: University of Chicago Press, 1954), Angus Campbell et al., *The American Voter* (New York: John Wiley & Sons, Inc., 1960); and George Gallup's lament that, "No amount of factual evidence seems to kill the bandwagon myth," in his "Polls and the Political Process," *Public Opinion Quarterly*, XXIX (Winter, 1965–66), 546.

are speaking of the long-term danger to confidence in democratic procedures that emerges from the overproduction of pseudo events.

There is another aspect to the confidence problem. Pollsters argue that they inform leaders of public sentiment; they deny that leaders slavishly pander to that sentiment: "No poll I have ever been witness to has made the candidate a different man, has changed his position on an issue, has made him into what he is not." [57] We have cited examples, however, that question the accuracy of this facile assurance. Was Edward Kennedy's projected illusion of experience an adequate substitute for the experience itself? How real was Robert Griffin's occupancy of the center against his more liberal opponent in Michigan in 1966? Is Senator John Tower the moderate he appeared in Texas in 1966? Was John Volpe's style a natural one in his Massachusetts election as governor in 1960, or a pose? Did Richard Nixon prove himself an honest politician in his "Checkers" speech in 1952, or merely a capable performer? Was Ronald Reagan well-read in California in 1966, or merely widely read? Was Nelson Rockefeller the popular choice for the 1968 Republican presidential nomination or the only alternative for anti-Nixon Republicans? The questions are endless and, contrary to the arguments of the research consultants, the answers are indefinite.

Opinion-polling is an industry without standards. Reputable pollsters periodically call for a code of ethics; a few even gather and announce joint agreements not to leak polls to the press, to make clear their margins of error and sample sizes to private and public clients, and so forth. But not all pollsters enter into these agreements and a few who do scarcely abide by them. So long as candidates remain ignorant of the purposes, procedures, and limitations of campaign surveys, a few members of the industry will continue to sell shoddy services. The standard will remain, "Let the Buyer Beware." Unless cheap, unreliable polling is to drive out the good, both client-candidates and the electorate must acquire functional literacy in this technique of mass persuasion.

[57] Harris, "Polls and Politics in the United States," p. 8.

4

CAMPAIGN COMMUNICATION: THE TACTICS OF MASS PERSUASION

One of America's most successful campaign management partnerships has likened the political campaign to a "war" for men's minds: "It starts with the battle plan. That is the strategy. Then there is the execution. That is the tactics." [1] Our discussion thus far has been concerned with the strategic considerations which involved professional managers and researchers as they plan, organize, finance, and probe. The payoff of their elaborate preparations to merchandise candidates comes in the campaign setting. Indeed the increasing influence of professional campaigners in American politics stems primarily from the politician's growing recognition that the key to a persuasive campaign lies as much in contriving the setting to his own advantage as in direct attempts to alter voters' choices. In this chapter we describe the techniques of that contrivance by examining the various media of campaign communication.

CAMPAIGN COMMUNICATORS AND AUDIENCES

In the competitive environment of an election candidates vie for public exposure. Each assumes that the more people attend to his messages, the greater his chances for victory. The candidate regards exposure as tantamount to influence; hence the campaign for exposure is as avidly waged as those for personnel, money, and information.

[1] Herbert M. Baus and William B. Ross, *Politics Battle Plan* (New York: The Macmillan Co., 1968), p. 115.

In modern political campaigns exposure is not easily won. Each candidate's appeal competes for the voter's attention with the exhortations of other candidates and with nonpolitical sources—product advertising, the day's news, documentaries, live coverage of men circling the moon, variety entertainment, each radio station's "Top Forty Tunes," and sundry other communications bombard the human senses. Stump speakers no longer monopolize public attention and enthrall rally crowds with golden-throated oratory. Changes in the content and character of mass communications and in the public's leisure-time habits make it more difficult for candidates to reach constituents. The task has become so technical that politicians recruit communications specialists to wage the exposure campaign; these specialists include public relations men, advertising executives, filmmakers, television producers, computer programmers, and marketing firms—the operators of the industrial complex commonly called the "mass media." [2]

Media specialists have been involved in political campaigns for decades but they became a significant force in American elections only in 1952. The advertising agency of Batten, Barton, Durstine and Osborn (BBDO) played a major role in Dwight Eisenhower's election to the presidency. It was BBDO, for example, who arranged and purchased the time for Richard Nixon's famous "Checkers" speech. During the campaigns of the 1950s media specialists executed the strategies of the candidate and his managers; they rarely planned an entire campaign with the struggle for exposure as a top priority. In the 1960 presidential contest elaborate preparations emerged to build a total campaign around the mass media, principally television. Carroll Newton, a former BBDO executive, argued that Richard Nixon should be "marketed" as a presidential candidate by creative television, relying on thorough research, testing of attitudes, and appropriate media techniques. But Nixon turned to more traditional communication techniques and failed to execute the elaborate media plan. Yet the idea of a creative media campaign remained. By 1964 "market" psychology prevailed: instead of thinking in terms of constituencies and voting districts, campaign managers oriented them-

[2] An excellent discussion of the rise of the public relations man in politics as a result of technological innovation in communications is Stanley Kelley, Jr., *Professional Public Relations and Political Power* (Baltimore: The Johns Hopkins Press, 1956).

selves to market areas of the United States; approximately 10,000 spot announcements were broadcast in the 1964 presidential contest to the nation's top seventy-five markets. In 1966 the Spencer-Roberts firm used television extensively to transform actor Ronald Reagan into a governor. The same year Jack Tinker & Partners, a New York advertising firm, prepared an elaborate and successful media campaign for Nelson Rockefeller. Two years later one advertising agency (Papert, Koenig, Lois) was prepared to place advertising costing $2 million during the Indiana, Oregon, California, and Nebraska primary campaigns in the ill-fated effort to make Robert Kennedy the Democratic nominee for president.[3]

So rapid has been the influx of media specialists into American elections that many specialists pride themselves that they, not the candidates, are the chief campaign communicators. Don A. Tabbert's nomination as the Republican candidate for Congress from his Indiana district in 1964 suggests that this lofty self-appraisal is not too exaggerated. A local advertising agency (never before involved in politics) used radio and television almost exclusively to saturate the electorate with Tabbert's appeals in the final two weeks of the campaign. Running against the candidate of the Republican organization and without backing of Indianapolis newspapers, Tabbert spent $18,-000 on television spots describing his career as U.S. attorney, on radio announcements (by a network voice, a heavy, folksy voice, a young voice, and a housewifish voice), and on 50,000 copies of a brief brochure. Tabbert's opponent relied on traditional media techniques and was defeated.[4]

The emphasis on the mass media illustrated by the Tabbert campaign results from a realistic assessment of how Americans learn about political events. In 1960, for example, the Survey Research Center of the University of Michigan gathered data from a nationwide panel on voting habits. They asked, "Would you say you found out about the campaign this year more by talking to other people, or from things like newspapers and television?" Of those responding more than 80 per cent named the mass media over interpersonal contacts.

[3] Max Marshall, "The Impact of Television on Politics," *Freedom of Information Center Report* No. 203 (Columbia, Mo.: School of Journalism, University of Missouri, July, 1968), p. 4.

[4] "Radio-TV Only Media Used by This Candidate," *Broadcasting*, June 15, 1964, p. 24.

Thus as the art of communication has become more complex because of expanding technology and as politicians have learned more about voter behavior, the media specialist has emerged as a key member of any candidate's entourage. His aim today is to work directly with the candidate and not through intermediate aides as was the case in the 1950s. As one such specialist puts it, "The specialist is, after all, putting words into the candidate's mouth that must sound natural." [5] Hence he must know the candidate well and specialist-client relations must be as close as the manager-candidate relations or pollster-candidate relations discussed previously.

The campaign communicators, then, are media specialists who work closely with and through the candidates. Who constitutes the audiences for these messages? To answer that question we must first note who uses and believes the various media; then, within these groups, we must identify the targets for persuasive communications.

Studies by communications scientists produce generalizations concerning what types of people use the various media. Surveys dating back to 1959 indicate that increasing proportions of Americans get most of their news from television rather than from radio, newspapers, or magazines; in 1959, for example, 51 per cent named television as their principal news source; the proportion rose steadily in each study and 64 per cent cited television in 1967.[6] Television is a "low effort" medium in the sense that relatively little thought or energy enters into its viewing. Although women watch television more frequently than do men, other sociodemographic characteristics do not distinguish viewers from nonviewers. So large is the viewing audience that exposure cuts across such sectors of the population as age groups, educational levels, economic strata, and races. The American television news audience is a representative microcosm of the total population. In 1967, for example, 28.5 per cent of American adult males had an eighth grade education or less and 30.7 per cent of adult male television viewers of network news programs had that educational background; 43.9 per cent of adult men and 43.7 per cent of adult men viewers of television news had gone to high school; 27.7 per cent of adult men and 25.6 per cent of adult male viewers of network news

[5] Gene Wyckoff, The Image Candidates (New York: The Macmillan Company, 1968), p. 39.

[6] Elmo Roper and Associates, "The Public's View of Television and Other Media: 1959–1964, 1967," Television Information Office.

coverage had attended college. The same close parallel between television viewers and the American public as a whole holds true for other sociodemographic characteristics.[7] Differences that do emerge are small: television viewing is highest among persons with only a high school education, with an annual income of $4–5000, and among the ghettos of black and impoverished America.[8]

Radio is less frequently used for either news or entertainment than is television by women and younger Americans who comprise a large portion of the listening audience. The printed media—newspapers and magazines—are "high effort" media compared to television and radio. The contrast is so sharp that only a small proportion of heavy readers of newspapers and magazines are part of regular television news audiences. Studies reveal that level of education is positively correlated with the use of the printed media. This stems in part from the fact that the skills necessary to newspaper and magazine readership come through education. Moreover, greater education, particularly at the college level, prepares citizens for roles which afford more opportunities for exposure to the printed media; both newspapers and magazines are more likely to have job-connected information for the business and professional man than for the craftsman or laborer.[9]

Although these generalizations about exposure patterns are derived from studies of how Americans obtain news about the world, they also apply to the ways Americans pay attention to political campaigns. Table 4-1 presents data on the sources most used by Americans to learn about the presidential campaigns of 1952–64. Note that television is a major source of campaign information, either alone or in combination with other media.

Not only do Americans rely heavily on the televised media for news, they are more likely to believe what they see than what they read in newspapers. In recent surveys almost half of persons interviewed list television as the "most believable" medium as opposed to less than a

[7] From data of the Brand Rating Index reported in Robert MacNeil, *The People Machine* (New York: Harper & Row, Publishers, 1968), pp. 3–4.

[8] Bradley S. Greenberg and Hideya Kumata, "National Sample Predictors of Mass Media Use," *Journalism Quarterly*, XLV (Winter, 1968), 641–46, 705; Thomas H. Allen, "Mass Media Use Patterns in a Negro Ghetto," *Journalism Quarterly*, XLV (Autumn, 1968), 525–31.

[9] Merrill Samuelson, Richard F. Carter, and Lee Ruggels, "Education, Available Time, and Use of Mass Media," *Journalism Quarterly*, XL (Autumn, 1963), 491–96; Bruce H. Westley and Werner J. Severin, "A Profile of the Daily Newspaper Non-Reader," *Journalism Quarterly*, XLI (Winter, 1964), 45–50, 156.

TABLE 4-1

Media Exposure to Political Campaigns in Presidential Election Years, (percentage distribution)

MEDIA	1952	1956	1960	1964
Read newspaper articles about the election				
Minimum to regularly	79.0%	68.6%	79.5%	78.4%
None	21.0	31.4	20.5	21.6
	(N = 1,707)	(N = 1,760)	(N = 1,780)	(N = 1,437)
Listened to speeches or discussions on Radio				
Minimum to regularly	69.7%	45.4%	41.9%	47.9%
None	30.3	54.6	58.1	52.1
	(N = 1,703)	(N = 1,758)	(N = 1,814)	(N = 1,441)
Read about the campaign in Magazines				
Minimum to regularly	40.2%	31.1%	40.8%	39.0%
None	59.8	68.9	59.2	61.0
	(N = 1,703)	(N = 1,751)	(N = 1,808)	(N = 1,438)
Watched programs about the campaign on television				
Minimum to regularly	51.3%	73.8%	86.6%	89.1%
None	48.7	26.2	13.4	10.9
	(N = 1,654)	(N = 1,758)	(N = 1,818)	(N = 1,446)
Source of most campaign information:				
Newspapers	22.9%	24.3%	22.3%	24.5%
Radio	28.1	10.6	5.3	3.7
Television	31.9	49.4	60.9	57.8
Magazines	5.2	4.6	4.3	6.9
Newspapers and radio	2.2	.6	.1	.2
Newspapers and TV	1.0	1.2	1.7	1.8
Radio and TV	1.2	.2	.2	.4
Magazines and one other	.9	.2	.5	1.1
Any other combination	.2	.5	.2	.4
Did not follow campaign	6.4	8.4	4.5	3.2

Source: From data of the Survey Research Center, University of Michigan. Provided through the facilities of the Inter-University Consortium for Political Research.

third who list newspapers; generally only about one in ten Americans credits either radio or magazines with being "most believable." [10] Moreover, these same studies reveal that Americans think television is less biased, more colorful, and more complete than newspapers or radio. Certain sociodemographic factors are correlated with the degree of credibility Americans see in the various media. Larger proportions of women than men believe a television news report more than they do their newspaper. In sample surveys less educated persons are more likely to believe a television news story over a newspaper version. Younger persons accept television versions as believable; older respondents prefer newspaper accounts.[11] Persons especially trusting of television include females of relatively low education and income, associated with "working-class" status, perhaps on the farm, largely indifferent to politics, and without partisan identification. Those assigning high credibility to newspapers are generally men with at least some college, residing in an urban area, professional or in a reasonably high-status occupation, participants in organized groups, and of weak partisan identification. Finally, farmers are inclined to place high credibility on radio as an information source.[12]

These, then, are the types of persons that attend to and believe the principal media. Knowing patterns of exposure helps the media specialist identify his campaign audience. That audience falls basically into two groups. The first consists of persons using and believing the printed media. The likelihood is that these citizens use multiple media, that they attend to television as well as to newspapers and magazines. These are probably members of special interest groups, concerned and informed about issues, and possessing moderate to strong loyalties to one of the two major political parties. On election day these media types vote in large proportions and probably for a candidate they decided upon early in the campaign. For these reasons the appeals aimed at persons in this group are designed to reinforce their existing commitments, not to convert them.

[10] Harvey K. Jacobson, "Mass Media Believability: A Study of Receiver Judgments," Journalism Quarterly, XLVI (Spring, 1969), 20–28; Richard F. Carter and Bradley S. Greenberg, "Newspapers or Television: Which Do You Believe?," Journalism Quarterly, XLII (Winter, 1965), 29–34.

[11] Bradley S. Greenberg, "Media Use and Believability: Some Multiple Correlates," Journalism Quarterly, XLIII (Winter, 1966), 665–70, 732.

[12] Bruce H. Westley and Werner J. Severin, "Some Correlates of Media Credibility," Journalism Quarterly, XLI (Summer, 1964), 325–35.

It is the second, increasingly growing, group that occupies the attention of professional media men. This audience relies on the electronic media for information about the world—principally television, sometimes radio. The mass media campaign is not directed to the informed voter but to the eyes and the ears of the voter who does not care very much.[13] This voter is a member of a vast audience built primarily by commercial television and radio for purposes of marketing products. As noted above, that audience includes Americans of all sociodemographic backgrounds. But within it are large numbers of persons who usually isolate themselves from all other media—citizens of low to moderate income, with high school educations, little interest in politics, more experience in evaluating television, film, and recording personalities than in deciding ambiguous public issues. Many, but not all, possess the characteristics ascribed to the alienated voter in Chapter 2.[14] The audience of the electronic media is the target of the media campaign. This is the audience to which Richard Nixon played when he opened his presidential campaign in September of 1968 by purchasing sixty-second spots on *Rowan and Martin's Laugh-In, Monday Night at the Movies, The Outsider, Wild Wild West,* and the daytime soap opera, *Edge of Night.* It is a target audience described by one television specialist as "moderately more sophisticated and somewhat better informed than that of a generation ago" but "passive and incurious about the world"—one, in sum, that "because it is not particularly interested in many subjects and issues, . . . will apparently accept what it is told about them more or less trustingly." [15] Let us examine the channels campaign communicators use to reach their target audiences.

CHANNELS OF CAMPAIGN COMMUNICATION

The media used by political campaigners ranges from the most tacky of signs erected in a neighbor's yard to slick television commercials that sell by understatement. We shall look at five categories of communication channels employed in American campaigns—personal ap-

---

[13] MacNeil, *The People Machine*, pp. 198, 222.
[14] Jack McLeod, Scott Ward, and Karen Tancill, "Alienation and Uses of the Mass Media," *Public Opinion Quarterly*, XXIX (Winter, 1965–66), 583–94; Leslie W. Sargent and Guido H. Stempel III, "Poverty, Alienation and Media Use," *Journalism Quarterly*, XLV (Summer, 1968), 324–26.
[15] MacNeil, *The People Machine*, p. 17.

pearances, the campaign organization, displays, the printed media, the auditory media, and television. The professional campaigner's selection of a particular media, or combination of media, to carry the candidate's appeal depends on the audience sought and the purpose of the message. If, for example, the target audience consists of the uninformed, uninterested, and independent voters, television plays a prominent role. For such targets the mass media are helpful in promoting name recognition (making a candidate known to large numbers of people), projecting an appealing image, or turning out voters on election day. Some aspects of campaign communication, however, are directed not at the mass but at differentiated groups with special concerns in hopes of getting endorsements, financial support, and votes. Direct mailings, door-to-door canvassing, newspaper advertising, and regional television are adaptable to these more selective appeals. As needed, they can provide special literature for medical doctors or a taped radio program for farmers. Selective media differ from the mass media as a rifle might differ from a shotgun. Finally, the candidate has the audience of his own supporters, volunteers, and workers. Constant attention must be paid to lifting their sagging morale. Much of the typical paraphernalia of campaigns—billboards, yard signs, bumper stickers, buttons, and so forth—are designed more to counter the lethargy of the committed than to influence undecided voters.

PERSONAL MEDIA

Even in the age of television public appearances by a politician carry his message to voters. A candidate for a lower-level office (legislative seat, city council, or school board, for example) frequently builds his entire campaign around relatively inexpensive appearances; candidates in congressional and statewide districts take pains to assure that their public presentations mesh well with sophisticated media techniques.

The candidate's appearances take various forms. The prepared speech repeated endlessly is perhaps the most common. Campaign mythology says that the purpose behind these formal presentations is to enable the candidate to "speak out on the issues." But, the speeches are not designed to change people's minds or even to give an in-depth view of the candidate's position. The function of discussing issues is more latent than manifest. By quoting facts and details on a variety of issues the candidate leaves the impression that he possesses the knowledge, sophistication, and acumen to hold public office. Indeed, rather than trying to communicate the content of his speech to his audience, he may purposely talk above them and create the aura that he is prepared to deal with highly complex matters. In 1968 Richard Nixon had a set presentation, "The Speech," delivered extemporaneously, as if unprepared; actually the address had evolved gradually during the primaries and was much the same message in September that it had been in January, but to small-town audiences it was a natural, unrehearsed statement from the heart.[16] In sum, candidates endeavor to communicate not substance, but style and image in their speeches.

Staged rallies also occupy an important place in any campaign. In shopping centers and factories, in football stadia and baseball parks, opening campaign headquarters and dedicating statues, at whistle-stops and airport fly-ins these appearances stimulate the supporters turned out by professional managers. (Spencer-Roberts prepared innumerable rallies for Nelson Rockefeller in 1964.) The professional managers plan minute details of rallies, including who sits on the platform with the candidate, who introduces him, the number of noisemakers that should be available, the exact moment to release balloons, and whether each reporter covering the event prefers a 7-to-1 or 12-to-1 martini. Again, this maximum contrivance of setting is designed to publicize style, not substance.

Press conferences are handy ways of exposing candidates to the fourth estate, usually under favorable conditions. Candidates traditionally grant several "background" interviews to permit reporters to probe them on salient issues. Some candidates, particularly those who think the reporters covering their campaigns secretly favor the opposition, avoid such conferences. The Spencer-Roberts firm, for example, banned any press conferences with Ronald Reagan in the 1966 California gubernatorial election. Reagan was suspicious of and hostile to the press; his managers feared an outburst from their star that might alienate the journalists. Richard Nixon's managers in 1968 courted the working press assiduously by caring for reporters' creature comforts with hotel accommodations, yacht trips, water-skiing, limousine transportation, and endless rounds of cocktail parties. Nixon himself, however, remained aloof and granted only brief interviews as he

---

[16] Theodore H. White, *The Making of the President 1968* (New York: Atheneum Publishers, 1969), p. 378.

stepped from his airplane, limousine, or hotel. By holding the press at arm's length Nixon's managers sought to convey the image of a calm, efficient, deliberate, and cautious approach to the crises of the times.[17]

Personal appearances in local elections frequently take the form of coffees with the candidate. Acquaintances of the candidate invite friends, usually on a neighborhood basis. Beyond a light discussion of issues these coffees serve the more important function of recruiting campaign workers. Formalized coffees are frequently filmed for television. The result is a seemingly leisurely approach providing the candidate the opportunity to field, usually flawlessly, the inquiries of housewives, dowagers, and coeds.

Formal speeches, rallies, press conferences, and coffees are traditional ways of exposing the candidate to the public, primarily to convey a positive impression of his personality, manner, and sincerity. In recent campaigns professional managers have developed a variation that brings these conventional middle-brow formats up to date. Speeches and rallies are risky if the candidate, faced with a hostile audience of militant students or racial minorities, might "blow his cool" and show anger, outrage, or lack of sympathy. When the audience cannot be selected to the candidate's advantage, campaign managers employ a new tactic of "confrontation." The candidate facing a hostile crowd simply challenges one or more of his hecklers to share the rostrum. If he has the native talent and has been properly coached, he convinces detractors that he is sincerely interested in a rational discussion of the militants' grievances, that he understands their plight, and that he is courageous and spontaneous. Governor Claude Kirk managed to win election in Florida as a Republican by confronting his detractors in this fashion. After his election, and on the advice of professional managers, he continued the confrontation tactic and won nationwide acclaim when he successfully "faced down" black militant leader Rap Brown. In the 1968 presidential contest the Democratic nominee for vice-president, Senator Edmund Muskie, confronted numerous student militants at rallies on college campuses. Muskie maintained control in each situation and usually won the

[17] Lewis Chester, Godfrey Hodgson, and Bruce Page, *An American Melodrama: The Presidential Campaign of 1968* (New York: The Viking Press, 1969), pp. 677–89, discusses the Nixon treatment of the press in detail. For a comparison, see White, *The Making of the President 1968*, pp. 381–82.

respect of his audience. The novelty of the technique guaranteed valuable television exposure on evening news programs.

ORGANIZATIONAL MEDIA

By organizational media we refer to the offices within the campaign organization that communicate with voters on the candidate's behalf —precinct workers, speakers' bureaus, and endorsement groups.

We observed in Chapter 2 that research into voting behavior has indicated that some voters decide to vote for candidates because they have been influenced by friends. Since the enthusiasm of an amateur volunteer wins votes, candidates at all levels rely heavily on grass-roots workers to carry their message, particularly in primaries, where turnout is small and the number of candidates usually large. It is impossible to measure precisely how intricate the network of grass-roots volunteers is in any election, but the evidence suggests that it is extensive. In September, 1964, for example, a Gallup poll reported that Republican party workers had contacted 7,100,000 households on behalf of the Goldwater candidacy; Democrats had contacted 3,800,000 for the Johnson-Humphrey ticket.[18] If party workers contact only their own sympathizers, of course, the extensive network indicated by these figures is meaningless; Republicans who had already decided on Goldwater and were later contacted by volunteers on Goldwater's behalf would add nothing. There is evidence, however, that in 1964 Republican workers had an effect on voting decisions that was independent of voters' party loyalties; one survey indicates, for example, that of Independents contacted by Republicans, one-half voted for Goldwater and of Independents not contacted only 29 per cent chose Goldwater. Similarly, of Democrats contacted by Republicans 15 per cent voted for Goldwater; of those Democrats not contacted only 9 per cent chose Goldwater. In sum, "we can conclude that this organizational work did influence votes, and that it represented genuine Republican success." [19]

Speakers' bureaus contribute relatively little to the drive to win converts. In a television era only the candidate can really speak for

---

[18] Thomas W. Benham, "Polling for A Presidential Candidate," *Public Opinion Quarterly*, XXIX (Summer, 1965), 192.

[19] John H. Kessel, *The Goldwater Coalition* (New York: The Bobbs-Merrill Co., Inc., 1968), pp. 287–89.

himself as far as the audience-electorate is concerned. But the speakers' bureau (a staff of individuals ready to speak anywhere at any time for the cause) does serve a purpose. Speakers travel to local headquarters to raise the morale of workers. In presidential elections the Republican party has a "truth squad" consisting of Republican congressmen who follow Democratic candidates from town to town. The device garners publicity which undercuts the appearance of the Democratic standard-bearer and the Republican speakers stir up local supporters with arguments to counter the Democratic presence. The staff of a speakers' bureau is more effective in local referenda than in partisan elections. Prestigious citizens armed with slides, charts, films, and other material to sell a bond issue, a charter amendment, or a tax increase speak at Rotary or Lions Club luncheons. The speakers endeavor to convert highly impersonal propositions into personal issues.[20]

Many voters judge a candidate by the people who endorse him. Consequently, campaign managers seek endorsements from prestigious groups not so much because of the votes represented by group members but because the endorsing groups can be added to the general network for delivering the campaign message. Whitaker and Baxter, the campaign managment firm, always seeks endorsements for candidates and causes from a wide variety of groups. In their planning the mobilization of "natural allies" is an essential feature of the campaign.[21] Managers publicize the endorsements through news stories and brochures to interested associations and attempt to prompt new endorsements from other organizations. Sometimes, however, it is best to keep endorsements quiet. Spencer-Roberts, for instance, walked a delicate line in electing Ronald Reagan governor of California in 1966. Spencer-Roberts had to win endorsements from moderate groups without alienating the members of the right-wing John Birch Society which supported Reagan. To accomplish this Reagan had to disavow certain aspects of the Birch philosophy, so Spencer-Roberts issued a mimeographed statement that criticized Robert Welch, the society's founder but avoided indictment of the Society or its members. The charge against Welch helped mute the extremist label pinned on Reagan by Democrats, yet retained the votes

[20] Baus and Ross, *Politics Battle Plan*, p. 360.
[21] Kelley, *Professional Public Relations*, pp. 58–59.

and money of Birchers.[22] Edward Kennedy's managers recognized the value of individual endorsements in his 1961 campaign for the U.S. Senate. Prior to the Democratic primary the Kennedy team conducted a door-to-door signature drive to obtain the endorsement of Democrats, Republicans, and Independents. The 200,000 pledges permitted Kennedy's managers to publicize the broad endorsement by members of all parties in Massachusetts.[23]

DISPLAY MEDIA

Any discussion of campaign media would be remiss to ignore such items as bumper stickers, billboards, yard signs, placards, buttons, and other visual aids. Candidates distribute propaganda novelties to build morale and to promote name recognition. Edward Kennedy's campaign for the U.S. Senate in 1961 suggests the magnitude of these operations. Kennedy forces purchased 500,000 bumper stickers, distributed a million tri-color printed handouts, spent $47,000 on billboards and another $43,500 on bumper stickers, buttons, lapel tabs, streamers, ribbons, and other novelties. A further indication of the importance politicians place on such media is the fact that the twenty candidates for Congress in the bay area of California in 1962 devoted 16 per cent of their campaign budgets to signs, billboards, and the like.[24]

Displayed messages such as "Dump the Hump," "Clean Gene," "Make Love, Not War," or "We Try Harder," are really directed at the in-groups who already sympathize with the purposes of the campaign. Few opinions or votes are changed by such displays. But they do put supporters (and the opposition) on notice that the campaign is under way. Sympathizers feel they are effective (even though they may not be) when they distribute pencils, bumper stickers, buttons, and cards bearing their candidate's name. The opposition, particularly amateurs, are intimidated by elaborate displays into fearing they may be "outspent."

Outdoor advertising—billboards and placards—dots the landscape

[22] Joseph Lewis, What Makes Reagan Run? (New York: McGraw-Hill Book Company, 1968), p. 131.

[23] Murray B. Levin, Kennedy Campaigning (Boston: Beacon Press, 1966), pp. 175–76.

[24] Ibid., pp. 276–79; David A. Leuthold, Electioneering in a Democracy (New York: John Wiley & Sons, Inc., 1968), p. 104.

in every election. Many campaign managers swear it is effective not only in raising the spirit of the troops but in advancing name recognition. At a cost of but 8–18¢ per 1,000 voters reached, billboards are an inexpensive channel of mass advertising. Placards on telephone poles, fence posts, and tree trunks are even cheaper. If properly tied into the overall campaign theme, billboards give a rationale for voting for the candidate that lingers in the voter's mind. In his successful campaign for Congress in 1966, for example, Republican George Bush in Texas effectively combined the use of billboards and television. Measurement of the effects of the outdoor displays revealed that voters surveyed had not only noticed the principal theme, "Vote for Bush and Watch the Action," but were able to recall it long after the campaign.

An effective display format for reaching the informed and involved voter who is not yet committed is the visual aid. The first systematic employment of visual aids as a nationwide campaign technique occured in the 1952 presidential election. Republican strategists developed films, slides, and taped presentations for service organizations, businessmen's clubs, women's associations, church groups, and employee organizations. Particularly effective were cartoons that carried the Republican message in a light vein. These visual aids appeared throughout the country and reached an estimated audience of 3 million. One firm, the John Deere Company, provided a crew to show such films on a full-time basis (thus making a non-monetary but substantial contribution to the Republican effort).[25]

PRINTED MEDIA

The most widely used of the printed media are campaign literature, political biographies, and newspaper publicity and advertising. Each possesses useful features as a campaign technique.

Campaign Literature

Campaigners spend a sizable portion of their time and money distributing literature about the candidate and his cause. In 1962 26 per cent of all expenditures by congressional candidates in

[25] Kelley, *Professional Public Relations,* pp. 164–65.

California's bay area went to print, distribute, and mail literature and handouts.[26] Similar levels of expenditure for propaganda leaflets occur in other winning and losing campaigns. Pierre Salinger, once President John F. Kennedy's press secretary, sought the Democratic nomination for the U.S. Senate from California in 1964. Salinger had never held elective office and faced a formidable opponent in State Controller Alan Cranston. To capitalize on his association with the popular Kennedys, Salinger's managers allocated funds to prepare and distribute a black-bordered picture of Jack Kennedy carrying a plea to support candidates "in the tradition of our martyred President." Although in questionable taste, the tactic helped Salinger defeat Cranston by 140,000 votes.[27] In Nelson Rockefeller's unsuccessful effort to win the 1964 California Republican primary the Spencer-Roberts firm relied heavily on printed material; they spent $120,000, for example, on a single mailing of quotes from Barry Goldwater (entitled "Who Do You Want in the Room with the H Bomb?") to demonstrate the Arizona Senator's "trigger-happy" approach to foreign affairs; they also distributed a regular pro-Rockefeller newsletter with a circulation that rose to 25,000.[28]

There are two basic types of printed literature. The first carries general appeals aimed at a mass audience through direct mail techniques. In a highly mobile population like that of America, candidates seldom rely solely on personal contact with prospective voters (either direct or through their organized workers). Radio and television are the most publicized ways to reach a mass electorate, but direct mail can also be significant. If professional campaigners specialize in direct-mail techniques, the results can be startling. Direct mail figured prominently in the upset when write-in candidate Henry Cabot Lodge, then in Saigon as ambassador to Vietnam, defeated Barry Goldwater, Nelson Rockefeller, and others in the 1964 New Hampshire Republican presidential primary. The Lodge effort was managed by Paul Grindle, a New England businessman who had used direct-mail techniques to build a successful scientific instruments firm. Grindle turned his professional talents in direct mailing to the task of distributing 96,000 letters in a first mailer and obtaining 8,600

[26] Leuthold, *Electioneering in a Democracy*, p. 101.
[27] Lewis, *What Makes Reagan Run?* p. 83.
[28] Theodore H. White, *The Making of the President 1964* (New York: The New American Library, 1966), pp. 150–53.

pledges of support in return. A second mailer drew an even larger response. Lodge ultimately received 33,000 write-ins in the primary of which as many as 26,000 may originally have been contacted through mailings.[29] Direct mail played a similar role in the 1966 Democratic gubernatorial primary in Pennsylvania. The imaginative merchandising techniques of professional campaigner Joseph Napolitan converted an unknown, Milton Shapp, into a credible candidate. Napolitan distributed 1,000,000 sixteen-page brochures entitled "The Man Against the Machine" (the central theme of Shapp's campaign against the Democratic organization). At a cost of seven cents to produce and distribute, these general audience brochures were an economical way to gain access to a vast constituency.[30]

The second type of printed literature is aimed not at the mass audience, but at specific interest groups. This clientele literature frequently is distributed by direct mail (as in Winthrop Rockefeller's campaigns for the governorship of Arkansas discussed in Chapter 3), but it is hard to distinguish group members when managers have only general mailing lists. Hence other means are needed to reach sectional, religious, occupational, racial, economic, and professional audiences. One technique is to have the interest group itself do the distributing. In the 1968 presidential campaign the AFL-CIO's Committee on Political Education (COPE) distributed a brochure on behalf of the Democratic party to union members. The tri-color brochure countered the rising support for third-party candidate George Wallace by recounting that "George Wallace's Alabama" ranked forty-eighth among states in per capita income and per pupil expenditure on schools, forty-ninth in welfare payments, and had one of the highest illiteracy rates in the nation. In his term as governor, the union brochure noted, Wallace had not changed these conditions yet he wanted to be president. One cannot say whether the leaflet was effective but it did reach its intended audience. Another way for distributing clientele literature is to use a large mercenary or volunteer organization to distribute pamphlets in person. In winning his reelection as governor of New York in 1966 Nelson Rockefeller's managers prepared brochures on the governor's programs for mental retardation, labor, the arts, and so forth. For each

[29] Ibid., pp. 136–38.
[30] James M. Perry, *The New Politics* (New York: Clarkson N. Potter, Inc., 1968), pp. 59–64.

kind of brochure a worker was paid to see that it reached the intended audience. Similarly, Spencer-Roberts flooded low-income white areas with a brochure reminding voters that Ronald Reagan had once been president of the Screen Actors Guild and asking, "Can a Union Man Be Elected Governor?" The leaflet helped counter the charge that Reagan was antiunion; it adroitly ignored Reagan's support for Section 14B of the Taft-Hartley Act permitting states to pass "right to work" laws, which was opposed by labor unions.[31]

Richard Nixon's 1968 campaign had a "participation mailer" to give the citizen the impression he was actually influencing the candidate's thoughts. In Republican headquarters throughout America visitors were encouraged to ask questions, recorded on tape, to be sent to the candidate. Then a computer programmed with Nixon's positions on significant issues would prepare a "personalized" letter to be mailed to the questioner.

There is little evidence available on the effectiveness of general audience and clientele literature delivered by direct mail, special groups, or the candidate's organization. Americans' mail boxes are certainly glutted with "junk" advertising; much of it is thrown away, despite a survey conducted by the Direct Mail Advertising Association which reported that 85 per cent of those questioned had "no general dislike to direct mail." [32] We have no reason to believe that campaign literature wins votes, although emotional appeals in printed materials have proved effective in limited cases.[33] Yet campaign managers rely on printed material, particularly to promote name recognition and to reinforce the themes touted by personal appearances, campaign workers, and radio and television messages. There is evidence that literature promotes voter turnout. One study of a local charter revision election revealed that of persons not contacted, only one-third voted; of those contacted by mail, 60 per cent voted; and three-fourths of those contacted personally voted.[34]

[31] Lewis, *What Makes Reagan Run?*, pp. 149–50.

[32] Baus and Ross, *Politics Battle Plan*, p. 339.

[33] G. W. Hartmann, "A Field Experiment on the Comparative Effectiveness of 'Emotional' and 'Rational' Political Leaflets in Determining Election Results," *Journal of Abnormal and Social Psychology*, XXXI (1936), 99–114.

[34] Samuel J. Eldersveld and Richard W. Dodge, "Personal Contact or Mail Propaganda?" in Daniel Katz et al., eds., *Public Opinion and Propaganda* (New York: Henry Holt and Co., 1954), pp. 532–42.

Campaign Biographies and Tracts

In every political contest, particularly those for the presidency, books detail the lives of respective candidates. Sometimes the content is laudatory, sometimes it is critical, but in either event the biographies are intended not only to make money for the author, but also to shape the image of the office-seeker, to reinforce loyalties, and to condition voters' perceptions.

Campaign biographies played a prominent role in the presidential election of 1964. For example, six million copies of J. Evetts Haley's anti-Johnson diatribe, *A Texan Looks at Lyndon,* were published and distributed; seven million copies of John Stormer's *None Dare Call It Treason,* also anti-Johnson, were printed. In general the 1964 election witnessed the publication of an unprecedented number of books and pamphlets designed to criticize or expose.

Political tracts also carry candidates' messages. In 1964 Barry Goldwater's *Conscience of A Conservative* was a best-seller; Johnson forces countered with the president's *My Hope for America.* It is doubtful that either book changed voters' minds or constituted a lasting addition to the literature of American political thought. In most cases such books reach the already informed and committed and merely reinforce the direction and intensity of their predispositions.[35]

Newspapers and Political Campaigns

Professional campaigners use newspapers for image-building publicity, advertising, and editorial endorsements. We said in Chapter 1 that campaign managers promote a positive image of their candidate. Recall we likened a candidate's image to the impression voters have of his inner character, an impression constructed from his physical appearance, style of life, bearing, conduct, and manner. A man displays an image by assuming a role in life. Selective aspects of his personality suitable to that role are emphasized and permitted public exposure; those not so suited are underplayed, compensated for

[35] Charles A. H. Thomson, "Mass Media Performance," in Milton C. Cummings, Jr., ed., *The National Election of 1964* (Washington, D.C.: The Brookings Institution, 1966), pp. 138–42.

by revealing "other sides" of the man, or simply ignored. The image is not, therefore, that of the "whole man," but of dimensions of personality appropriate to the role and its setting. All the mass media may be used to portray candidate images, but professional campaigners charged with the task of conveying positive pictures of their candidates—the image specialists[36]—are particularly fond of newspapers, radio, and television for this purpose.

Newspapers publicize candidates in ways that convey to the reader an impression of the candidate's credibility and character. In covering opposing candidates, for example, the placement of the news stories about each makes a difference. A critical story on a front page one day is not easily offset if a candidate's denial appears on a back page. Headlines also make a difference; "Humphrey Picketed" leaves a different impression than "Humphrey Speaks." The types of stories about candidates contributes to their images. Citizens are pleased to know their would-be mayor visited a children's hospital but seldom approve of his failure to pay a traffic ticket when he was in law school. The tone and content of news stories subtly build or destroy a reputation while reporting the candidate's deeds and misdeeds, describing his appearance or style, and extolling or lamenting his character.

All this is not to suggest newspapers characteristically distort their electoral coverage in deliberate attempts to favor one candidate over another. Analysis of America's fifteen most prestigious dailies in the 1960 and 1964 elections indicate that they devoted almost equal space to both sides even though nine of the fifteen supported Nixon editorially in 1960 and eleven endorsed President Johnson in 1964. No clear coloring of coverage emerged in story content in either year, although there is some suggestion that editorial positions on foreign affairs worked to Johnson's advantage in ten of the prestige papers in 1964.[37]

[36] Wyckoff, The Image Candidates, p. 11; Joe McGinniss, The Selling of the President 1968 (New York: Trident Press, 1969), pp. 26, 38.

[37] See Guido H. Stempel III, "The Prestige Press Covers the 1960 Presidential Campaign," Journalism Quarterly, XXXVIII (Spring, 1961), 157–63; Guido H. Stempel III, "The Prestige Press in Two Presidential Elections," Journalism Quarterly, XLII (Winter, 1965), 15–21; Jim A. Hart, "Election Campaign Coverage in English and U.S. Daily Newspapers," Journalism Quarterly, XLII (Spring, 1965), 213–18; and David S. Myers, "Editorials and Foreign Affairs in the 1964 Presidential Campaign," Journalism Quarterly, XLV (Summer, 1968), 211–18.

Columnists are particularly adept at image-building. In major New York City dailies, for example, they played a major role in advancing John Lindsay's candidacy for mayor. A content analysis during the 1965 election reported that thirty-seven of fifty-seven columns were either favorable to Lindsay or against his opponents. His positive reputation soared as columnists described him as the potential Republican candidate for president in 1968, as vying for governor of New York with Robert Kennedy in 1970, as representative of "a new generation of educated and public-spirited men," and as a probable "landslide" victor.[38]

Campaign managers recognize the image-building potential of newspaper publicity and cultivate every opportunity to present their candidates in favorable lights to publishers, editors, reporters, and columnists. Sometimes, however, their candidate makes the wrong kind of news. Reporters covering Barry Goldwater in 1964, for example, found him personally attractive, but his policy pronouncements and his off-the-cuff remarks at news conferences always caused difficulty. If the journalists reported accurately his quick rejoinders (like his statement that the U.S. should bomb North Vietnam), they knew they were not doing justice to the candidate's total stand. For a period they probed for safe quotations to report what they thought he had meant in a belligerent remark, but they turned ultimately to direct quotes. This proved devastating and the Goldwater camp soon avoided frequent meetings of their candidate with the press. Goldwater had won the battle for exposure but the effects of his remarks were causing him to lose the war.[39]

Image-building publicity is not sufficient to communicate the candidate's message in newspapers, particularly if the publicity is not favorable. Consequently, campaign expenditures for paid newspaper advertising are heavy. Such expenditures are justified by campaigners on the basis of studies indicating that 80 per cent of pages carrying national advertising, for example, are opened and scanned by the average reader and that men and women of all ages, incomes, educational attainments, and regions pay attention to newspaper ads.[40]

[38] Donald R. Shanor, "The Columnists Look at Lindsay," *Journalism Quarterly*, XLIII (Summer, 1966), 287–90.

[39] White, *The Making of the President 1964*, p. 133.

[40] The Newspaper Information Committee, *A Study of the Opportunity for Exposure to National Newspaper Advertising* (New York: Bureau of Advertising, ANPA, 1966).

Whereas newspaper advertising normally has been employed for direct appeals to voters, specialists make increasing use of space for image-advertising. Picture material is well suited to image projection. In a sample of ninety newspapers during the 1960 presidential campaign, for instance, Democrats used pictures in almost 60 per cent of their advertising. Most of these ads were directed simply at promoting name recognition, but almost one-fourth had an image appeal as well. One ad pictured Jacqueline Kennedy on the phone reminding all women to listen to a special broadcast for wives and mothers. Republicans used fewer image ads, but a prominent one captured a principal theme of Nixon's managers; it portrayed Nixon pointing a finger at the Soviet Union's Premier Nikita Khrushchev during their "debate" in Moscow when Nixon toured that country and left the impression that Nixon was master of the situation.

Other advertising formats include endorsements of the candidate by prestigious persons, linking the presidential candidate to local office-seekers, and ads directed to special interests. To appeal to special interests, candidates always place advertising in Negro and foreign language newspapers. Newspaper advertising, at least in presidential elections, is usually concentrated in the last two weeks of the campaign.[41]

Editorial endorsements typically favor Republican candidates, particularly in presidential contests or in gubernatorial, senatorial, and congressional races outside the South. From 1940 to 1960, for example, from one-half to two-thirds of the dailies in the United States (with from 70 to 80 per cent of total circulation) endorsed the Republican presidential standard-bearer. In 1964 there was a sharp reversal as only 35 per cent of dailies endorsed Barry Goldwater, 42 per cent endorsed Lyndon Johnson, and 23 per cent remained un-committed.[42] The normal pattern returned in 1968. That editorial endorsements are neither a necessary nor sufficient condition for elec-toral victory is demonstrated by the many candidates at local, state,

[41] James J. Mullen, "Newspaper Advertising in the Kennedy-Nixon Campaign," *Journalism Quarterly*, XL (Winter, 1963), 3–11; James J. Mullen, "Newspaper Advertising in the Johnson-Goldwater Campaign," *Journalism Quarterly*, XLV (Summer, 1968), 219–25; James J. Mullen, "How Candidates for the Senate Use Newspaper Advertising," *Journalism Quarterly*, XL (Autumn, 1963), 532–38.
[42] Edwin Emery, "Press Support for Johnson and Goldwater," *Journalism Quarterly*, XLI (Autumn, 1964), 485–88; Richard L. Bishop and Robert L. Brown, "Michigan Newspaper Bias in the 1966 Campaign," *Journalism Quarterly*, XLV (Summer, 1968), 337–38.

and national levels who win over editorial opposition. This is not to say that endorsements or newspaper coverage have no influence. Indications are that editorial endorsements provide cues for voters, especially in nonpartisan local elections and in state and local referenda where party loyalties are less relevant. In California elections held between 1948 and 1962, for example, newspapers endorsed the winning candidate in local elections 84 per cent of the time, for state senate 65 per cent of the time, and in 63 per cent of elections for the state assembly.[43] Indeed, the principal proposition that emerges from studies of the campaign effects of newspaper readership is that newspapers influence (through stories, advertising, and editorials) the marginally interested voter. Under conditions of low involvement the voter has few guidelines for what to believe or how to vote. In these circumstances readers frequently acquire knowledge of issues, form attitudes, and vote on the basis of newspaper content.[44]

AUDITORY MEDIA

We have said that the modern political campaign is a mediated one; instead of direct contact with the electorate, the candidate's character and appeals reach voters through organized partisans, displays, and the printed media. Even more significant in this century are the electronic media: radio and the telephone channel the candidate's words; television adds the illusion of the candidate's presence.

Campaigning By Radio

With the advent of radio in the 1920s politicians gained a means of achieving instantaneous transmission of appeals to individual members of a mass electorate. No longer did they have to wait for staged rallies, recruited volunteers, billboard erection, and the publication or distribution of literature and newspapers. Now they could speak directly to the people. The first candidate to use radio effectively was President Franklin Roosevelt in 1936. The addition of

[43] James E. Gregg, "Newspaper Editorial Endorsements and California Elections, 1948–62," *Journalism Quarterly*, XLII (Autumn, 1965), 532–38; Jules Becker and Douglas A. Fuchs, "How Two Major California Dailies Covered Reagan vs. Brown," *Journalism Quarterly*, XLIV (Winter, 1967), 645–53.

[44] James E. Brinton and L. Norman McKown, "Effects of Newspaper Reading on Knowledge and Attitude," *Journalism Quarterly*, XXXVIII (Spring, 1961), 187–95.

radio to campaigns was followed by significant increases in turnouts in presidential and congressional elections.[45] By the second decade of radio's popularity it seemed destined to play the dominant role in future elections. Then, with the emergence of television, politicians ceased to emphasize radio as a campaign medium. Only in recent elections has its utility been rediscovered by professional campaigners.

In recent presidential contests Republicans especially have re-emphasized radio as a campaign medium. Barry Goldwater's managers in 1964 broadcast a five-minute "Goldwater Report" each evening from October 28 to election eve on 300 stations of the Mutual Broadcasting System. In addition radio spot announcements were used extensively for national, state, and local tickets urging citizens to vote a straight Republican ticket "From Goldwater to ————" (the name of the last-named local candidate on the ballot in a particular area). But John Mitchell, Richard Nixon's campaign manager in 1968, exploited radio more fully than in any campaign to date. He found the medium so effective that he remarked after the campaign that if it were to do over again, his only change would be to spend more money on radio. Among Mitchell's techniques were rebroadcasts of five-minute excerpts from Nixon's acceptance speech before the Republican convention calling for "New Leadership"; the presentation of long, detailed speeches on key issues that were not well-adapted to television, but that sounded tightly reasoned and well-informed on radio; the broadcast of radio messages from Nixon's campaign plane while the candidate was flying over a particular region thus permitting Nixon to tailor his remarks to special clienteles; and numerous appearances by key Republicans on interview programs, call-in shows, and talk programs.

Radio has certain advantages over other campaign media. It reaches an audience largely missed by either newspapers or television. The average suburban commuter spends ninety minutes of every working day isolated in his automobile. Radio is his link with the world. Millions of housewives listen to radio during their daily chores. The elderly, who grew up with radio, depend on news broadcasts for information about politics. And the transistor has a sizable audience of young adults still "hooked" on radio as they grow out of their rock-and-roll teens. Radio is also far less expensive for political advertising than is television. Candidates for minor local offices find it more economical to reach their limited electorate by radio than to pay exorbitant television rates to carry their message to counties in which they are not running. Radio often provides free image-building publicity. Interview and "talk" shows are the staple of public affairs programming on radio. Managers exploit radio shows that rely on listeners to phone in their views by organizing volunteers to flood the station with calls favorable to their candidate. And candidates not particularly marketable on television may come off well as radio performers. In 1960, for example, viewers of the first of the Kennedy-Nixon debates on television generally credited Kennedy with "winning"; but persons who had listened only to radio thought Nixon had done the superior job. Since radio news programs depend heavily on taping "actualities" (the voices of persons in the news), candidates try to make news for stations. In his first campaign for mayor of Los Angeles in 1961 Sam Yorty bought little radio time but had taped interviews played on numerous public affairs programs. Since his opponent, Mayor Norris Poulson, was supported heavily by the metropolitan newspapers, the free radio time was exploited by Yorty as an essential communication channel to his campaign audience.[46] Finally, one professional campaign manager argues that radio is the best place for the "hard sell," particularly when that includes attacks on an opponent that a candidate does not want answered—the "hit and run." Missouri's Senator Stuart Symington faced such a radio attack in his first campaign for the U.S. Senate in 1952. His opponent's radio advertising charged that Symington's position on issues paralleled that of Vito Marcantonio, a New York congressman. Marcantonio's position was labeled the "Communist line." The link of Symington to communism, however, proved too tenuous for voters; they elected Symington even though Eisenhower carried the state for Republicans.

Telephones and Turnout

So well publicized is the role of the newspaper, radio, or television as a medium of mass communication that we overlook the most popular channel for conducting business, transmitting informa-

[46] Charles G. Mayo, "The Mass Media and Campaign Strategy in a Mayoralty Election," *Journalism Quarterly*, XLI (Summer, 1964), 353–59.

tion, providing entertainment, and influencing opinions—the telephone. Professional campaigners, however, do not overlook it. Indeed, campaign managers who specialize in organizing telephone campaigns are well paid; they compile lists of telephone subscribers (both general lists and lists for special clienteles), establish central headquarters, and recruit personnel for round-the-clock manning of phones. Using arrangements with phone companies to place unlimited numbers of local and long distance calls for a set fee (the WATS line or Wide Area Telephone Service), the specialists try to influence voters and get them to the polls.

The principal technique using the telephone to survey voters is the playback of a recorded message. Here an operator dials a number, gets an answer, and switches on a recorded message by a candidate. If the listener has been notified to expect the call (perhaps by letter), he may have the illusion he is actually speaking with the candidate; even in the absence of this illusion he is flattered by the attention. George Romney's managers in Michigan market-tested several variations of the basic technique including a message from Romney alone, one from Romney introducing a congressional candidate who would speak to the phone listener, and one providing a number to be called should the citizen have any questions or complaints. In the 1966 election the Romney organization completed calls to 145,758 households in three key congressional districts. Romney's managers felt that the calls supplied the margin of victory for their candidate in two of those districts. At a cost of 4–5¢ per call the telephone could play an even greater role as a relatively inexpensive campaign medium in the future.[47]

Recent campaigns provide examples of how effective the telephone can be in getting voters to the polls. In the 1968 Democratic gubernatorial primary in Texas eleven candidates vied for the nomination. The leading contenders were the current lieutenant governor (Preston Smith), former ambassador to Vietnam (Eugene Locke), and a twice-defeated candidate for governor in past elections (Don Yarborough). Far down the line was a politician-rancher, Dolph Briscoe, who had been out of elective politics for several years. Briscoe's managers hired an eastern firm which specialized in telephone campaigns to conduct a "blitz" on election eve. In the counties in which the blitz was conducted the turnout for Briscoe exceeded all

[47] Perry, *The New Politics*, pp. 102–3.

poll predictions by significant margins and Briscoe finished fourth among all candidates, missing the run-off primary.

The telephone blitz was not a new technique. It had been particularly effective on a national scale in Richard Nixon's 1960 presidential campaign. Since then it has become a standard method of achieving high voter turnouts in "soft areas." Nixon's managers used the technique on behalf of his write-in candidacy in the 1964 Oregon presidential primary and Spencer-Roberts employed the blitz for Nelson Rockefeller in the 1964 California Republican presidential primary.

The telephone is a tool for campaign research as well as for stimulating turnout. In seeking the Republican nomination to win his reelection as mayor of New York City in 1969, John Lindsay's managers established a phone brigade to make calls to 100,000 registered Republicans. Each Republican rated Lindsay and his opponent, John Marchi, on a scale from one to five; names of persons giving Lindsay positive ratings were stored in a computer with addresses, telephone numbers, ages, income, and ethnic backgrounds. The computer printout was used to provide lists of voters to contact on election day. One estimate placed the pro-Lindsay responses at only one of every three, a portent of his ultimate loss to Marchi in the Republican primary.[48]

TELEVISION MEDIA

Despite the increasingly imaginative use of direct mail, image-advertising in newspapers, radio publicity, recorded messages, and telephone blitzes, it is television that distinguishes modern campaign communication from that prior to the invasion of the professional campaigners. We will focus on two aspects of the television revolution in campaigning—the considerations in its selection as a campaign medium and the professional approach to image-making on television.

The Uses and Costs of Televised Campaigning

Professional managers cite several instances where television is the only appropriate media around which to organize a campaign.

---

[48] James M. Perry, " 'Politically, The Mayor Is Not Doing So Well,' " *The National Observer*, June 9, 1969.

The most universally cited is the election involving an unknown candidate running against an incumbent. The newcomer must rely on normally inactive citizens to overcome the traditional support that regularly elects the incumbent. Because the newcomer is unknown and is appealing to persons with little active interest in politics, his managers know that voters will not come to his public appearances, peruse his literature, note his displays, or read about him in newspapers. He must therefore wage his campaign in the voters' homes when residents settle down to be entertained. As the great entertainer television provides the political neophyte a means for shattering the inattention of his desired audience.

But incumbents also use television extensively, particularly the incumbent who has not made a strong impression (or has made a negative impression) on his constituents and faces stiff opposition. In Senator John Tower's reelection campaign in 1966 (see Chapter 3) a television campaign was designed with precisely these goals in mind—to awaken Texans to Tower's accomplishments and to replace a negative image with a positive one. The result was a slick and successful advertising campaign (prominently featuring the candidate and his attractive family) planned and executed by the Rives-Dyke advertising agency of Houston.

Primary elections are particularly well suited to television campaigning. In the absence of anchoring partisan loyalties and clear-cut issues, most primaries degenerate into popularity contests between candidates who enter the campaign as relative unknowns. Recent American political history is replete with examples of men who have become credible candidates because of clever television campaigns in primaries; Milton Shapp in his 1966 bid to become the Democratic nominee for governor of Pennsylvania, Ronald Reagan in his triumph over San Francisco Mayor George Christopher in 1966, and the case of Don Tabbert of Indiana are illustrative. Sometimes similar conditions prevail in general elections, particularly in contests for lesser offices. A new star appeared on the Missouri political horizon in the 1968 election for attorney general when John C. Danforth, a Republican, upset the Democratic candidate by massive use of well-produced television spots in the final two weeks of the campaign. His victory made him the first Republican to win statewide office in Missouri in two decades and resulted in a *Newsweek* designation as one of the four most promising politicians for the 1970s.

One final instance when television campaigning seems most appropriate occurs when a candidate faces a hostile press (or when it seems to him that the press is hostile). Television permits him to hurdle reporters or editors and reach voters directly. We described earlier how the Spencer-Roberts firm deliberately shielded Ronald Reagan from reporters, preferring Reagan's presence on television to outline his positions. Similarly, Sam Yorty's managers hurdled hostile editorial writers by taking advantage of television in the Los Angeles mayor's race in 1961 against Norris Poulson. In addition to paid half-hour talks by Yorty on camera, his managers missed no opportunity for publicity through televised news conferences, interviews, and panel shows.[49]

Television is not always appropriate, especially for those candidates who leave a poor television impression. In the Yorty-Poulson race, Poulson's managers—the Baus and Ross agency—discouraged televised appearances of their candidate because his voice was scarcely audible as a result of a throat ailment. Ultimately Poulson went on television despite his managers. An impression of the showing can be gained from a survey of voters undertaken by a commercial polling organization after the election. Of Yorty voters 73 per cent said they felt television was the most effective medium in winning votes for their candidate, but only a bare majority of the Poulson voters thought that television had assisted his campaign.

Whether a candidate uses television or not depends in large measure on the costs of producing the television package, buying television time, and preempting other programs. Production costs alone are sizable. Professional campaigner Joseph Napolitan allocated $120,000 alone to Guggenheim Productions for spots and films used in Milton Shapp's campaign in Pennsylvania in 1966. Napolitan easily surpassed that cost in the documentary about Hubert Humphrey which he commissioned to be shown on election eve in 1968. But the high production costs resulted in equally high quality and effectiveness, like that of the segment in which Humphrey played with his mentally retarded grandchild and observed in tears that

[49] Mayo, "The Mass Media," p. 358.

through her affliction he had learned the power of human love. Skimping on production costs, suggests Napolitan, is false economy: "The truth is that you just can't make good, cheap films." [50]

Television time is also expensive. Rates depend on the time-period purchased. The larger the number of viewers likely to be reached at any given hour, the higher the cost. A full hour on network television would cost no less than $100,000 during prime viewing hours. A one-minute spot announcement during NBC's series, *The Virginian*, would cost $23,000. In New York City twenty seconds of prime time costs in the neighborhood of $3,000, but in Los Angeles "only" half as much.

And campaigners pay for the right to preempt programs normally shown in the desired time period. Campaigners usually pay the production costs of the programs they preempt, a cost that can easily exceed the production figures for the candidate's own film and the original costs for air time.

The Political Imagery of Television

In connection with our discussion of newspapers we introduced the image-building functions of the mass media. Professional managers take advantage of television's capacity to communicate images and impressions more effectively than facts or reasoned judgments. Television is now the preeminent medium of image politics. To understand its use we need to examine the character of television.

Television specialists do not think of their enterprise in terms of its ability to inform, educate, indoctrinate or even entertain. Rather, "it is the audience-delivery business, the business of selling time to advertisers." [51] Television sponsors buy time and the broadcasters guarantee a large audience in exchange for the price of the commercial message, more particularly, a large audience of persons aged eighteen to thirty-four (those with the most buying power in the United States). Each audience member subjectively selects which programs he watches and which products he purchases, largely without communication with other members. The convergence of individual selections constitutes the mass behavior so vital to American television

[50] Chester et al., *An American Melodrama*, p. 754; Perry, *The New Politics*, p. 54.
[51] MacNeil, *The People Machine*, p. 12.

and merchandising.[52] Television producers compete ruthlessly to win mass attention and deliver it to advertisers.

To compete in audience-delivery television executives respond to what they think viewers want—entertaining programming presented in an endless repetition of variety, dramatic, and comedy formats. The viewers of these programs make up the audience that advertisers receive when they pay for sponsorship; candidates pay $10,000 for this same audience when they preempt five minutes of *The ABC Wednesday Night Movie*. To receive the full value of his dollar, therefore, the candidate must hold the attention of an audience that is conditioned to entertaining formats (even news programs must adjust to the entertainment criterion—witness NBC commentator David Brinkley's effective, but often forced, wit). In short, politicians compete not only with opponents, but also with other television programs in a purchased time period. The conventions of the market prevail, over those of politics.

Politicians employ numerous techniques to adjust to the demands of video campaigning. These techniques are usually based on an appeal to the tastes, rather than the convictions, of Americans, for television advisers are convinced that personalities and not issue stands or political parties win votes. The overall ploy is contrived spontaneity, the effort to appear uninhibited, candid, open, and credible without running the risk of an unrehearsed performance. Contrived spontaneity has made idols of ordinary performers—Johnny Carson, Andy Williams, Jerry Lewis, and Dean Martin to name but a few; campaigners feel that it also works for them. By thoroughly rehearsing "extemporaneous" performances, testing the delivery while on the road, and editing film versions of seemingly "live" events, television specialists give candidates the planned informality they seek.[53]

A tragic example of the overuse and potential dangers of planned spontaneity occurred in California in 1964. In January Senator Clair Engle decided to seek reelection despite the fact that he had undergone serious brain surgery in August, had a paralyzed arm, and could hardly walk or talk. He announced his candidacy in a forty-two second

[52] Herbert Blumer, "The Mass, the Public, and Public Opinion," in Bernard Berelson and Morris Janowitz, eds., *Reader in Public Opinion and Communication* (New York: The Free Press, 1966), pp. 43–50.
[53] Kurt Lang and Gladys Engel Lang, *Politics and Television* (Chicago: Quadrangle Books, Inc., 1968), pp. 178–79.

television film which had been repeatedly filmed and minutely edited to contain little indication of disability. The appearance of health submerged the actuality of illness. Engle died before the primary, but the incident suggests the possibilities that lie in manufacturing false images.[54]

In 1968 contrived spontaneity reached its zenith as a political art form in the "Hillsboro Format" employed by Richard Nixon. This format, first tried by Nixon when he announced his candidacy in Hillsboro, New Hampshire, showed the candidate meeting with panels of citizens. Each panel consisted of persons of a particular occupation (housewives or farmers), interest (teenagers), or race or ethnic background (Negroes). Panel members asked Nixon unrehearsed questions; he provided his positions on various issues in an informal, easy-going style. The entire panel show was usually taped as an hour show, then edited to a half hour for television. Panel composition was adjusted to local situations—adding local journalists, mixing housewives with lawyers and laborers, or the like. When they were criticized for editing the programs, Nixon's managers switched to live coverage, but carefully screened the questioners in advance. Ultimately the Hillsboro Format was expanded to include auditorium performances before all-white, suburban teenagers. In their regional showings these television broadcasts were used as a forum for local appeals. As is true of most television productions for politics, the Hillsboro Format was carefully developed by a media specialist— Frank Shakespeare, a CBS executive later named by President Nixon to be head of the Voice of America.

The Hillsboro Format was a triumph of form over content. It took advantage of two characteristics of television—the emphasis on visual effects and the primacy of the candidate's personality. Television specialists are particularly sensitive to visual as well as verbal communication; tapes and film, insist television news directors, are as vital to telling a story as is a reporter speaking directly to the camera.[55] Since the visual aspect is what distinguishes television from other media, producers try to exploit it fully. Color television adds a new dimension to the visual that campaigners are just beginning to recognize. A comparison of color and black-and-white programming sug-

---

[54] MacNeil, *The People Machine*, pp. 136–37.
[55] R. Smith Schuneman, "Visual Aspects of Television News: Communicator, Message, Equipment," *Journalism Quarterly*, XLIII (Summer, 1966), 281–86.

gests that color adds a greater emotional impact to the medium, decreases the importance of the spoken word on television, and makes the viewer more a participant and less an observer. In advertising color television commercials elicit more recall than those in black-and-white.[56] Richard Nixon's 1968 television campaigning capitalized on the growing use of color. One observer noted that in 1960 Nixon's "clean masculine quality" did not come through on black-and-white television; in his debates with John Kennedy the television camera emphasized Nixon's worst features—deep eyewells, heavy brows, thick beard, transparent skin, and a "smile made meaningless by the grin of all the commercial announcers who appear with similar white teeth showing." [57] On color television in 1968, however, Nixon appeared more natural; the range of contrasts provided by color pictured a personable man with a tanned, cheerful, and almost glowing countenance. To achieve a radiant candidate a Nixon television advisor urged in a memo: "An effort should be made to keep him in the sun occasionally to maintain a fairly constant level of healthy tan." [58] Even after the election, Nixon continued to be concerned with his television image. To maintain his appearance, according to one report, he dieted to keep from looking jowly, refurbished his suntan regularly, and wore carefully tailored suits. To sharpen his performance at televised news conferences, Nixon avoided notes and rostrum to appear cool, informed, and fearless in the face of the pressures of office.[59]

Media specialists employ the visual impact of television to publicize their candidate's personality. They realize that viewers, exposed to numerous entertainment series featuring attractive television stars, are strongly affected by the performer's style. Research, for example, reveals that viewers prefer personal news sources like Walter Cronkite, Chet Huntley, or local commentators to nonpersonal ones like *Time* or *Newsweek*. They regard personal sources as accurate, sincere, re-

[56] T. Joseph Scanlon, "Color Television: New Language?" *Journalism Quarterly*, XLIV (Summer, 1967), 225–30; Eric Schaps and Lester Guest, "Some Pros and Cons of Color Television," *Journal of Advertising Research*, VIII (June, 1968), 28–39.

[57] Theodore White, *The Making of the President 1960* (New York: Atheneum Publishers, 1961), p. 275.

[58] McGinniss, *The Selling of the President 1968*, p. 73; MacNeil, *The People Machine*, p. 139.

[59] Hugh Sidey, "The Presidency," *Life*, July 11, 1969.

sponsible, and impartial; they are willing to trust the word of commentators.[60] Campaign specialists endeavor to take advantage of the intimate personal relationship between television performers and viewers by making the candidate a television personality, an image candidate. To understand this professional approach to image-making we need to look closely at candidates' personalities and images, the research underlying image-making, and the strategies and techniques of television campaigns.

The politics of personalities and images. We suggested earlier that images are the conceptions of qualities that people associate with certain objects, products, or individuals. Sophisticated advertising techniques enable viewers to perceive in candidates the qualities they really want in themselves; thus the candidate does not project desired qualities but serves instead as a suitable receptacle for "elements of projection that reside in the viewer rather than in the person viewed." [61] Ideally the candidate as a receptacle will be pleasant, not abrasive; have a clear, but not too specific, personality; be self-assured, even cocky, but not pretentious; be articulate, but not erudite or glib; be courageous but also cautious; and appear handsome, but not too pretty. Similarly, certain cigarettes are associated with male virility and various cosmetic products assume the image associated with a sexy tigress. The late Robert Kennedy sought identification with youth through television reports that showed him surfing, shooting rapids, skiing, and mountain climbing (all covered by television as news features).

To provide the proper receptacle for viewer projections the image specialist deliberately places candidates in settings that present a selective view of the aspiring politician's most attractive attributes. The television adviser exploits the best features of the candidate's personality to form the "television personality." By research, rehearsal, and controlling and staging events the candidate is never allowed to expose his naked personality.[62]

The candidate's television personality is a composite of how he performs on the medium, his political role, and his personal qualities. The performance aspect refers to his acting accomplishments. John F.

[60] Leslie W. Sargent, "Communicator Image and News Reception," *Journalism Quarterly*, XLII (Winter, 1965), 35–42.

[61] Lang and Lang, *Politics and Television*, p. 189.

[62] Wyckoff, *The Image Candidates*, pp. 54–8; MacNeil, *The People Machine*, pp. 158–59.

Kennedy, for example, was a polished television artist. The political role refers to the impression he gives of his ability as a politician—his astuteness, his grasp of issues, his knowledge, or his demonstration that he can control any situation. Nelson Rockefeller always manages in television appearances to be knowledgeable, acute, and capable. The candidate's personal qualities refer to the feelings and emotions that he exhibits, feelings and emotions his audience is able to share sympathetically. In 1968 George Wallace tapped the resentment among his followers to federal government of any kind by flailing away at the Supreme Court, the "conspiracy" of "national Republicans and Democrats to circumvent the Constitution", and the "Big City, Eastern" press. In seeking reelection as governor of California against Ronald Reagan (an accomplished performer with pleasing personal qualities) Edmund "Pat" Brown labored hard to display the attributes he thought Californians admired. He swam daily, dieted, and lost twenty pounds in an effort to look lean and dynamic. But at sixty-one he could not compete with his more attractive opponent.[63] To upset the favored Shirley Temple Black in a special election in California's Eleventh Congressional District in 1967, Pete McCloskey practiced hard to improve his performer image; an arresting, crisp style replaced his flat, subdued monotone and he compared well with the former movie star's now matronly image.[64]

It is best to be accomplished in all three aspects of the television personality, but this is not always the case. Lyndon Johnson played his political role well, yet never communicated the personal qualities Americans demand of their presidents. Barry Goldwater displayed the desirable personal qualities, but performed poorly on television. Sometimes, however, viewers are so captivated by one of these elements of public personality that they ignore deficiencies in the others. Dwight Eisenhower played the political role badly and was hardly an accomplished television performer, yet his personal qualities compensated for these faults. The success of a television campaign depends in large measure on how these three elements are interwoven to give the viewer the impression that he is intimately associated with an attractive person.[65]

[63] Lewis, *What Makes Reagon Run?*, p. 124.
[64] Rodney G. Minott, *The Sinking of the Lollipop*, (San Francisco: Diablo Press, 1968), pp. 89–90.
[65] Lang and Lang, *Politics and Television*, pp. 186–211.

Image research. To appear to be the type of personality the voters want, it is necessary first to know what voters want. This is where image and research specialists join forces. Just as advertisers learn what consumers want and are willing to buy before marketing a product, image-makers ask pollsters to determine what electorates look for in both ideal and acceptable candidates. Before preparing his effective image documentary on Milton Shapp in the 1966 Democratic gubernatorial primary in Pennsylvania, Joseph Napolitan conducted four statewide polls; he learned that voters associated the Democratic party with machine bosses bent on robbing the public treasury. Napolitan contrasted the negative image of the party with a positive image of Shapp in the documentary, "The Man Against the Machine." [66]

Precampaign polls can help uncover a theme for an image campaign. Polls during the campaign reflect the impact of television exposure and hence provide an estimate of the effectiveness of image-building. Moreover, they suggest what should be done if the painstakingly built and flawless image is threatened. In 1964, for example, Lyndon Johnson's advisers refused to respond to attacks by Republicans on the integrity of the president's friends ("cronies" as labeled by Goldwater). But in early October Walter Jenkins, the president's confidant, was arrested in the basement of the Washington YMCA, a gathering place for homosexuals which had been under police surveillance. Once the story was publicized the question was, what effect would this have on the campaign? Pollster Oliver Quayle surveyed a cross section of voters by telephone and found no detectable shift of opinion. Quayle advised that the event be ignored in Johnson's campaigning. It was and the Jenkins case became only a footnote to the election.[67]

Some candidates fail in their attempts to build a positive image without the benefit of opinion polls. Barry Goldwater in 1964 failed to clarify his position on the Social Security issue (he had been labeled as trying to destroy the system), even though public polls indicated confusion over his program. In other cases candidates engage in elaborate research, but conduct their television campaigns independently of the findings. Prior to his nomination in 1968, Richard Nixon's managers commissioned extensive polling research under the

[66] Perry, *The New Politics*, pp. 52–53.
[67] White, *The Making of the President 1964*, pp. 439–43.

auspices of political scientist David Derge of Indiana University and the Opinion Research Corporation. Panels of 500 respondents each were established in thirteen key states. Three waves of personal interviews and several telephone polls took place from July through October. In addition, George Romney's chief researcher, Walter DeVries, consulted with the Republican senatorial and congressional campaign committees. But all the intelligence gathered had little effect on general strategy, and, although researchers advised shifts in tactics during the closing days of the campaign as it became clear that Nixon's early lead was evaporating, no substantial adjustments ensued.[68]

The strategies and techniques of image-making. The subtleties and expense involved make it mandatory to plan video campaigns well in advance of the time television is actually used. The general strategies are clear. First, purchase the maximum audience possible.[69] Second, select formats suited to the viewing habits of the audience (perhaps spot announcements that only interrupt, not preempt, favorite programs) and to the image material or performance capabilities of the candidate. Third, employ entertaining and dramatic material approximating the most arresting of normal programming (it helps if candidates conduct themselves like Efrem Zimbalist, Jr.). Fourth, use television time to emphasize only qualities, issues, and identifications bearing on the imagery; don't squander it on side matters.

Advertising firms, film producers, and television technicians share in planning strategy, purchasing television time, negotiating preemptions, coaching candidates, and preparing image material. In the relatively short history of video campaigning certain specialists have built national reputations for political image-making: Batten, Barton, Durstine, and Osborn (in the 1952 and 1956 Eisenhower campaigns); Doyle Dane Bernbach (which provided a creative and controversial approach to spot political commercials in 1964 and 1968 on behalf of Democratic presidential candidates); Joseph Napolitan (in Milton Shapp's 1966 Pennsylvania campaigns); Jack Tinker & Associates (who prepared Nelson Rockefeller's imaginative commercial spots in 1966);

[68] Chester et al., *An American Melodrama*, pp. 618–19, 630–31; White, *The Making of the President 1968*, p. 387.
[69] Stanley Kelley, Jr., "Campaign Debates: Some Facts and Issues," *Public Opinion Quarterly*, XXVI (Fall, 1962), 355–58.

the Ben Kaplan agency (which arranged John Kennedy's confrontation with Baptist ministers in Houston in 1960 giving Kennedy the opportunity to silence the issue of his Catholicism); Papert, Koening, Lois (on behalf of Robert Kennedy); Carl Ally (who worked for Senator Eugene McCarthy); Gene Wyckoff (television writer and producer who worked on behalf of Nixon in 1960, Rockefeller in 1964, and Henry Cabot Lodge in 1960); and Fuller & Smith & Ross (involved in the 1968 Nixon campaign). When the expense of this type of expertise is added to production, time, and preemption costs, we can understand why the Republicans were prepared to spend $8 million on television in 1968 to elect the thirty-seventh president of the United States.

Naturally planning an image campaign depends on the candidate available and the setting. When Doyle Dane Bernbach planned the mass media campaign for Lyndon Johnson in 1964 it sought not merely to win an election, but to win by a landslide. The agency decided not to picture Johnson in commercials but to "let him be President" in his personal appearances. Television spots attacked Senator Goldwater's credibility by clever portrayals of his stands on nuclear responsibility, Social Security, civil rights, and liberal Republicanism. Pritchard, Wood, Inc., working for the Republicans, aimed their guns at the ethics of the Johnson administration. But, the Republican effort floundered in the closing days of the campaign because of inability to clear television time and a cutback on television expenditures to balance the campaign budget once it became clear that defeat was inevitable. In the Dallas-Fort Worth area, for example, a crucial week in the campaign saw only two programs and no commercials aired on behalf of Republicans.[70]

In contrast to the muted finish of Goldwater's media campaign in 1964, Richard Nixon's efforts have always relied on a last minute television "blitz" or saturation. In 1960, for example, he finished with a four-hour telethon on the ABC network (at a cost of $200,-000) which ranged from discussing complex issues to a chat with Ginger Rogers. In 1968 he closed his campaign on election eve with several showings of a sentimental documentary combined with a live telethon in which former Oklahoma football coach Bud Wilkenson asked Nixon questions phoned in by such personages as "little Mary

[70] Karl A. Lamb and Paul A. Smith, *Campaign Decision-Making* (Belmont, Cal.: Wadsworth Publishing Co., 1968), pp. 194–201.

Rhodes of Pasadena."

In preparing the 1968 media plan for Hubert Humphrey's presidential bid, Doyle Dane Bernbach relied on computers to estimate the relative value of repeating commercials in a given frequency on given subjects (say disarmament) in given cities after first showings. But conflicts with Humphrey's media adviser—Joseph Napolitan—and limited funds threw scheduling badly awry. Yet effective ads were produced including one that offered a sign, "Spiro Agnew for Vice President," above a sound-track of tittering and laughter with the closing remark being, "This would be funny if it wasn't so serious." [71]

Each of the television specialists mentioned above has developed innovative, imaginative, and controversial formats for merchandising candidates. For convenience we consider, first, those maximizing the effectiveness of paid advertising and, second, those that achieve exposure through free publicity.

Advertising Techniques and Formats

The first election in which television played a major role was the presidential contest in 1952. The formats employed were conventional but they foretold the pattern of the future. Although Richard Nixon's "Checkers" speech proved effective, specialists frowned on having candidates speak directly to the audience. The direct-to-camera format was often dull, (particularly if the candidate read a speech) nonentertaining, and not suited to ineffective candidate-performers. Television advisers substituted the device of televising live candidate appearances before rallies. But this format required preempting whole television shows. Moreover, candidates frequently ran into problems if the teleprompter failed (Eisenhower once uttered into an open microphone, "How the hell does this thing work?") or if their speeches ran too long. Adlai Stevenson, the Democratic candidate, had a different problem: he could not time his witty oratory for full impact on the audience at home. To meet these problems a new format was born; filmed appearances of candidates. Republicans, for example, had Eisenhower respond to questions asked by an off-camera voice: "Mr. Eisenhower, what about the high cost of living?" Reply: "My wife Mamie worries about the same thing. I tell her it's our job to change that on November 4." These

[71] Chester et al., *An American Melodrama*, pp. 637–39.

gems, prepared by Ted Bates and Company, appeared as commercial "spots," thus reaching a captive audience without requiring the preemption of popular television fare. Staged conversations between party leaders lauding the candidate and damning the opposition provided a format for five- or fifteen-minute programs. The telethon, a program lasting two to four hours, had candidates responding to questions called in by citizens. Finally, filmed documentaries were an effective device, particularly that shown by Republicans on election eve purporting to be a report to Eisenhower on the activities of the Citizens for Eisenhower Committee; it covered citizens filmed against attractive backgrounds (including a ten-year-old leader of "Tykes for Ike") explaining why they supported Eisenhower (and closed with the General and Mamie cutting a victory cake).[72]

Since the 1950s basic advertising formats have changed little; what has changed are the techniques used to create visual interest, to give the audience a sense of participation, and to provide effective video entertainment. As a result political television exploits short time periods (twenty-second and one-minute spots, perhaps five-minute trailers) during the early portions of a campaign and saturates the audience with half-hour documentaries and lengthy telethons on election eve.

In the 1950s political spot advertising usually featured the candidate in some informal pose. There was little effort to create a one-minute film, spotted around the television dial, to persuade through shock, titillation, or humor. (An exception was one 1952 Republican spot that depicted two American soldiers in Korea bewildered by the futility of the war; when one was killed his friend charged at the enemy in a hopeless gesture of anguish and a voice entoned, "Vote Republican.") In the 1960s however, entertaining political spots on television became commonplace in local, state, and national elections. In the process their showing constituted pseudo events that sometimes generated more controversy than the candidate or issues. The leading example was a spot produced by Doyle Dane Bernbach in 1964 for the Johnson campaign.[73] To discredit Goldwater's position on nuclear warfare and the testing of nuclear weapons the agency devised

[72] Kelley, *Professional Public Relations*, pp. 184–95.
[73] Thomson, "Mass Media Performance," p. 127; Kessel, *The Goldwater Coalition*, pp. 237–39; Bernard Rubin, *Political Television* (Belmont, Cal.: Wadsworth Publishing Co., Inc., 1967), p. 185.

the following spot: a small girl picks petals from a daisy as she sits in a meadow; a background voice begins a countdown; the countdown ends, a nuclear explosion is heard and a mushroom cloud appears; the voice says, "These are the stakes: To make a world in which all of God's children can live or go into the dark." A second spot on the same theme showed a little girl with an ice cream cone as a motherly background voice explained that Strontium–90, a fallout element from nuclear testing, is found in milk and that Barry Goldwater voted against the Test Ban Treaty. Naturally Republicans protested, playing directly into the hands of Democratic tacticians. The "Daisy Girl" spot, for example, was aired only once but generated free publicity on networks and in editorials because of the controversy; Americans eagerly tuned to other Democratic spots to see if they too would be sensational! But Republicans learned their lesson; in 1968 they used an anti-Humphrey commercial (linking Humphrey to urban rioting in a causal way) that brought not only Democratic wrath but also bigger audiences for future Republican spots.

By the late 1960s local and statewide candidates capitalized on the use of political spots. Jack Tinker & Associates (a firm that had succeeded in giving Alka-Seltzer a "fun" image and in changing the color of Braniff airplanes) created arresting commercials for Nelson Rockefeller's campaign to be re-elected as governor of New York. Instead of taping commercials the agency used a sound-on-film technique that produced a higher quality product, especially for color television. Although Rockefeller was the product the agency merchandised, he never appeared in the spots. A typical sixty-second commercial, for example, gave the viewer a picture of a road as seen from the front end of a moving car, the broken white center line moving to the sound of the throbbing engine and a voice declaring, "If you took all the roads Governor Rockefeller has built, and all the roads he's widened and straightened and smoothed out; if you took all those roads and laid them end to end, they'd stretch all the way to Hawaii." The road ends as though on a Hawaiian beach, the car turns around to the strains of Hawaiian music and begins a return trip, and the voice adds, "All the way to Hawaii and all the way back." The Tinker spots added a final polish by having television actor Ed Binns (more well-known for huckstering Busch Beer and Gillette razors) do the narration. The result was an entertaining series of spots run 208 times in New York City alone reminding voters of the governor's accomplishments.[74] Similar political commercials have been used in other statewide contests and have proved highly effective in introducing political newcomers, particularly to viewers in the outlying rural areas who depend almost solely on television for entertainment.

The five-minute trailer (so called because it is scheduled at the end of a regular television program and preempts commercial time rather than program time) has also grown more sophisticated. In 1960 television producer Gene Wyckoff devised a five-minute film made up of still pictures to provide a "heroic" image for Henry Cabot Lodge, the Republican vice-presidential nominee. Finding Lodge almost impossible as a television performer, Wyckoff used still photographs to capture the former ambassador to the United Nations in striking, forceful poses. The five-minute production, "Meet Mr. Lodge," was resurrected in 1964 by leaders of the write-in campaign for Lodge in the New Hampshire primary. Even as a dated film it had an impact on viewers and aided Lodge's upset of Rockefeller and Goldwater.[75] As governor of California Ronald Reagan filmed five-minute pieces, "Reports to the People," in preparation for his reelection campaign, thus avoiding embarrassing questions in live press conferences.

The staged conversation, or panel show, remains much as it was in the 1950s. Edward Kennedy used the format successfully in his bid for the U.S. Senate in 1961 by directing it to a particular kind of voter. Recognizing that only the more interested and informed viewers would sit through panel presentations, he used discussions between Professor Robert Wood of Massachusetts Institute of Technology, James McGregor Burns of Williams College, and others to provide the illusion of endorsement by the intellectual and informed community of Massachusetts.[76] In seeking the Texas governorship in 1962 John Connally aimed his panel shows at another audience— housewives. By scheduling a televised "Coffee with Connally" every morning he reached the morning game show and soap opera audience. In 1964 Barry Goldwater aimed at a similar audience with a morning "TV Brunch with Barry" in which he conversed with a panel composed of the widow of a pilot killed in Vietnam (Goldwater gave his

[74] Perry, *The New Politics*, pp. 107–8, 113–21.
[75] Wyckoff, *The Image Candidates*, pp. 49–51.
[76] Levin, *Kennedy Campaigning*, p. 155.

views on the war), an elderly woman dependent on Social Security (to help him explain his stand), a mother concerned about the school-bussing issue, and so forth. And to clarify his stand on using nuclear weapons, Goldwater held a televised conversation with General Eisenhower at the general's farm in Gettysburg, Pennsylvania. During the program Eisenhower dutifully endorsed Goldwater, pointing out that it was "tommyrot" to think that the Republican candidate wanted to use atom bombs. Finally, of course, the major innovation in the panel format came with Nixon's Hillsboro Format described previously.

As we noted in discussing Richard Nixon's "blitz" theory of video campaigning, telethons are a useful technique for last-minute saturation of the television audience. Telethons are excellent examples of contrived spontaneity. In Nixon's closing telethon of 1968, for example, the moderator, Bud Wilkenson, introduced David Eisenhower, grandson of the former president. "I think," prompted the football strategist, "that you have a message for us." As had been planned, the younger Eisenhower reported that the general, ill in the hospital, urged voters to elect Dick Nixon. Not all telethons are so well rehearsed; if truly spontaneous they can lead to disaster. Campaigning in the 1960 West Virginia presidential primary, for example, Hubert Humphrey squeezed out $750 for a telethon on a local station, but had no money to arrange its production (including screening of calls). So Humphrey faced the cameras, telephone in hand. An initial call set the tone as a scratchy-voiced elderly lady barked: "You git out! You git out of West Virginia, Mr. Humphrey!" The call left Humphrey reeling and largely inarticulate. To add to the humility an operator came on the line demanding that Humphrey hang up to clear the wire for an emergency. An observer remarked, "From that point on the telethon lost all cohesion—proving nothing except that TV is no medium for a poor man." [77]

Next to the spot commercial the filmed documentary is the most entertaining format for political appeals. If properly produced it can compete favorably with the best of dramatic programming. Such production incorporates the tested techniques of show business: (1) Devise a symbolic scene representing the film's basic theme and repeat it at appropriate points to remind the audience of the desired image. In a documentary on Richard Nixon the producer built the

[77] White, *The Making of the President 1960*, pp. 111–12.

candidate's image as being experienced in international negotiations by repeating scenes of an air force transport allegedly flying him to foreign countries (actually the scene had been filmed for a Jerry Lewis movie, *Geisha Boy*). (2) Instead of revealing too much about the candidate, give the impression that he can control situations without actually showing him doing so. Indeed, keep the candidate off the screen! To indicate, for example, that Richard Nixon could talk directly to the Russians, the film producer provided a shot of what appeared to be Russian antenna (actually culled from an old movie called *Rat Patrol*) and added Nixon's voice so that the audience had the impression the former vice-president was indeed speaking directly to the Soviet people.[78] (3) Maximize visual effects by allowing pictures to speak for themselves; write the narrative script after the film is complete, thus adapting the spoken to the visual rather than the reverse; and steer away from the politician's tendency to use the same words and phrases over and over; in personal appearances the politician must be redundant to gain attention, but this is not true for film. (4) For dramatic emphasis of dull material, employ striking musical backgrounds. In 1968 Republican films depicted people starving in America to the tune of impressive drum rolls and Nixon's voice asking "Have we come all this way just for *this?*"

Like spot commercials some political films stir controversy in their own right and attract newspaper, commentator, and general interest. In 1964 the Citizens for Goldwater produced a film, "Choice," to portray the declining moral fiber of Americans. The decline was tied to the bad examples supposedly set by Democratic leaders in such areas as over-indulgence and racial integration. One scene showed a black limousine with Texas license plates moving at dangerous speeds as empty beer cans were thrown from the driver's window; the link to Lyndon Johnson's alleged preference for fast driving was clear. Barry Goldwater repudiated the film before it was ever shown publicly as "nothing but a racist film." As was the case with the "Daisy Girl" commercial, however, the film's notoriety served its purpose without being televised.

Each of the advertising formats described can be, and is, used well in advance of elections to publicize potential candidates. When entering the race for the Republican nomination for president in 1968, for example, Nelson Rockefeller undertook a massive spot com-

[78] Wyckoff, *The Image Candidates*, pp. 23–36.

mercial effort throughout the country intended to build his popularity in public opinion polls. Similarly Ronald Reagan, a noncandidate for the Republican nomination until the convention, achieved maximum exposure in May and June of 1968 by the showing of a clever documentary depicting the rise of the "principled nonpolitician." But the uses of paid advertising for candidate build-ups is limited; free publicity is the preferred communication method for that purpose.

Publicizing Candidates

Aside from personal appearances and paid advertising, a candidate is visible only to the extent that the news media make him so. One of the long-term effects of the growth of the news media in this country has been to convince Americans that anything important will be in the news. Important people, goes the myth, make news; unimportant people do not. To be a credible candidate an aspiring politician must make news. To aid him in this task he hires public relations personnel—specialists in publicizing events, products, and people. In recent elections public relations specialists have taken advantage of three trends in television to publicize candidates—the quest of the news media for entertaining events to report, the ritualistic television coverage of public events like party conventions, inaugurations, and space shots, and the desire of television stations to perform a "public service" by staging debates between candidates.

Manipulating the news. Campaign specialists thrive on the image publicizing properties of television by generating material for news reports (live, film, and taped), documentaries, interviews, panels, and guest shots on celebrity shows. Brief exposure on an evening news program is particularly prized. Robert Kennedy maintained that thirty seconds on the evening news was worth more than a story in every newspaper in the world. The Baus and Ross agency regards thirty seconds on television news as more valuable than a half-hour paid ad on television.[79] The reason is simple enough: exposure on a news program legitimizes the candidate; anyone can buy commercial advertising.

The conventions of television journalism make it relatively easy for public relations personnel to contrive pseudo events for television reporters. Competition on the television news beat finds each station

[79] Baus and Ross, *Politics Battle Plan,* p. 321.

striving to attract a large audience with interesting and entertaining stories; television's appetite for such news dovetails well with the candidate's thirst for image exposure. The values of television journalism are those of show business, not of candid, probing, or informative reporting; the pseudo event delivered on a platter is frequently the pap the television news department seeks, particularly if the event is amusing, visually arresting, or conveys a sense of human experience. Television news departments are organized not as news-gathering agencies but as disseminators of material uncovered by wire services, newspapers, magazines, or free-lance reporters. The stars of television news (Chet Huntley, David Brinkley, Walter Cronkite, and Frank Reynolds nationally or Ray Miller, Eddie Barker, or Ron Wilson on local outlets) are less reporters than messengers with neither the information nor the time to elucidate on the nonmeaning of pseudo events.[80]

The techniques for achieving free news coverage are quite familiar. If a network or local television filming crew accompanies the candidate, permit it to choose its own shots. If not, the candidate's advisers should produce tapes and provide them to stations. To take full advantage of broadcast times, events should be scheduled early in the day so films can be processed for evening viewing; Nixon's managers in 1968, for example, scheduled his personal appearances in the morning and minimized nighttime rallies. It also helps to place the candidate in situations that will attract the television newsman's attention; recall our earlier example of how vice-presidential candidate Muskie confronted hecklers to gain news coverage. When Senator Edward Kennedy's Senate subcommittee investigated poverty among Alaskan Eskimos in 1969 it was no coincidence that a cameraman just happened to be available in the frozen clime to photograph Teddy visiting barren shacks. An incumbent president, governor, or mayor can always command news attention simply by informing the press that he has an announcement. John Kennedy, Lyndon Johnson, and Richard Nixon are presidents who have used such a ploy; Ronald Reagan, George Romney, Claude Kirk, and George Wallace have done so from statehouses. And when all else fails, public relations men have

[80] William A. Wood, Electronic Journalism (New York: Columbia University Press, 1967); Ralph L. Lowenstein, "The 1968 Campaign: TV Lost Its Cool," Freedom of Information Center Report #006, (Columbia, Mo.: School of Journalism, University of Missouri, November, 1968.)

been known to gain the cooperation of reporters in staging photographs of events the cameramen missed on their first occurrence.[81]

A candidate's media specialists also exploit television documentaries for publicity. Election year documentaries usually take great pains to be glib, objective, and superficial. Each candidate gets a few minutes exposure; the skilled public relations man strives to see that his candidate's film sequence reinforces the selected image. Network and locally prepared documentaries reflect the primary convention of television—to present material in a sufficiently entertaining fashion to command a large audience. Public relations men understand this and coach candidates to be amusing, humorous, and congenial, so that the filmed segment will appear on the screen, not on the cutting-room floor.

Television interviews by a single reporter or on a panel show such as *Meet the Press* or *Face the Nation* constitute another news channel for free publicity. Edward Kennedy in 1961 announced his candidacy for the senate on *Meet the Press* and at the same time advanced his candidacy with some voters simply because he was important enough to be invited to the prestigious program. Sometimes these interviews backfire. Governor William Scranton of Pennsylvania appeared on *Face the Nation* in 1964 to announce his candidacy for the Republican presidential nomination (at that time Goldwater seemed a certain winner). Scranton, thinking he had Eisenhower's endorsement, decided to challenge the Arizonian's conservatism and chose the CBS program for the kickoff of his campaign. But just prior to the program Eisenhower phoned Scranton to warn that he endorsed nobody. Scranton, shaken by the Eisenhower nondecision, did not announce; instead he was flustered, indecisive, and hesitant before the television cameras. Later, when Scranton did announce his candidacy, the memory of his television disaster lingered on in the minds of Republican leaders.[82]

Finally, candidates acquire free exposure on variety shows. Johnny Carson's *Tonight* show and Joey Bishop's nighttime venture have been publicity vehicles for Richard Nixon, Robert Kennedy, John Lindsay, and other politicians. Locally produced variety shows in Detroit, Philadelphia, Los Angeles, and other cities provide similar

[81] Walter Wilcox, "The Staged News Photograph and Professional Ethics," *Journalism Quarterly*, XXXVIII (Autumn, 1961), 497–503.
[82] White, *The Making of the President 1964*, pp. 176–96.

opportunities for gubernatorial, congressional, and mayoralty candidates. The ultimate in guest performances was Richard Nixon's 1968 spot on NBC's *Laugh-In,* asking, "Sock it to ME?"

Special events publicity. Television routinely reports such major political events as party conventions, election returns, and inaugural ceremonies. The networks cover presidential and congressional offices; local and regional outlets cover statewide, county, and municipal contests. Public relations specialists move quickly to get free exposure for their candidates. The way a governor or congressman conducts himself at a party convention reaches his constituents via television. Even if he is not a candidate for national office, a good performance buttresses the career ambitions of a local politician. Speaking from the rostrum (placing a name in nomination, giving a seconding speech, or debating the party platform) can mean nationwide exposure. Being interviewed by a floor reporter means being alone in the limelight. It is not uncommon, therefore, for a politician's press agent to plant a rumor and force news reporters to track down the candidate for televised "clarification." Televised convention coverage is indispensable to the party's presidential candidate. It gives supporters throughout the country the opportunity to reidentify with their party through the ceremony, intrigue, and contrived symbolism of the event. Moreover, the candidate's acceptance speech climaxes the convention and provides an opportunity to reach millions of viewers. Convention managers purposely schedule events, including acceptance speeches, for the prime-time viewing audience. In 1968 Richard Nixon understood that the acceptance speech leaves a lingering impression and painstakingly prepared a rousing address aimed at home viewers as well as convention partisans; so polished was the performance, so precise was the timing, and so elaborate the staging that excerpts from the taped speech made effective spot commercials throughout the campaign.[83]

Election night coverage, particularly of primary election returns, provides another windfall of free exposure. The winning candidate inevitably holds televised personal interviews and press conferences and makes a victory statement. And in presidential primaries losers appreciate the opportunity on television to inject confidence into loyal supporters before moving on to the next state primary. After his loss to Robert Kennedy in the 1968 Indiana primary, for example, Eugene

[83] Lang and Lang, *Politics and Television,* pp. 78–149.

McCarthy raised the flagging spirits of his workers by besting Kennedy in a split-screen interview conducted by CBS commentator Walter Cronkite. McCarthy went on to defeat Kennedy in Oregon, but lost the California primary.

Televised debates. The televising of debates between John F. Kennedy and Richard M. Nixon in the 1960 presidential election contributed a new avenue for image exposure. It is now routine for candidates, particularly underdogs, to challenge their rivals to televised debates. Sometimes the challenge is sincere, but more often it is merely an artful dodge: the candidate makes the routine challenge expected of him, then quarrels endlessly about the time, place, and specific arrangements for the confrontation. Thus the televised debate has not become an institution of American campaigning, but the symbolic gesture of the challenge has. Yet there are other examples of televised confrontations of candidates besides the Kennedy-Nixon debates. Indeed, John Kennedy debated Hubert Humphrey in the West Virginia presidential primary in 1960. Other notable "debates" include that between Democrat Pierre Salinger and Republican George Murphy in the senate race in California in 1964, one between Edward M. Kennedy and Edward McCormack in the Democratic senatorial primary in Massachusetts in 1961, a joint appearance by Ronald Reagan and Edmund "Pat" Brown in the California gubernatorial contest in 1966, another by Robert Kennedy and Gene McCarthy prior to the California Democratic presidential primary in 1968, and a unique split-screen appearance by Governor Ronald Reagan and Senator Robert Kennedy on a CBS special, *Town Meeting of the World,* in 1967.

"Debate" is clearly an inappropriate designation for the exchanges between candidates at these sessions. They are not arguments on issues, but confrontations of images. Candidates direct themselves not to one another but to the viewing audience, particularly to the undecided voters. John Kennedy understood this well in the first of his debates with Richard Nixon in 1960. While Nixon endeavored to rebut each of Kennedy's arguments like a debater seeking points, Kennedy performed to the television audience, largely ignoring Nixon and repeating many of the themes made in his personal appearances throughout the nation.

What the candidates say is less significant than how they look. Style, not content, prevails. Nixon expresses the point well in his *Six*

Crises when he discusses a lost election: "I believe that I spent too much time in the last campaign on substance and too little on appearance: I paid too much attention to what I was going to say and too little on how I look." In the Salinger-Murphy debate Salinger hoped to demonstrate to 3.5 million Californians that Murphy did not know enough to be a senator. Murphy, however, was more interested in appearances—in looking like a senator rather than in talking like one. Salinger looked pudgy, self-indulgent, irritable, and shady, but Murphy smiled, radiated, and portrayed an image of sincerity and courtliness. Instead of responding to Salinger's arguments, Murphy (like Kennedy in 1960) reiterated the points he had made throughout the campaign. Salinger (Kennedy's press secretary in 1960) complained, "I guess this just shows the futility of trying to come to grips with anyone as slippery as my opponent." [84]

Debates are intended to seem spontaneous, but a candidate should be carefully rehearsed. Before his debates with Nixon in 1960 John Kennedy had aides fire questions at him to sharpen his faculties and briefed himself on matters likely to be raised by questioners. His brother Robert, however, did not take this precaution before his appearance with Ronald Reagan in 1967. The format had Kennedy in New York and Reagan in California responding to questions asked via satellite by students in London. A crucial exchange involved views on the Vietnam war. Prior to the program Reagan's staff had prepared a memo on the war question; he studied it and rehearsed a question-and-answer session. Kennedy had not prepared. Thus while Kennedy acted diffident and indecisive as though trying to win favor with the students, Reagan played his role before the fifteen million Americans watching the program by fielding questions astutely and with humor.

The setting and arrangements for the debate are crucial and campaign managers endeavor to arrange them to the advantage of their respective candidates. Nixon's advisers in 1960 insisted on several repaintings of the backdrop so that Nixon's picture would contrast properly, demanded lighting adjustments, and fretted over air conditioning because of their candidate's tendency to perspire heavily. And the format is always a matter for contention. Candidates are

[84] Lewis, *What Makes Reagan Run?*, pp. 88–90.

usually questioned by a panel of journalists, students, housewives or whatever. In the 1968 McCarthy-Kennedy debate, the Minnesota senator preferred a direct confrontation with Kennedy; Kennedy, however, liked the panel format provided by a joint appearance on ABC's *Issues and Answers* telecast. Because of McCarthy's tendency to respond to reporters' questions rather than to address the audience and his hesitancy to attack sharply, Kennedy appeared more forceful and decisive.

The first rule of all campaigning (ATTACK) holds true for televised debates. The key is to seize the initiative and put the opponent on the defensive. John Kennedy did this both to Hubert Humphrey and Richard Nixon in 1960 debates and George Murphy put Pierre Salinger off balance in 1964 this way. But if the attack appears vicious or unfair it can rebound. Edward McCormack discovered this in his debate with Edward Kennedy in 1961. Attempting to discredit his opponent as a serious candidate by asserting that Kennedy's only qualification was that he was the president's brother, McCormack charged, "If his name was Edward Moore, with his qualifications, with your qualifications, Teddy, if it was Edward Moore, your candidacy would be a joke; but nobody's laughing because his name is not Edward Moore. It's Edward Moore Kennedy. . . ." But, the style was too belligerent, the attack too pointed. Kennedy's flush and the cracking of his voice won sympathy, not scorn, for the president's brother.[85]

Finally, studies of the effects of televised debates suggest that few voters change their minds as a result of watching debates, but that a significant number crystallize their decisions (that is, the undecided reach conclusions). One analysis of the 1960 Kennedy-Nixon debates, for example, concludes that Kennedy won the votes of a substantial portion of Americans who, before the debates, had not yet made up their minds for either candidate; but these dramatic gains by Kennedy were not matched among voters who had made a choice prior to the debates. The undecided voters were for the most part Independents, generally indifferent to the election's outcome, not well informed, or Democrats who were put off by Kennedy's youth or religion. Among this group Kennedy's image improved significantly;

[85] Levin, *Kennedy Campaigning*, pp. 182–232.

reservations about his youth particularly were removed by his capacity to "best" the older and more experienced Nixon.[86]

We can conclude by suggesting that, as a publicity device, televised debates influence the images voters have of the contenders. But the particular group that is most susceptible to such image-making is composed of indifferent and undecided citizens who may not vote at all unless stimulated by a dramatic campaign event like a televised confrontation. This reserved conclusion about the effects of televised debates raises a larger question to which we address ourselves in the closing chapter: What are the effects of political campaigns on voting behavior and attitudes? We have described the professionalization of campaign management, the sophistication of campaign research, and the diverse media for campaign communication. We must now turn to the cumulative impact of this technology of modern campaigning on our democratic elections.

[86] Lang and Lang, *Politics and Television*, pp. 218–47; Russell Middleton, "National TV Debates and Presidential Voting Decisions," *Public Opinion Quarterly*, XXVI (Fall, 1962), 426–28.

5

PROFESSIONALLY MEDIATED CAMPAIGNS: EFFECTS AND CONSEQUENCES

We said in Chapter 1 that a campaign consists of the activities of an individual (or group) in a particular context directed at manipulating the behavior of a wider number of people to his (their) advantage. So defined, campaigns involve a series of communications in specific settings between campaigners and their constituents. In American elections campaigners rely heavily on professionally developed skills to gather relevant information about the electorate in order to devise strategies and contrive the setting to the advantage of client-candidates. Instead of direct, spontaneous, personal contact between candidates and voters, we find professional management firms, pollsters, and communications specialists mediating between political leaders and followers. Our tasks in this final chapter are to estimate and explain the effects of the professionally mediated campaigns on voter behavior and to speculate about the consequences of modern campaign technology for democratic elections. Since the bulk of research explaining campaign effects (both experimental and survey research) has focused on the efforts of persuasive communications to change personal attitudes, we will report the results of that research. We will also examine a line of inquiry which suggests that campaigns do not change voters' attitudes (and are not intended to), but do influence voters' behavior by shaping human perceptions. Finally, we will discuss the impact of the management-pollster-television complex on democratic elections.

A THEORY OF ATTITUDINAL EFFECTS

Since political campaigns consist largely of persuasive communications, we can begin to explain their impact, large or small, by reviewing the findings of communications research into the types of effects persuasive messages have on personal attitudes.

PERSUASION AND ATTITUDE CHANGE

There are few questions as intriguing for behavioral scientists as those dealing with the influence of persuasive communications on human behavior: Does mass advertising sell products? Can propaganda win the war for men's minds? Is brain-washing possible? Can campaigns condition voting? Can we teach loyalty and devotion to the state? Interest in these questions has spawned a plethora of studies in the last quarter century.[1] We should first note the premises that underly these investigations. The leading assumption is that a person's attitudes direct his behavior by predisposing him to respond in certain ways to a stimulus—positively, negatively, or with indifference. As latent feelings which mediate between the demands on an individual and his response to those demands, underlying attitudes are revealed in the consistent behaviors people display toward given objects (perhaps expressed as opinions, votes, or purchases).[2] A prime example is the partisan leaning of a citizen that results in his voting for his party's candidate regardless of the issues or circumstances involved.

The assumption that attitudes guide behavior carries with it the implication that to change behavior a leader must first change the attitudes related to it. In keeping with this view students of political campaigns have catalogued the ways attitudes are affected by the diffusion of campaign information and appeals. The assumption that the purpose of election campaigns is to win votes principally by altering

---

[1] See, for example, Carl I. Hovland, A. A. Lumsdaine, and F. D. Sheffield, *Experiments on Mass Communication* (Princeton, N.J.: Princeton University Press, 1949); Carl I. Hovland, Irving L. Janis, and Harold H. Kelley, *Communication and Persuasion* (New Haven: Yale University Press, 1953); Elihu Katz and Paul F. Lazarsfeld, *Personal Influence* (New York: The Free Press of Glencoe, Inc., 1955).

[2] Richard F. Carter, "Communication and Affective Relations," *Journalism Quarterly*, XLII (Spring, 1965), 203–12.

attitudes lies at the base of much of the research about campaign effects and, as we shall see, has conditioned many of its conclusions. Although existing studies suggest different categories of attitude-change, we can summarize their conclusions by describing the converting, modifying, and creative effects of campaign communications.[3]

A campaign's effects are *converting* when persons committed to a given party, candidate, or cause forsake that commitment in favor of opposing appeals. If empirical studies are correct, conversion occurs relatively infrequently. We say "if" because we must draw our conclusions from studies of communications effects conducted well before the full advent of professionally mediated campaigning. For example, the study most often cited to demonstrate the general absence of conversion effects was conducted during the 1940 presidential election. Utilizing a representative sampling of voters in Erie County, Ohio, it compared the vote intentions of respondents in the precampaign period with their intentions in October. Only 2 per cent had converted from Republican to Democrat and 6 per cent from Democrat to Republican.[4] Comparable research (including a study of the 1948 presidential election in Elmira, New York, and others using nationwide samples in the 1952 and 1956 presidential contests) underscore the relative immunity of partisan loyalties to campaign conversion.[5] Hence, we conclude tentatively that if attitude-change in the form of partisan conversion must precede vote shifts (a questionable assumption, as we shall see later), campaigns win few votes.

The *modifying* effects of campaigns consist of altering the intensity of personal attitudes without necessarily changing their direction (conversion). Thus, a stern Democrat may become moderate in his partisanship. Although modifying effects can take several forms, *reinforcement* (a strengthening of intensity) of held convictions is the most common. Indeed, to the extent that steadying the morale of

---

[3] The most complete summary is Joseph T. Klapper, *The Effects of Mass Communication* (New York: The Free Press of Glencoe, Inc., 1961). See also Otto N. Larsen, "Social Effects of Mass Communication," in Robert E. L. Faris, ed., *Handbook of Modern Sociology* (Chicago: Rand McNally & Co., 1964), pp. 348–81.

[4] Paul F. Lazarsfeld, Bernard Berelson, and Hazel Gaudet, *The People's Choice* (New York: Columbia University Press, 1948), p. 102.

[5] Bernard R. Berelson, Paul F. Lazarsfeld and William N. McPhee, *Voting* (Chicago: The University of Chicago Press, 1954); Angus Campbell, Philip E. Converse, Warren E. Miller, and Donald E. Stokes, *The American Voter* (New York: John Wiley & Sons, Inc., 1960).

supporters is vital to victory, reinforcement is a prime objective of politicians (recall our discussion of Table 1-2). The reinforcement effect probably applies to the majority of the electorate exposed to campaign propaganda. There are cases, however, in which voters lose their enthusiasm for a favored candidate, perhaps even growing undecided at some point, but ultimately voting for him when election day brings an end to their wavering. Such a *diminishing* of attitudinal intensity (referred to in various studies as partial conversion, minor change, neutralization, or wavering)[6] is sufficiently common to worry contending candidates. In the 1940 study, for example, 15 per cent of voters wavered but returned to their original choice. A third type of modification, *crystallization*, occurs when voters enter a campaign undecided between candidates and finally reach a choice congenial to their unconscious leanings. Exposure to campaign propaganda provides the mildly interested voter with a rationale for choice by "identifying for him the way of thinking and acting that he is already half aware of wanting." [7] If crystallization results in voting rather than merely thinking about it, *activation* of attitudes has occured. A candidate does not win converts by activating complacent supporters, but he can win close elections by instilling interest. In Erie County in 1940 researchers estimated that 14 per cent of the voters were activated in this manner. Studies of more recent presidential elections provide evidence that campaigns conducted through mass communications channels (newspapers and television) activate attitudes and stimulate turnout among users of such media; non-users—less interested in politics to begin with—vote in lower proportions. Increases in turnout rates are associated with newspaper readership, but radio listening is independent of turnout; it does not seem that the advent of television campaigns has produced higher turnout rates.[8]

The *creative* force of persuasive communications refers to the latent effect campaigns have in forming attitudes where none previously existed. This effect is not easily measured because it is not readily apparent, but persons do acquire attitudes through campaign exposure. The most obvious examples occur not in politics, but in commercial

[6] See Lazarsfeld et al., *The People's Choice*; Klapper, *Effects of Mass Communication*; and Larsen, "Social Effects of Mass Communication."

[7] Lazarsfeld et al., *The People's Choice*.

[8] William A. Glaser, "Television and Voting Turnout," *Public Opinion Quarterly*, XXIX (Spring, 1965), 71–86; Angus Campbell, "Has Television Reshaped Politics?" *Columbia Journalism Review*, I (Fall, 1962), 10–13.

advertising designed to build brand loyalties in children. Professional political campaigners, whose goal is usually victory in the short run rather than long-term structuring of attitudes, seldom strive to create party loyalties and usually concentrate on tapping existing loyalties. However, media specialists often fashion candidate images for creative purposes. We shall have more to say of the creative functions of campaigns when we discuss their latent effects at a later point.

    The types of attitude change generated by persuasive campaign communications can be summarized as follows: modifying effects are the most likely, with the order of their relative occurrence being reinforcement, crystallization and/or activation, and neutralization; long-term creative effects occur in unknown magnitudes; and conversion is relatively rare. Finally, there is another possibility—that campaigns do not alter commitments, their direction, or their intensities at all. Past studies lead us to suspect that a small, but measurable, group of voters regularly remain totally unaffected by political campaigns. This group is largely confined to the apolitical strata of the community—those without political opinions or interest who shield themselves from the campaign through indifference and who seldom vote. Surveys indicate that this potential "no effect" group ranges from 3 to 10 per cent of those surveyed in recent national elections, but may be much higher in local and state contests.[9]

THE LAW OF MINIMAL CONSEQUENCES

If we accept for the moment the proposition that political campaigns influence votes only by first influencing voter attitudes, then we must conclude from the above typology of attitudinal effects that the fundamental impact of election campaigns is to reinforce, crystallize, or activate long-term voter loyalties; campaigns are therefore relatively ineffective when it comes to winning adherents from the opposition. And, as we suggested in Chapter 1, if the majority of voters with fixed convictions make up their minds even before the campaign begins, vote switches resulting from campaign appeals—no matter how professional and sophisticated the campaign—will be unusual. This general view is capsulized in the "law of minimal consequences," which states that the conversion potential of mediated appeals "is progressively reduced by the presence, within the communication situation,

[9] Campbell et al., *The American Voter*, p. 124.

of a host of intervening conditions, each one of which tends by and large to minimize the likelihood of a response disjunctive with prior inclinations." [10] To understand how this law operates when the function of campaigns is to change attitudes in order to switch votes, let us look at these limiting conditions in the communication setting of the political campaign. We can then consider the more provocative possibility that these same conditions do not restrict the potential influence of the professionally mediated campaign principally because modern campaign technology is aimed not at attitude change but at perceptual shifts.

Limiting Conditions in the Communication Setting

Mass communications, including those in a political campaign, are but one set of influences contributing to attitude-change; any message is but one stimulus working amid others in a total situation. Studies of communications effects suggest that the overall impact of accompanying stimuli is to reduce the conversion potential of communications and negotiate a reinforcement effect. Researchers have designed experiments and sample surveys to identify the factors operating in the communication setting that limit the direct effects of mass communication—those related to the audience, the social situation, the source, the message, and the media.[11]

Personal. One of the principal reasons that mass communications obey the law of minimal consequences is that an individual's existing attitudes are a defense against the persuasive demands made on him. As predispositions instilled during childhood by such socializing agencies as family, school, church, and peers, they are durable and fairly resistant to change. Because of these personal interests people tend to expose themselves to communications congenial to their existing attitudes and to avoid messages that challenge those attitudes. Moreover, even if exposed to conflicting communications, people perceive and remember arguments favorable to their own side while filtering or forgetting the opposition's pleas. Predispositions, then, give rise to

[10] Kurt Lang and Gladys Engel Lang, *Voting and Nonvoting* (Waltham, Mass.: Blaisdell Publishing Co., 1968), p. 4.

[11] See particularly Klapper, *Effects of Mass Communication*, pp. 98–132 and Arthur R. Cohen, *Attitude Change and Social Influence* (New York: Basic Books, Inc., 1964).

selective exposure, perception, and retention; to the extent that such selectivity operates, people attend to communications that reinforce existing beliefs.[12] From the standpoint of the political candidate selectivity implies that the people he is most likely to communicate to are those already predisposed to vote for him; conversely, those whose votes he wishes to win from the opposition are least likely to be in his audience.

Existing attitudes are not the only personal factor limiting the direct effects of persuasive communications. In some cases the level of intelligence of audience members can be important. Experiments conducted with troop indoctrination programs in World War II, for example, suggest that persons with high intelligence tend to be influenced by communications relying on intricate logical arguments (apparently because of a capacity to draw inferences) and pay relatively little attention to communications based on unsupported generalities or incorrect, illogical, or irrelevant arguments.[13] If valid, these hypotheses suggest the advisability of campaigners designing arguments with various levels of sophistication to reach the audiences of the printed, audio, and video media.

There is also experimental evidence that some individuals, because of personality traits, are especially susceptible to persuasive messages regardless of content. "Authoritarian" personalities (persons who adhere rigidly to conventional middle-class values, have uncritical views of people in authority, condemn outsiders, concern themselves with power and "toughness," or think in rigid categories) appear susceptible to persuasion by authority figures; people with low self-confidence and self-esteem are more easily influenced by mass communications.[14] Finally, an individual's cognitive style (how a person looks at the world, deals with information, and infers meaning) and his cognitive need for clarity, meaning, organization, integration, and reasonableness of experiences are related to his persuasibility. People with strong

[12] Klapper, *Effects of Mass Communication*, pp. 19–27.

[13] Hovland et al., *Experiments on Mass Communications;* Hovland et al., *Communication and Persuasion.*

[14] T. W. Adorno et al., *The Authoritarian Personality* (New York: John Wiley & Sons, 1961), Part One, p. 228; Eleanor L. Norris, "Attitude Change as a Function of Open or Closed-Mindedness," *Journalism Quarterly*, XLII (Autumn, 1965), 571–75; Irving L. Janis et al., *Personality and Persuasibility* (New Haven: Yale University Press, 1959).

cognitive needs who are quick to draw clear distinctions (sharpeners) pay more attention to communications and may undergo more attitude-change than persons with equal needs who simplify and ignore distinctions (levelers). But, if the cognitive needs are weak, the presuasibility of sharpeners and levelers is reversed. Interestingly enough, sharpeners seem particularly responsive to ambiguous communication; this suggests that campaign appeals—often the essence of ambiguity —may be particularly effective in meeting the needs of individuals who strive to project their own meanings into the message (a point related to the task of image-making discussed in Chapter 4).[15] Generally, however, the evidence regarding persuasibility as a function of personality is too sketchy to provide definitive conclusions on which candidates might base their actions.

Social. As targets of campaigns, voters exist not as isolated individuals but as members of social groups. Each group has norms, standards, and prejudices which guide the member to select messages and arguments in keeping with group appeals. Thus social groups contribute to the reinforcement effects of mass communications.

Within the social group individuals encounter the opinion leadership of respected members. These opinion leaders are more likely than are the average members to attend to a variety of mass communications, then interpret their messages for others. Consequently, personal influence reduces the direct impact of mass communications by intervening between the citizen and the politician's appeals.[16] To say that the direct effects of mass communication are reduced by interpersonal ties, however, is not to say that mass communications are without reinforcing or converting impact. In fact, studies of how information is diffused in America indicate that television and radio play the major role in delivering news of average importance (such as a candidate's position on a given issue) while interpersonal communication is the most important source for news stories of extraordinary significance (like President Lyndon Johnson's decision not to seek reelection in 1968). Even during working hours more people tend to learn about news events in a private home than in any other setting, making television the most frequent source of first exposure, but increasing the likelihood that the message will be interpreted through interpersonal

[15] Cohen, *Attitude Change and Social Influence*, pp. 48–55.
[16] Katz and Lazarsfeld, *Personal Influence.*

exchange.[17] Thus, the combination of mass and interpersonal communication constitutes a significant channel for persuasive efforts.

٭ *Source.* It stands to reason that the reputation of a candidate helps determine his effectiveness in persuasive communications. Numerous studies support this common-sense notion. Sources with reputations for high credibility, for example, stimulate more attitude-change in the desired direction than do sources of low credibility. And with respected sources, the greater the discrepancy between the citizen's position and the one advocated, the greater the degree of attitude-change (in this case in the direction of neutralization of the citizen's position). Interestingly enough, however, the advantage of high over low credibility tends to disappear over time; a "sleeper" effect occurs in which people dissociate the content of the message from the source and remember what was said without thinking about who said it.[18] A political campaigner could capitalize on this fundamental feature of image-advertising in the television spot commercial: Democrats who viewed Republican commercials (a low credibility source) would, in ensuing weeks, retain only the content of the spot while deemphasizing the source.

The Message. A political candidate states his positions through speeches, television spots, brochures, and similar media. Experimental studies of responses to communication messages underscore a point we made in the last chapter; that the form of the message is frequently far more significant than its content. For example, the order of presentation of arguments makes a difference. When conflicting views are presented in succession a "law of primacy" occurs, but the last view can still be made the most effective if the communicator contrasts his position sharply with those preceding. Richard Nixon has long recognized this rule, probably instinctively, as a campaigner. In press conferences and public addresses he frequently presents a series of positions on a major issue—Vietnam, crime, civil rights—then states his own view prefaced by "I say this . . ." or "I want to make *my* position very clear." Other rules of thumb revealed by empirical study and practiced instinctively by many politicians include: attitude-change in a desired direction is more likely to occur if the communicator states a conclusion instead of permitting the audience to draw their own;

[17] Richard J. Hill and Charles M. Bonjean, "News Diffusion: A Test of the Regularity Hypothesis," *Journalism Quarterly,* XLI (Summer, 1964), 336–42.
[18] Cohen, *Attitude Change and Social Influence,* pp. 23–36.

among interested supporters the most important points are best saved until the end of a presentation but among the disinterested they should come early; before a sympathetic audience (a rally of partisans) a communicator can be effective while presenting only one side of an argument, but if the audience is hostile or of mixed feelings (such as a captive television audience) both sides of an argument should be presented; and, aggressive or threatening presentations arousing fear frequently stimulate defense attitudes that limit the message's effectiveness.[19]

The media. The effectiveness of communications in changing attitudes also depends on the channel used to convey them. Both laboratory experiments and sample surveys (unfortunately conducted before the era of professionally mediated campaigns) emphasize that informal personal appeals are more effective than formalized mass presentations. Television and films are the most effective of the mass channels, with radio and printed media following in that order.

Although relying on scanty evidence, students of communications regard each of the mass media as possessing unique advantages for certain types of persuasion. The visual media—television and film—promote a sense of greater personal participation and command more complete attention of a viewer than do other media. One thesis argues that the visual media, because they do not depend upon patterned or sequential presentations as does the printed media, permit the audience to project their own predispositions and interpretations into the message content. Hence, the suitability of television for conveying images—each viewer fills in the content of the image to suit his own needs, interests, and fantasies.[20] The auditory media, such as radio, permit greater structuring of content to the advantage of the communicator but have the disadvantage of being only casually attended to by listeners. Printed media, such as newspapers, aid the communication of complex arguments, but require more effort beyond mere exposure than do either television or radio. The great advantage of personal contact is that the communication can be tailored continuously to the reactions of the individual listener or the large audience.[21]

[19] Carl I. Hovland et al., *The Order of Presentation in Persuasion* (New Haven: Yale University Press, 1957).

[20] Marshall McLuhan, *Understanding Media* (New York: New American Library, 1964).

[21] Klapper, *Effects of Mass Communication,* pp. 110–12.

Limiting Conditions in Voting Behavior

The personal predispositions and personalities of individuals, their social ties, the credibility of sources, the form of the message, and the media employed all limit the independent effectiveness of communications in changing attitudes and, through attitudes, behavior. These factors operate in any communication setting—a televised appeal for the United Fund, a minister's exhortations to his congregation, a teacher's lecture to students, or even a football coach's half-time pep talk. And of course they operate in political campaigns. In fact, research has revealed them to be so influential (particularly personal predispositions) that they often result in the overwhelming majority of voters reaching decisions before the campaign begins, leaving the appearance that most voters are not affected by political campaigns (at least in presidential elections). Let us now turn to the significant factors that shape voting behavior and minimize the efficacy of political campaigns.

Personal. The leading theory of American voting behavior contends that electoral choices reflect the interplay of two sets of forces—long-term predispositions of voters and short-term influences (such as candidates and issues) peculiar to a given election. Of the former, none are so crucial as the standing commitments of citizens to the two major parties. The evidence is that "three Americans out of four freely classify themselves as Democrats or Republicans, and most of those who call themselves Independents grant that they are closer to one party than they are to the other." [22] As with any attitude, partisanship varies in intensity as well as direction. Strong and moderate partisans are not likely to be won over by the opposition, but the weakly identified and the Independents (these two groups comprise about one-fourth of the electorate) are open to persuasion and in close elections they may provide the winning margin for a candidate. Although there is no one-to-one relationship between partisan identification and voting choices, partisan attitudes color a voter's perspective on candidates, issues, and campaign events. Thus, as in most communication settings, a predisposition conditions the exposure,

---

[22] Angus Campbell, "Some Findings of Voter Research," *Voting Research and the Businessman in Politics* (Ann Arbor, Mich.: The Foundation for Research on Human Behavior, 1960), p. 3.

perception, interpretation, and retention of campaign messages and the likelihood is that party loyalty will be reinforced rather than weakened or reversed. On the average only a fraction (less than 10 per cent) of voters change from one party to another in a campaign.[28]

Partisanship is not the only personal attitude that influences those voters who settle on their final vote by the time candidates are nominated in presidential elections. Some ideological predilections also serve this purpose. Certainly many conservatives in both political parties in 1964 were dedicated to the candidacy of Barry Goldwater long before his nomination. But, in a nation where less than 15 per cent of citizens sampled can even distinguish between liberal and conservative views, ideological predilections are not biasing tendencies of the same intensity as party identifications. Another personal factor associated with voting is the constellation of attitudes linked with a person's social and economic status in the community (SES). Closely tied to party identification (Democrats are located somewhat lower on SES scales than are Republicans), status consciousness contributes to the reinforcing effect of campaign appeals.

In addition to party identification, ideology, and socioeconomic status, we should also consider the degree of a citizen's interest in politics as a factor limiting the impact of the campaign. If voters simply do not follow the campaign, we can expect only minimal consequences from minimal exposure. Interest in election campaigns varies widely from year to year. In 1960, for example, the Survey Research Center of the University of Michigan asked of a nationwide sample, "Some people don't pay too much attention to election campaigns; how about you? Are you very interested, fairly interested, slightly interested, or not at all interested?" Almost three of every four respondents were "very interested" and fewer than 5 per cent "not at all" interested. Yet four years later less than half of respondents were "very interested." Generally we can say that the higher the proportion of citizens who follow a campaign, the less the impact of predispositions on the outcome and the greater the effect of persuasive communications. The reason is that under normal circumstances the people who follow campaigns most avidly are partisans who have made up their minds; a campaign in which there is high interest, however, captures the attention of people of low political

[28] Berelson et al., *Voting*, p. 345.

involvement—the Independents without partisan commitments or awareness. Since the marginally involved enter the electorate without the anchoring of party loyalties, they are most susceptible to persuasive appeals built upon images.[24]

Social. Group membership also helps to determine the effectiveness of campaign stimuli. In a study of the 1948 presidential election in Elmira, New York, researchers noted that the partisan character of political discussion within groups affected voting changes; the more an individual was exposed to members of the opposition party within his group, the more likely he was to change his vote to the opposition. If there was no intragroup conflict, each member was likely to vote with the group consensus. If a person was a member of two or more groups with differing political outlooks, the resulting cross-pressures on him as a voter (from his friends and co-workers, from friends and family, and so forth) tended to make him delay his final vote decision until late in the campaign; and the more intimate the conflict, the later the decision. Citizens whose voting fluctuated most between the two parties were those who did not discuss politics in their groups and who seemed to have no obvious cue for their behavior.[25]

Social groups consist of more than the face-to-face contacts among co-workers, friends, families, or peers. Certain categories of individuals with a similiar characteristic (Catholics, the middle-aged, urban dwellers, or farmers, for example) must also be considered. Although certain tendencies appear in the voting behavior of persons within each category, these are not always consistent and no cause-and-effect relation should be inferred (living in a central city does not cause a person to vote Democrat, for example). Generally, however, the voting patterns of sociodemographic groups are sufficiently clear to pose problems for any campaigner who tries to appeal to specific segments of his constituency. In national elections, at least, women tend to favor Republican candidates slightly more than do men; younger and older persons divide their vote between the parties in no clearly discernible fashion; Democrats draw votes from the Irish, Polish, Italian, and Slavic ethnic groups and Republicans from Americans of English, Scottish, Welsh, German, and Scandinavian ancestry; since World War II black Americans have shifted substantial voting support to

[24] Angus Campbell et al., *Elections and the Political Order* (New York: John Wiley & Sons, Inc., 1966), pp. 136–57.

[25] Berelson et al., *Voting*, pp. 118–49.

the Democrats; suburban America is divided in its support, leaning slightly Republican, as do small towns and rural areas outside the South; Democrats garner urban votes; Catholics and Jews tend toward the Democratic party and Protestants lean toward the Republican; and the high-status occupations, the upper-income groups, and the better-educated segments of the population lend disproportionate support to Republicans.

Political. Personal predispositions, we said earlier, are resistent to change in a specific campaign; and we have seen that these basic attitudes are frequently interlocked with the citizen's social life and sociodemographic characteristics. Together these long-term personal and social elements direct voting behavior. But there are also short-term political conditions peculiar to each campaign that interact with long-term forces and, as indicated by survey research, reinforce voter predilections rather than convert them. Among these short-term factors are the voter's orientations toward competing parties, candidates, issues, and the campaign media.

By *party orientations* we refer not to the partisan identifications of voters but to the images voters have of the two parties in a specific campaign. Voters usually, but not always, possess favorable images of the parties with which they identify. In 1956, for example, surveys indicated that both strong and weak Democrats held positive views of how well they thought the Democratic party could manage governmental affairs; and, expectedly, Republicans (both strong and weak identifiers) evaluated Republican management of government positively. But 1964 was a different story. Only a minority of Democrats gave positive comments (49 per cent) about their party's management of government and only 41 per cent of Republicans evaluated the incumbents of their own party favorably. Thus while party allegiance has a great impact on party images, conflicts between personal attitudes and perceptions can occur.

Similarly, partisans usually have positive *candidate orientations*, that is, favorable images of their party's candidates. But even more so perhaps than in the case of party orientations, attitudes and perceptions may be in conflict. In 1964, for example, about one-third to one-half of Republicans expressed negative comments about their candidate's character and background, personal attraction, position on domestic and foreign policies, and quality as a representative of their party. Did the Republicans who expressed unhappiness at the

Goldwater candidacy change their partisan attitudes and then vote Democratic (as would be suggested by the theory of attitudinal effects which states that communications changes behavior by first changing attitudes)? The evidence is that they did not. Nearly 49 per cent of Republicans unhappy with Goldwater's candidacy did vote Democratic, but their basic Republican identification remained. In effect, these Republicans voted their perceptions, not their attitudes (a point . we shall return to again).

Issue orientations refer to the voters' positions on conflicts they regard as important in the election. Again, these positions usually conform to those of the parties with which the voters identify, But, as in the case with party and candidate orientations, partisan attitudes and issue perceptions may differ for individual voters. A clear example of this occurred in the 1960 presidential election when large numbers of Protestant Democrats voted for the Republican candidate because of the religious issue of whether there should be a Catholic (Kennedy) in the White House.[26]

In sum, voters' perceptions of the short-term forces mentioned thus far—parties, candidates, and issues—normally conform to their long-term predispositions. To the extent that this is the case, information and impressions communicated to voters in the course of a campaign simply reinforce the voting choices they have already made on the basis of their partisan leanings. Under these conditions campaigns change few minds. Yet we have urged that voter perceptions are not always simple results of personal attitudes. A conflict between fundamental loyalties and immediate perceptions generates a delay in making voting decisions. For those who are undergoing such conflict as well as for those who are indifferent to the campaign until its closing weeks, the source of information on which to base their ultimate voting decision is frequently the mass media. What do we know of the effects of media exposure on voters?

The most general proposition relating *media orientations* to voting behavior is that the persons who actually expose themselves most are those who are least likely to shift their voting intentions during a campaign. By the same token, however, "the more exposure to the

[26] Denis G. Sullivan, "Psychological Balance and Reactions to the Presidential Nominations in 1960," in M. Kent Jennings and L. Harmon Zeigler, eds., *The Electoral Process* (Englewood Cliffs, N.J.: Prentice-Hall, Inc., 1966), pp. 238–64.

campaign in the mass media, the more correct their perception of where the candidates stand on the issues." [27] The greater the discrepancy between the preferred party candidate's stand on issues and the voter's, the less likely (in these instances) that the voter's perceptions will be distorted by his party allegiance. Therefore, although most interested voters who follow the campaign in one or more media have already made up their minds (and simply reinforce those decisions), those few who are experiencing conflicts between personal attitudes and perceptions are likely to be influenced by campaign messages, perhaps resulting in a neutralization effect.

In any event the evidence indicates (see Table 4-1, p. 116) that the campaigns are relatively well monitored through the media. In 1964, for example, 19 per cent of citizens sampled by the Survey Research Center followed the campaign in four different media, 36 per cent followed it in three, 30 per cent in two, 12 per cent in one, and only 3 per cent used no media at all. Interestingly enough, however, in that campaign the number of media used bore no relation to when voters made up their minds on the candidates; thus, 60 per cent of those using two or more media made up their minds after the nominating conventions, but so did almost the same percentage of those using one medium (50 per cent) or no media (52 per cent).[28]

As we observed in the last chapter, of the media available for following a campaign Americans increasingly rely on television for campaign information. The evidence regarding the effects of television (as opposed to the total campaign effort) on changing votes is scanty. In one study of the 1964 presidential campaign 46 per cent of respondents reported having seen television commercials for Goldwater and 39 per cent had seen commercials for Johnson; 29 per cent of those who saw a half-hour Goldwater television show reported they knew a great deal more about what he stood for because of it and 17 per cent who saw his commercials said they learned about Goldwater by doing so. But, as the study concludes, "opinion was already fairly well crystallized, and not much change resulted." [29] And, in 1960 44 per cent of a sample conducted by Elmo Roper reported the Kennedy-Nixon

[27] Berelson et al., *Voting*, p. 252.
[28] Jerome D. Becker and Ivan L. Preston, "Media Usage and Political Activity," *Journalism Quarterly*, XLVI (Spring, 1969), 129–34.
[29] Thomas W. Benham, "Polling for a Presidential Candidate: Some Observations on the 1964 Campaign," *Public Opinion Quarterly*, XXIX (Summer, 1965), 196.

debates had "influenced" their votes, 5 per cent ascribed their final decision to the debates alone. Even if we accept these figures as accurate reflections of television's impact, however, "the net change caused by the debates was only 2 per cent of the total vote." [30] Thus the available evidence on the attitudinal effects of media orientations in general, and of television exposure in particular, does little to negate the law of minmimal consequences.

A THEORY OF PERCEPTUAL EFFECTS

On the basis of what we have said about the attitudinal effects of persuasive communications and the limiting conditions present in any communication setting (particularly in the campaign setting of presidential elections), we can reiterate that the law of minimal consequences applies to professionally mediated political campaigns in so far as they are directed at winning votes by changing attitudes. Yet there remains the fact that a small proportion of voters (perhaps one-third of voters in national elections and far higher proportions in primary, statewide, and local contests) decide between competing candidates during the course of the campaign. Nor can we ignore the fact that in presidential and congressional elections, where party loyalties ordinarily play an overriding part in voter decisions, voters frequently select candidates from the opposition (as did the Democrats who voted for Eisenhower in the 1950s and Nixon in the 1960s or Republicans who voted against Goldwater in 1964). We must conclude that despite the limiting conditions that minimize the consequences of election campaigns, there remains an area of impact not easily explained by the theory of attitudinal effects. Let us, then, turn to an alternative explanation of voting behavior, a theory of perceptual effects.

PERSUASION AND PERCEPTION

In most communications studies the concept of persuasion is narrowly defined. Since attitudes toward persons, objects, and situations are

---

[30] Richard S. Salant, "The Television Debates: A Revolution That Deserves A Future," *Public Opinion Quarterly*, XXVI (Fall, 1962), 341; Stanley Kelley, Jr., "Campaign Debates: Some Facts and Issues," *Public Opinion Quarterly*, XXVI (Fall, 1962), 351–66.

either positive, neutral, or negative, communications studies usually define a persuasive communication as one intended to change an attitude to a position opposite to that held before exposure to the message (usually positive to negative or vice versa). In this view the intended effect of persuasion is conversion; communications that change the intensity of an attitude—reinforcement, neutralization, crystallization, or activation—are, almost by definition, "ineffective." [31] In studies of political campaigns the implied definition of persuasion, i.e. overcoming a resistant attitude, is taken for granted. Thus since political campaigns change few people's minds, the conclusion is that they have only marginal influence on voting behavior.

Now we have seen that there are many reasons why persuasive communications seldom overcome resistant attitudes. Perhaps the most important is that to possess an attitude implies commitment; that is, having an attitude means that the individual is to some degree involved in his stand. The more highly involved or committed he is to his stand (the greater the intensity of his attitude), the more likely he is to reject all alternative views; conversely the lower his involvement, the more noncommittal he is toward other positions. The highly involved individual contrasts opposing views with his own and resists any persuasive effort to change; the less-committed person, however, assimilates alternative positions into his own point of view and accepts any one of a broad range of options as suitable behavior, without necessarily changing the attitude with which he has a low degree of involvement.[32]

To the extent that this thesis of the relation of attitudes and ego-involvements is correct, it offers a slightly different way of looking at the nature of persuasion. We saw earlier that one reason mass persuasion falls short of converting attitudes is that existing predispositions provide perceptual defenses against challenging stimuli. With low involvement or noninvolvement, however, these perceptual barriers are not as formidable or are entirely absent. In such cases of lesser involvement the intent of persuasion is not to change attitudes directly, but rather to break through the weak perceptual barriers and convince the individual of alternative ways of acting, each of which conforms to his basic predispositions instead of being contrary to them. In a

---

[31] Larsen, "Social Effects of Mass Communication," p. 361.
[32] Carolyn W. Sherif, Muzafer Sherif, and Roger E. Nebergall, *Attitude and Attitude Change* (Philadelphia: W. B. Saunders Company, 1965), pp. 11–17.

political campaign, for example, this might mean altering the perceptions of a loyal Republican so that he sees in the Democratic candidate the qualities he has learned to associate with being an effective leader, thus giving him the rationale for voting for the opposition despite his long-term predisposition. Certainly many lifelong Republicans chose Lyndon Johnson over Barry Goldwater in precisely this fashion in 1964.

Following this reasoning, then, the purpose of persuasion is not to change the attitudes of the committed, but to shift the perceptions of voters with low involvement. If persuasive communications are successful, the audience learns the messages and modes of behavior acceptable to the persuader without being converted, a process labeled "learning without involvement." [33] In these instances the qualities of the mass media, particularly television, are influential. First, the form of messages takes precedence over their content. Studies indicate, for example, that the perceptions of noninvolved or only slightly involved persons vary significantly with changes in the order of arguments, communication style, and the prestige of the source.[34] Second, imagery is crucial. It is important that the content of a message or the qualities of a product or candidate be sufficiently ambiguous that members of an audience can project into it the percepts relevant to their own cognitive needs. As the Erie County study revealed, "A campaign argument will be particularly successful if a variety of meanings can be read into it." [35] In advertising it is possible to take a product which for years has been perceived as "reliable," slightly alter its appearance (perhaps through packaging, slogans, or associating it with energetic housewives), and have it perceived as "modern" (but no less reliable). Although we lack evidence to support the thought, one could speculate that in 1968 the "New Nixon" was a product of changed perceptions; seen as "shrewd" in 1960, the "whole man" in 1968 emerged as "credible" (but no less shrewd). Finally, message repetition plays an important part in shifting perceptions. Since perceptual persuasion is aimed at persons with low involvement in an issue, it is an audience that pays little attention to the commu-

[33] Herbert E. Krugman, "The Impact of Television Advertising: Learning Without Involvement," *Public Opinion Quarterly*, XXIX (Fall, 1965), 349–56.

[34] Hovland et al., *Order of Presentation*, p. 136; Sherif et al., *Attitude and Attitude Change*, p. 16.

[35] Lazarsfeld et al., *The People's Choice*, p. 151.

nication. But repetition of a commercial or political spot helps over-come their lack of awareness as well as their weakened perceptual defenses.

The less important to a person the subject considered, the more likely is persuasion, or learning, without involvement. People are par-ticularly adept, for example, at learning trivia or nonsense material (as a meaningless string of words) of little significance to them. In many respects television advertising (including political spots) is nonsensi-cal or unimportant. Such "trivia are repeatedly learned and repeatedly forgotten and then repeatedly learned a little more. . . ."[36] As this happens some of the material is retained. Another possibility is that the learning-forgetting cycle alters the way we look at the product or candidate under consideration (suggesting, as it did for some in 1968, that Spiro Agnew didn't "sound" like a vice-president). A third pos-sibility is that, having shifted our perceptions and having acted ac-cordingly to our altered views, we gradually change our attitudes in the direction of our altered perceptions. That is, instead of the atti-tude-change-precedes-behavioral-change sequence posited earlier, the pattern may well be: perceptual shift, followed by behavioral change, and ultimately a delayed attitude-change. This seems particularly likely if we find the results of our behavior pleasing, that is, if the rewards of our action reinforce or rationalize that action. In political campaigns, therefore, the attitude-change we seek may lag several years behind the campaign itself, like the gradual movement of former southern Democrats to the Republican party after years of voting for Eisenhower, Goldwater, and Nixon.

In relating the process of perceptual change to politics we offer two points. First, perceptual shifts need not be limited to trivial or unim-portant matters. In fact, there are indications that predispositions related to deep prejudices may respond to perceptual shifts.[37] Second, a theory of perceptual effects is especially useful in discussing the con-sequences of political campaigns because many Americans have only low involvement in their political community, particularly below the level of presidential elections. Indeed, the evidence of various voting studies indicates that weak party identifiers and independents (ap-proximately the same population most influenced by campaigns), are slightly involved or uninvolved politically. The repetition of symbolic,

[36] Krugman, "The Impact of Television Advertising," p. 353.
[37] E. L. Hartley, *Problems in Prejudice* (New York: Kings Crown Press, 1946).

almost nonsensical, appeals by candidates and parties changes the way they look at politics and wins votes without really engaging fundamental predispositions. For the lesser involved of our citizens a campaign is effective to the degree that it gratifies inner needs rather than converts basic beliefs. Let us explore how this occurs.

A USES-AND-GRATIFICATIONS APPROACH

We saw that the basic element in the theory of attitudinal effects was the law of minimal consequences. The theory of perceptual effects rests on a different formulation, a uses-and-gratifications approach. By this we simply recognize that people use the mass media in their everyday lives, that they derive gratifications from their exposure to it (even from exposure to political programs in a campaign), and that a citizen contributes to an interaction between himself and the mass media. This leads us to ask what uses the media serve, what satisfactions accrue to that use, what are viewer preferences, and what political effects follow from exposure to preferred political programming.[38]

Information and Play Functions of Mass Media

For the most part studies of the attitudinal effects of exposure to political communications assume that people attend to political media to gain information about candidates, parties, and issues. It follows that if their motivation to learn about the campaign is high, they involve themselves in reading political news, listening to a broadcast, and watching political television. But voting studies consistently reveal that the people who are motivated enough to expose themselves to political information have already made up their minds; moreover, the persons who are most susceptible to the flow of persuasive information, the noninvolved, are least likely either to expose themselves to it or to vote.[39]

It is possible, however, to argue that the political media have substantial effects on lesser involved citizens even though these citizens do

---

[38] This approach is employed in a study of the 1964 British elections: Jay G. Blumler and Dennis McQuail, *Television in Politics* (Chicago: University of Chicago Press, 1969).

[39] Campbell et al., *Elections and the Political Order*, pp. 136–57; Verling C. Trodahl et al., "Public Affairs Information-Seeking from Expert Institutionalized Sources," *Journalism Quarterly*, XLII (Summer, 1965), 403–12.

not derive information from the media. This argument rests on the notion that, from the standpoint of an audience member, the function of the media is not to inform but to act as a source of subjective play. This notion, labeled the ludenic (or play) theory of mass communication, has several features that make it interesting to anyone concerned with explaining the effects of professionally mediated campaigns.[40]

The play concept is central to the theory. Play is pretending, an escape from the painful world of duty and responsibility; it occurs as an interlude in the work day, has the quality of fantasy in the sense that it is not ordinary or real, and is voluntary rather than obligatory. Finally, it is a disinterested activity that provides temporary satisfaction for its own sake; thus, although taken seriously by the player, it is not really important to him beyond the moment. Communication can be a form of play from which people derive communication-pleasure. For example, two people may converse and not expect anything from the interaction beyond the joy of the conversation itself (communication-pleasure) or they may undertake the conversation to resolve a dispute, change an opinion, or bring about some other goal (communication-pain).

Critics of mass culture have long recognized that mass communications is concerned primarily with providing entertainment, not information (recall, for example, our discussion in Chapter 4 of the use of entertainment in audience-delivery).[41] Play theory contends that where mass communications concerns entertainment, it is characteristically a matter of communication-pleasure that "brings no material gain and serves no 'work' functions, but it does induce certain elements of self-enchantment." [42] Hence listening to the radio, watching television, or reading a newspaper, magazine, or book usually occurs as play for its own sake, for immediate gratifications rather than for future rewards. As play (that is, as a voluntary, temporarily gratifying, disinterested, and unimportant interlude), media exposure does not

[40] William Stephenson, *The Play Theory of Mass Communication* (Chicago: University of Chicago Press, 1967).

[41] See the following: Elihu Katz and David Foulkes, "On the Use of the Mass Media as 'Escape': Clarification of a Concept," *Public Opinion Quarterly*, XXVI (Fall, 1962), 377–89; William R. Hazard, "Anxiety and Preference for Television Fantasy," *Journalism Quarterly*, XLIV (Autumn, 1967), 461–69; and Harold Mendelsohn, "Socio-Psychological Perspectives on the Mass Media and Public Anxiety," *Journalism Quarterly*, XL (Autumn, 1963), 511–16.

[42] Stephenson, *Play Theory*, p. 59.

demand intense or even moderate ego-involvement; indeed, when one is absorbed in the media, "all sense of self is absent" and "afterwards you may say how much you enjoyed it, but at the time there was no self-reference, no pride, no vanity, no sense of oneself, no wish, no being-with-anything, no intrusion of the self upon the news." [43] Thus, while deep concentration requires the motivation of those who are highly interested and involved in the real world, quiet absorption in the news is much less demanding.

Just as communication serves both work and play, pain and pleasure, so does politics. Professional campaigners, candidates, politicians, office-holders, and the politically motivated do the work; but for the general public, particularly the less involved, politics is only something to talk about (and to talk about only when it is fun). What each citizen derives from the mass media in a political campaign is not information (communication-pain), but entertainment (communication-pleasure). Alone as a member of a mass audience his senses are titillated and temporarily gratified. He does not internalize what he perceives in the sense that his attitudes are changed, but he remembers and forgets in the rote fashion of learning without involvement. In the process he comes to a vote decision congenial to his perceptions. The convergence of these individual decisions on election day constitutes the ultimate measure of the effectiveness of the mediated campaign.

As yet there has been no broadscale, systematic study of the effects of an American political campaign emphasizing the pain-pleasure, involvement-noninvolvement, and convergent selectivity variables suggested by play theory. What evidence we have of the usefulness of this approach is derived from a study of the effects of political television in the 1964 British general elections. Surveys in that contest were aimed at revealing why people watch political television and what types of program formats they prefer. Two general reasons for watching political television emerged. The first, surveillance of the political environment, was the type of information-gathering typical of highly motivated party identifiers who have already decided on their choice and are seeking reinforcement—to keep up with the issues of the day, judge what leaders are like, and see what the parties will do with power. The second, the excitement of the election, was charac-

[43] Ibid., p. 51.

teristic of the lesser involved who did derive some vote guidance from television. When it came to preferred political formats, voters generally sought challenging forms of political television, particularly televised debates, that heighten the excitement and drama of the contest.[44]

Para-Social Character of Campaign Communication

Our discussion thus far suggests that mediated campaigns perform a play function for lesser involved voters who derive communication-pleasure from them. As we said earlier the uses-and-gratifications approach involves the view that an individual contributes to an interaction between himself and the mass media. Mass media experts refer to this interaction as "para-social." [45] In brief, the mass media—especially television—expand the citizen's social world by giving him immediate access to whatever occurs anywhere in the world (thus, as one scholar says, creating a "global village").[46] Television heroes, celebrities, and hosts are personalities with whom audience members figuratively converse daily. A sense of participation with little demand for involvement makes para-social interaction pleasurable for its own sake.

Political television raises the possibility of para-social participation by viewers in election campaigns. The remarkable capacity of television to convey the images of conflicts, candidates, and political moods yet allow the viewer to perceive in those images what he expects to see, to "see for himself," results in citizens who are electronic participants in political events rather than mere targets for campaign messages. But the character of television itself shapes what they expect to see. No television viewer truly sees the "actuality" of the televised event, say a party convention or rally. Instead the picture on the screen is carefully contrived for dramatic effect by selection of what to focus on, camera angle, background, and timing. Perhaps an example from the nonpolitical realm will serve our purposes best, one that typifies television coverage of such diverse events as political

[44] Blumler and McQuail, *Television in Politics*, pp. 51–121.

[45] Kurt Lang and Gladys Engel Lang, *Politics and Television* (Chicago: Quadrangle Books, Inc., 1968), p. 20; Donald Horton and R. Richard Wohl, "Mass Communication and Para-Social Interaction," *Psychiatry*, XIX (August, 1966), 215–29.

[46] McLuhan, *Understanding Media*, pp. vii–xi.

rallies, space shots, urban riots, inaugurations, and state funerals. In 1960 the American Football League challenged the monopoly of the established rival, the National Football League. In its first few seasons the new league drew few spectators to its games. To survive it had to give the impression that its popularity was equal to that of the older league. Televised games were used to foster that impression. By congregating the small number of spectators on the fifty-yard-line and adroitly panning the camera across the "enthusiastic throng" at propitious moments, television transmitted the illusion of a packed stadium wildly cheering the gladiators on the field. Ultimately the league prospered and merged with its rival. Phony laugh tracks for comedy shows or tight camera shots of sparse crowds along parade routes provide the same illusion in other entertainment programming.

This capacity of television to structure what viewers assume to be truth from "actuality" coverage (the inferential structure of the medium) has far-reaching consequences for politics. The various media structure a political environment which people perceive only through the media. Moreover, the preconceptions, illusions, and impressions that affect voters' perceptions and ultimately their vote decisions have been influenced over the years by the mass media. Hence people perceive in the televised political campaign precisely what the media have led them to believe should be there. For highly motivated and involved voters whose attitudes are resistant to change in a single campaign, the media's reactivating and reinforcing of past loyalties has a cumulative impact which is not easily measured in studies of campaign effects. For the lesser involved the media, by para-social means, shape predispositions about what politics is about (crises and conflict) and the preferred qualities of political leaders (credibility and trustworthiness). Thus in the long term the mass media themselves create the conditions in which the image campaign can have its greatest impact.[47]

The Image Campaign as Para-Social Play

We have said that people participate in political communication via the mass media as in a form of play with relatively low involvement costs. Despite the efforts of news programs to practice objec-

---

[47] Lang and Lang, *Politics and Television*, pp. 300–310.

tivity and federal laws to assure an equitable distribution of free broadcast time between competing candidates, no communications media are neutral. Both news and campaign communications are symbolic in that they capture the outlines of an event or message in simple, easily grasped concepts. That conceptualization implies subjective selection and interpretation by newsmen, public relations personnel, media specialists, and others. The overall process results in a refraction or a reduction of fidelity in the transmission of content. As a result the citizen perceives only an approximation of the real struggle for power which is devoid of realistic detail and dramatic in outline. Having little contact with the political environment except through his para-social play with the mass media, he has no way of testing the reality of campaign messages even if he is motivated to do so.[48] Image campaigns make use of controlled refractions intended for voters in this situation.

We explained in Chapter 4 that an image campaign presents a candidate to the electorate in ways that emphasize appropriateness of style and ambiguity of content. If people see in an object what they project into it, image candidates must be sufficiently flexible receptacles to satisfy a wide variety of image predispositions. Image predispositions are the preconceptions people have of the qualities of an effective political leader. Because of its inferential structure, the source of the preconceptions is usually television. Television creates a myth of the ideal leader in two ways. First, coverage of political events gives viewers the impression that they can actually compare a politician's announced intentions with his behavior. By "eavesdropping" on a caucus of politicians at a party convention, for instance, viewers feel privy to what leaders are "really like." Or, if there are doubts about a politician's credibility, as there were following Senator Edward Kennedy's automobile accident in July, 1969, in which Mary Jo Kopechne was killed, viewers have an opportunity to take the full measure of the man's "maturity," "sincerity," and "honesty" as he makes a public report before the television camera. In short, television yields an impression of who can and cannot be trusted in politics, perpetuating the notion that the seemingly honest, sincere, and credible leader is trustworthy (witness the continuing concern of television reporters with the widening and narrowing of the "credibility gap" between

---

[48] Murray Edelman, *The Symbolic Uses of Politics* (Urbana: University of Illinois Press, 1964), pp. 122–23.

what politicians say and do).[49] Second, the ideal style for effective leadership is portrayed daily in television's endless parade of dramatic heroes, masters of ceremonies, and "personalities." Voters cannot help but compare the politician's performance with that of the professional entertainer.[50]

Which takes precedence in conditioning voting behavior—partisan or image predispositions? Available evidence yields no certain conclusion. In 1960 researchers examined the perceptions that two groups of political activists had of the presidential candidates, Richard Nixon and John F. Kennedy. One group was composed of 39 Young Republicans the other of 80 Young Democrats. It was assumed that if party loyalty distorted perceptions Republicans would react positively to Nixon and negatively to Kennedy while Democrats would react the opposite. If the stimulus of the candidate's image was effective, however, a mixed pattern was expected (Democrats and Republicans reacting positively or negatively to candidates regardless of party affiliation). The results tended to favor the image-determined view, but were not conclusive; members of both parties perceived Kennedy as more ambitious, aggressive, striving, active, and dynamic and Nixon as less ambitious, more easygoing, contented, passive, relaxed, and conforming. Yet members of each party tended to see their party's candidate as more complex, stable, and statesmanlike.[51] The cautious support for the image thesis drawn from the 1960 research paralleled the conclusions of a study undertaken at the time of the first widely televised presidential contest, that between Dwight Eisenhower and Adlai Stevenson in 1952. In that study 1,833 college students in California rated the two candidates on several qualities. Members of both parties rated both candidates as fine and great men, indicating an image impact. Television seemed to humanize Eisenhower by softening his soldier image and portraying him as more sensitive and withdrawn than his reputation indicated. Radio, on the other hand, helped convey a positive impression of Stevenson, apparently emphasizing his

[49] Kurt Lang and Gladys Engel Lang, "The Mass Media and Voting," in Eugene Burdick and Arthur J. Brodbeck, eds., *American Voting Behavior* (Glencoe, Ill.: The Free Press, 1959), pp. 217–35.

[50] Gene Wyckoff, *The Image Candidates* (New York: The Macmillan Company, 1968).

[51] Joseph E. McGrath and Marion F. McGrath, "Effects of Partisanship on Perceptions of Political Figures," *Public Opinion Quarterly*, XXVI (Summer, 1962), 236–48.

forensic skills.[52] A random sampling of Detroit voters in the 1960 presidential contest challenges the image thesis. These findings indicated that when rating the candidates on ten traits partisans tended to strive for perceptual congruence between their ideal and preferred-candidate images and did not perceive the candidate of the opposition in ideal terms. The image that Independents possessed of an ideal president corresponded with their perceptions of neither candidate.[53]

ᵼ For the moment, therefore, the conventional thesis that partisan predispositions are more significant than image predispositions in influencing voters has not been proved or disproved. But to justify the application of the law of minimal consequences to image campaigns there must be widespread partisanship in the American electorate. There is evidence, however, that partisanship is on the decline, particularly among the young. A Gallup survey in 1969 indicated that in the general public 28 per cent identified themselves as Republican, 42 per cent as Democratic, and 30 per cent as Independent. But, among college students 23 per cent were Republican, 33 per cent Democratic, and 44 per cent declared independence.[54]

There are other reasons to believe that the law of minimal consequences may not apply as rigidly under conditions of para-social play. In the area of selective exposure, for instance, the freedom of the citizen to choose his political television or ignore it) is decreased by the saturation use of spot announcements for image-advertising in a campaign; moreover, to the extent that such sophisticated commercials as those described in Chapter 4 are entertaining, they offer communication-pleasure. And critical readings of many of the studies from which the notion of selective exposure originally developed indicate that selectivity is not as limiting a factor as first advertised. For example, in the Erie County study in 1940, one of the first studies to minimize the converting effects of political campaigns, only Republicans evidenced selective exposure. Among Democrats 50.4 per cent paid attention primarily to Democratic propaganda and the remainder of Democrats exposed themselves mainly to Republican appeals. Simi-

[52] Ithiel de Sola Pool, "TV: A New Dimension in Politics," in Burdick and Brodbeck, eds., *American Voting Behavior*, pp. 236–61.

[53] Roberta S. Sigel, "Effect of Partisanship on the Perception of Political Candidates," *Public Opinion Quarterly*, XXVIII (Fall, 1964), 483–96.

[54] American Institute of Public Opinion, News Release, June 4, 1969.

larly, selective exposure was not overly apparent in the 1948 Elmira study. Finally, there is no conclusive evidence that people prefer information supporting their views to that opposing them; the conventional proposition that they do was generated from conflicting studies.[55]

Studies indicate that in a communication situation opinion leaders limit the direct effectiveness of mass appeals. Among less involved persons, however, a lack of audience interaction produces "pluralistic ignorance," a condition in which individuals do not know the opinions of others. In the absence of personal influence, therefore, these individuals frequently turn to the mass media to obtain cues for how to vote.[56]

Finally, the "not uncommon tendency to go overboard in blindly minimizing the effects and potentialities of mass communications" [57] frequently makes us ignore the latent effects of professionally mediated campaigns that are not readily apparent in a single election contest. We have already discussed one of these socializing effects—the inculcation of image predispositions, particularly the channeling of trust and distrust. Other effects should also be mentioned. Campaigns, for example, create and reinforce the images of what the two major parties stand for, even implying that two-party campaigns are the only legitimate ones in presidential politics and forcing a third-party candidate (like George Wallace in 1968) to accept the burden of proof that his American Independent party was somehow not "un-American." Political news between and during election campaigns sets the agenda by defining legitimate and significant issues for debate (as when the war in Vietnam became an issue prior to 1968). To reiterate, because so many Americans use and obtain gratifications from the mass media, it is their principal source of political reality; and because it is filled with secondhand pseudo events the mass of citizens can but imagine what politics is like while only the governing elites are privy to the reality.[58]

[55] David O. Sears and Jonathan L. Freedman, "Selective Exposure to Information: A Critical Review," *Public Opinion Quarterly*, XXXI (Summer, 1967), 194–213.

[56] Warren Breed and Thomas Ktsanes, "Pluralistic Ignorance in the Process of Opinion Formation," *Public Opinion Quarterly*, XXV (Fall, 1961), 382–92.

[57] Klapper, *Effects of Mass Communications*, p. 252.

[58] Lang and Lang, "The Mass Media and Voting."

Summary: A Field Theory of Campaign Effects

In this chapter we have posited two views of how voters react to professionally mediated campaigns as a result of their degree of political involvement. The citizen with a high degree of personal involvement is more than just interested, attentive, and excited; he actively prompts himself to read, discuss, and absorb information from the media while identifying with a political party. His political attitudes are fairly intense and stable and as a result the range of opposing views he is willing to accept is relatively narrow and there are few issues on which he is uncommitted. Any new idea in the form of a campaign stimulus must be compared and contrasted with basic predispositions, usually on the level of conscious attitude. Homeostatic theories of attitude-change tell us that if, in the process, a conflict between attitudes and perceptions occurs, a "strain toward consistency" will result in a balancing whereby there may be small shifts of attitude in the direction of the new view but outright conversion will be unlikely.[59] By selective exposure, perception, and retention, however, such conflicts are minimized and reinforcement rather than diminishment of an attitude with which the individual is deeply involved is more likely to occur. Involved voters, then, make up their minds prior to or early in campaigns and professionally mediated appeals do little to change their decisions.

The second type of voter is uninvolved or only slightly involved with political matters. His politically relevant attitudes are usually poorly articulated, of low intensity, and unstable. He probably does not identify with a party and attends to the campaign media for the gratifications it provides as entertainment rather than for information; the campaign is a form of para-social play in which his role, while not passive, is quiescent. Whereas the involved voter evidences concerned political activity, the uninvolved voter is politically inanimate, and sometimes only a spectator at the contest.[60] His relatively low involvement makes him the primary target of professional cam-

---

[59] Nathan Maccoby and Eleanor E. Maccoby, "Homeostatic Theory in Attitude Change," *Public Opinion Quarterly,* XXV (Winter, 1961), 538–45; Chester A. Insko, *Theories of Attitude Change* (New York: Appleton-Century-Crofts, 1967), pp. 112–284.

[60] Herbert E. Krugman, "The Measurement of Advertising Involvement," *Public Opinion Quarterly,* XXX (Winter, 1966–67), 584–85.

paigners. They bombard his weak perceptual defenses, attempting to effect modest shifts in perception, to reinforce those shifts by repetition of gratifying entertainment, and to activate sympathetic perceptions by providing a credible voting choice. Attitude-change is not the intent of such campaigns but a delayed attitude-change between campaigns (*after* the perceptual shifts in one campaign have resulted in voting choices) is a definite possibility. Thus, attitude-change results not from the balancing tendencies emphasized by homeostatic theories, but from the gradual learning, through repetition and practice, of a new way of looking at the world.[61]

A political campaign, like any social interaction, involves playing a variety of roles. The involved citizen plays an activist role while the uninvolved or only slightly involved citizen plays his part as a spectator, albeit a spectator drawn into the fray as a voter in the polling booth. The professional campaigner recognizes that an effective approach to the politically uninvolved individual must teach him a temporary political role. To guide the uninvolved citizen from his private role as businessman, worker, contractor, or clerk to his public role as voter, the professional campaigner contrives the campaign stage to his own advantage, employs the appropriate media, and endeavors to teach by example. The candidate is presented as the ideal leader in whom we can place faith and trust; his image remains sufficiently ambiguous to permit the gradually politicized voter to "fill in the gaps" by projecting his own private needs. The effects of political campaigns thus result from role-taking in a field of action; the roles assumed are those of candidates attempting to act as leaders and of highly involved, slightly involved, and uninvolved citizens moving toward their roles as voters. The professional campaigner's task is to see that his candidate's role successfully converges with those played by voters, a task in which he has had marked success in contemporary America.[62]

CAMPAIGNS AND DEMOCRATIC POLITICS

In this chapter we have confined ourselves to the effects of profes-

[61] Maccoby and Maccoby, "Homeostatic Theory," pp. 542–43; Insko, *Theories of Attitude Change*, pp. 12–91.
[62] J. Milton Yinger, *Toward a Field Theory of Behavior* (New York: McGraw-Hill Book Company, 1965); Bruce J. Biddle and Edwin Thomas, *Role Theory* (New York: John Wiley & Sons, Inc., 1966), pp. 3–63.

sionally mediated campaigns on voting behavior. We now consider another consequence of modern campaign technology—the impact of the invasion of professional managers, pollsters, and image-makers on the whole of the democratic process. We have alluded to this question in previous chapters; it is useful at this point to recapitulate and extend our evaluation of the new technology of electoral politics. Although our concern is primarily with American elections, the new technology extends far beyond our shores and what we say here may apply in other systems as well.[63]

The most publicized influence of professionally mediated campaigns on the electoral system has been in the area of campaign costs. The professionals are for hire, but at very high prices. Fewer and fewer politicians can afford the costs of candidacy. Perhaps good money drives out bad, but we are quickly approaching an era in which bad candidates with good money may drive out their more impoverished competitors. In an age when less affluent members of society are already disillusioned with a political arrangement which they perceive as shutting them out, it will hardly produce harmony to request that they play by the rules of an electoral game they cannot afford to enter. The conventional explanation of why protestors resort to violence has been that other channels of protest have been closed to them; great strides were made in the 1960s in the areas of civil rights, voting rights, and reapportionment legislation to open legitimate channels of representation. But this opening will indeed be narrow if exorbitant campaign costs make it impossible to field candidates who will appeal to protesting interests.

In the face of the rising costs of the new technology occasional voices demand regulation of spending, full disclosure of sources of funds, and public funding of election campaigns. It is unlikely, however, that these voices reflect the sentiments of a majority, particularly a majority of middle-class Americans. If asked, many Americans may

---

[63] British elections also feel the impact of modern campaigning techniques. The Conservative party in 1969 and 1970, for example, prepared to try to win back control of the government by gearing its campaign to the use of new techniques. In February, 1969 the party hired an advertising agency (Davidson, Pearce, Berry and Tuck) to handle the campaign. The agency's task was to identify target voters through surveys (MARPLAN was sub-contracted to conduct some of these), to create effective themes and slogans, and to plan a television campaign. Their initial budget totalled 2 million pounds. See David Wood, "Tory Election Campaign Set," Dispatch of the London *Times*, July 31, 1969.

criticize the high costs of campaigning for public office; the simple fact, however, is that the American public is generally indifferent to the problem and will readily tolerate higher campaign spending in the future. Indeed, the evidence of the Goldwater and Nixon campaigns of recent years indicates that individual Americans are bothered not by the amount of campaign spending but by how to raise the money. The large number of small donations in recent campaigns suggests that many citizens intuitively see campaign costs as a way of keeping the riffraff out of American elections; perhaps the financial contributors, large and small, prefer unregulated spending so long as it assures their interests a minimal control over elections. On the basis of the recent history of campaign funding in the United States, it seems unlikely that effective controls will be established that will truly open the new technology of elections to rich and poor alike.

Without question the new technology introduces not only the possibility but indeed the likelihood of systematic deception in electoral politics. Electronic editing, for example, by which a man can virtually be recreated on film or tape, is in only the initial stages of utilization. The time is near when a statement made weeks prior to a campaign could be introduced as if it were a response to a "live" question and blended into a televised appearance electronically.[64] The case of Senator Clair Engle described in the previous chapter merely hints at the potential.

Few campaign technicians deny the potential of their craft for deceiving the electorate but none will admit to having done so. Cases of deception may be isolated, but we would be naive to believe that deception will not occur. Campaign management is a competitive enterprise. To make a profit each agency must accumulate accounts. To entice prospective clients each agency must distinguish itself from its competitors. In the beginning this means offering special services and gimmicks of questionable effectiveness that dupe the unwary office-seeker; in the end it could mean a desperation for victory that would systematically mislead the electorate. If electoral victory becomes necessary to achieve business success, it is only reasonable to expect that some firms will employ questionable practices.

Can we anticipate some self-regulation of the industry to ward off

---

[64] David Gelman and Beverly Kempton, "New Issues for the New Politics: An Interview with Richard N. Goodwin," *The Washington Monthly*, I (August, 1969), 27–28.

deception? Nothing we have seen thus far would indicate optimism. No ethical codes have been accepted by all technical personnel to guide the behavior of the management-pollster-communicator complex. Many firms offer more than they can deliver; polls are still leaked, some findings even rigged; and agencies increasingly accept special interest groups as clients and attempt to "sell" policies to the very officials they helped elect by using the same image-advertising for policies that were found effective for candidates. Again, the costs of defeat for the professional campaigners (in time, money, contacts, accounts foregone, and so forth) are so great that few specialists are willing to declare any practice even unwarranted, let alone unethical. If the industry cannot regulate itself, can elected officials be expected to do so? The prognosis is not optimistic here either. As ties between candidates and campaign managers become more intimate, so must those between elected officials and the technicians of electoral politics. This is not to say that the former are mere mouthpieces for the latter, but it does suggest that as long as the services of campaign professionals are prized by officials relatively few federal, state, or local politicians will move quickly or vigorously in the direction of regulation.

Unregulated costs and techniques contribute to a more formidable problem—the future of American elections in the technological age. Democratic theory and folklore assigns a special function to elections in the governance of men: elections, it has been urged, provide citizens with their best single opportunity to achieve regularized popular control over policy-makers. Elections, so goes the tale, permit contenders to present opposing points of view on relevant issues so that the electorate can make an informed, rational choice. In reality the debate over issues has never been as meaningful nor has the interest of citizens been as intense as democratic theorists would like. For a long period the practitioners of an older, partisan politics rationalized the fact that the reality never measured up to the ideal by urging that the purpose of elections was not to debate policy issues, but to make choices between competing sets of party leaders who were supported by different coalitions of interests. But, in recent years —particularly 1968—this rationalization of what American elections should be has come under fire from diverse dissident elements— young Americans, black Americans, intellectuals, and others. For them elections are a vehicle for broadscale mass participation in the polity.

Through participatory democracy those dedicated to the reform of what they consider a deplorable system wish to convert elections into conflicts of principle (the "New Politics"); other interests are committed to the preservation of elections as conflicts of parties (the "Old Politics").

The new political technology thrives in this context of ferment and confrontation over the proper role of elections in a democracy. Ironically, the new technology, seemingly congenial to both the old and the new politics, adversely affects the interests of each. On the one hand, as we have seen in earlier chapters, party organizations find themselves increasingly dependent on management and consultant personnel, pollsters, and image-makers. The professional campaigners, instead of being the handmaidens of our major political parties, are independent factors in American elections. Parties turn to professional technicians for advice on how to restructure their organizations, for information about their clienteles, for fund-raising, and for recruiting new members. Candidates, winning nominations in primaries with the aid of professional campaigners rather than that of political parties, are increasingly independent of partisan controls. The old politics does not rest well beside the new technology.

On the other hand, the campaign professionals' orientation toward business and technology also threatens the very bases of the new politics. The skills of campaign professionals are directed at producing a candidate who is informed of his constituents' views, beliefs, characteristics, and habits and who is able to adapt himself to that constituency within the context of the campaign. All this is in keeping with the ideals of participatory democracy implied by the new political orientations. But when a candidate uses opinion surveys and image advertising to give the appearance of being the leader of a popular movement, he is a captive not only of the movement but of the technicians as well. He becomes a manufactured, contrived "personality" contending with rival contrived "personalities" for public office.

In a large sense the new technology of political campaigning portends a view of the electoral process quite different from that envisaged by practitioners of either old or new politics. Elections are approached neither as conflicts between parties nor as confrontations of principle. They are viewed instead as contests of personalities and, even more basically, they offer a choice between the sophisticated engineers working on behalf of those personalities. Many a candidate may argue, "No public relations man or ad man can make me any-thing other than I am." But the fact remains that these technicians can make a candidate appear to be what he is not and, if our theory of perceptual effects has any merit, the appearance counts for more than the reality.

Whether they like it or not Americans are moving toward the necessity of a searching reappraisal of the way they elect their leaders just as they are faced with the necessity of making searching evalu-ations of so many other areas of modern life. Several questions seem uppermost. First, how much freedom should professional campaigners have to saturate the mass electorate with partisan and image propa-ganda? Second, how far can we go in permitting candidacy for elec-tive office to be treated as an unregulated industry rather than as an open forum for increasingly crucial political discussion? Third, where does the democratic way lie between ignoring popular sentiments altogether and framing campaign appeals that are nothing more than the opinion polls writ large? Fourth, what freedom shall the journal-istic estate have in setting the agenda for political discussion? Fifth, where is the upper limit on "buying" public office in an era of modern technology and how, if at all, can equal opportunity for the use of that technology be assured?

It is the American governing practice to respond to such monu-mental questions piecemeal, changing present conventions and poli-cies by gradual increments rather than by wholesale revision. We suspect that the relationship between politics and persuasion, so markedly out of balance in modern America because of the advent of the new technology, will be redefined by much the same sort of "muddling through." In the main the new technology of political campaigning is but another facet of a broader technological society.[65] Effective regulation of the campaign industry will mean that, for the foreseeable future, professionally mediated campaigns will continue to reinforce and extend the symbolic dimensions of American elec-tions. Advocates of party government have generally been satisfied with the arrangements whereby elections offer primarily symbolic participation in the governing of the community; proponents of the new politics, however, demand a scheme in which the voter's partici-pation is more than symbolic. The impact of the new technology may

[65] Jacques Ellul, *The Technological Society* (New York: Alfred A. Knopf, Inc., 1964).

be to recast symbolic participation in a new guise, as para-social play that provides a more subtle illusion, but still not the substance, of transferring power from voters to attractive, trustworthy leaders. The shadows on the cave wall will be more precisely focused, but they will remain shadows.

APPENDIX A

Types of Campaign Management Personnel, Their Services, and Previous Involvement

Campaign Managers

Joseph Napolitan

Polling, advertising, issues research, publicity.

Eighty campaigns including Milton Shapp's (Dem.) for Pennsylvania governor, 1966, and presidential campaigns of John Kennedy and Lyndon Johnson; television aide to Hubert Humphrey in 1968 presidential campaign.

F. Clifton White

General campaign direction, particularly with party organization.

Nomination campaign for Barry Goldwater, 1964; organized efforts for Young Republicans; Richard Nixon's 1960 presidential campaign.

Lawrence O'Brien

General campaign direction.

Presidential campaigns of John Kennedy, 1960; Lyndon Johnson, 1964; and Hubert Humphrey, 1968.

Murray Chotiner

General campaign direction.

Richard Nixon's congressional, senatorial, gubernatorial, and presidential campaigns, 1946–68.

Robert Finch

General campaign direction.

Richard Nixon's presidential and California gubernatorial campaigns, 1960–68.

William J. Ronan

Issues research.

Nelson Rockefeller's reelection campaign for governor of New York, 1966.

Hal Evry

Use of motivation research and mass media.

Campaign of David Trapp (Dem.) for governor of Kentucky, 1967; George P. Mahoney's 1966 campaign for governor of Maryland against Spiro Agnew.

Joseph S. Miller

Public relations and lobbying.

Advice to Democratic Senatorial Campaign Committee.

Hal Short

General campaign direction.

Served Republican Sen. Thruston Morton of Kentucky, Republican Louis Nunn of Kentucky, and Rep. James C. Gardner of North Carolina in advisory and managerial capacities.

Campaign Management Firms

Whitaker and Baxter
(California and Chicago)

Full-service campaign management.

Numerous California campaigns, especially for Gov. Earl Warren, 1953–54; Shirley Temple Black for Congress, 1967; and in Michigan for Republican Sen. Robert Griffin, 1966.

Spencer-Roberts and Associates
(California)

Full-service campaign management.

Over fifty campaigns including Rep. Alphonzo Bell, 1960; Nelson Rockefeller in California's 1964 presidential primary; Sen. Thomas H. Kuchel, 1962 and 1968; Sen. Clifford Hansen (Wyo.), 1966; Rep. Donald Riegle, Jr. of Michigan; 1966; and Gov. Ronald Reagan of California in 1966. (All are Republicans.)

Baus and Ross
(California)

Full-service campaign management.

Richard Nixon's California primary and general election campaigns, 1960; Barry Goldwater's presidential primary in California, 1964; Democratic Gov. Pat Brown of California, 1966.

Robert McGee,
National Directors, Inc.
(California)

Full-service campaign management.   Max Rafferty's campaign to defeat Sen. Kuchel in the 1968 California primary; Rep. Edwin Reinecke, 1966, and Rep. Robert Mathias, 1967 (both California Republicans).

Civic Service, Inc.
(Missouri)

Full-service campaign management.   Congressional and senatorial campaigns, particularly for Thomas Curtis (Rep.) in Missouri, 1968, and Senator Robert Dole in Kansas, 1968.

Chicago Public Relations
Associates, Inc.

Political management, public   Gov. Richard Ogilvie's campaign for Illinois
relations.   governor, 1968 (Republican).

Collins-Knaggs and Associates
(Texas)

Management for Republican   Paul Eggers Republican campaign for governor
candidates.   of Texas, 1968; numerous legislative races, all Republican.

Read-Poland, Inc.
(Texas)

Management and consultation.   Gov. John Connally's campaigns in Texas, 1962–66; Democrat Waggoner Carr's effort to defeat John Tower, 1966, for U.S. Senate; statewide attorney general and commissioner races.

Rives, Dyke and Co., Inc.
(Texas)

Planning, press relations,   Republican John Tower's 1966 campaign for
advertising.   reelection to the U.S. Senate.

Communications Centers Inc.
(Chicago)

Management of mass   Active in several 1968 senatorial and guber-
communications activities.   natorial campaigns.

Publicom, Inc.

Legislative lobbying,   Numerous campaigns in the South, Midwest,
full-service campaign management.   and mountain states.

Matthew A. Reese and Associates
(Washington, D.C. and
Kansas City)

General management; specialization   Democratic candidates including Gov. Robert
in voter turnout.   Docking of Kansas, 1966–68; Sen. Thomas
Eagleton's Missouri primary victory, 1968.

Campaign Consultants

Robert Goodman
(Baltimore)

Management and advertising.   Spiro T. Agnew's campaign for governor of
Maryland, 1966; Lawrence K. Roos' campaign
for governor of Missouri, 1968.

Travis Cross and Associates, Inc.
(Oregon)

Public affairs consultation.   Adviser to Mark Hatfield, governor and U.S.
Senator, Oregon, 1959–68 (Rep.).

Harry Lerner
(California)

Advice on ballot proposition issues.   Numerous local campaigns; consultant for
Gov. Pat Brown's 1966 reelection campaign
in California.

Kaplan, Chamberlain Inc.
(Texas)

Public relations, consultation,   John Kennedy's presidential campaign in 1960
advertising.   in Texas; Waggoner Carr's 1966 effort to unseat
Sen. John Tower; numerous bond elections,
hospital district elections, Houston Mayor
Louis Welch's campaigns, state legislative
candidates, and candidates for Congress.

George Dillman
(Texas)

Campaign strategies.   Public relations for Kennedy-Johnson in Texas,
1960; speech writer for Texas Gov. John
Connally; vice-chairman for public relations
for Johnson-Humphrey in Texas, 1964.

William F. Haddad
(New York City)

Campaign strategies.   Sen. Robert F. Kennedy's 1964 campaign.

William Keisling
(Pennsylvania)

Public relations.   Republican Gov. Raymond Shafer's 1966 Pennsylvania campaign.

Robert C. Walker
(California)

Organization building.   Worked on behalf of Shirley Temple Black, 1967 campaign for Congress; consulted on organization of Republican machinery in Houston, Texas; was executive director of Nixon for President organization, 1968.

Campaign Consultants, Inc.
(Boston)

Research and direct voter contact.   Organized telephone contact campaign for George Romney's presidential primary campaign in New Hampshire, 1968.

The Hyde Agency
(Texas)

Advising, public relations.   Active in 1961 campaign of Sen. John Tower in Texas, 1962 Texas gubernatorial election, and "Texans for Goldwater" in 1964.

Campaign Specialists*

Doyle Dane Bernbach

Television advertising.   Chief agency for 1964 Johnson-Humphrey campaign.

Jack Tinker & Associates

Television advertising.   Prepared television spots for Nelson Rockefeller's reelection campaign as governor of New York, 1966.

John F. Kraft, Inc.

Opinion surveys.   Provided polls for Republican candidates including Sen. John Tower, Texas, 1966; Rep. George Bush, Texas, 1966.

Kudner Agency

Advertising.   Advertising formats, literature kits, billboards, etc. for 1952 Eisenhower-Nixon ticket.

* For a more detailed listing of polling specialists see Appendix B.

Batton, Barton, Durstine, and
Osborn

Advertising.   Television campaign for Eisenhower-Nixon,
                                  1952.

Richard A. Viguerie

Direct mail.   Fund-raising for Max Rafferty's 1968 campaign
                                  for the Republican nomination for U.S. Senate.

Market Opinion Research

Research services.   Opinion research for candidates in thirteen
                                  statewide elections and fifty congressional
                                  districts in 1968.

Datamatics

Computer research services.   Employed computer analysis of demographic
                                  data for its parent organization, Spencer-
                                  Roberts, in California and Indiana races in
                                  1968.

Edward Howard and Co.

Public relations.   Involved in 1968 Nixon-Agnew campaign and
                                  1967 campaign of Seth Taft for mayor of
                                  Cleveland.

Gene Wyckoff

Television production.   Prepared documentaries on behalf of Richard
                                  Nixon, 1960; Henry Cabot Lodge, 1960; Nelson
                                  Rockefeller, 1964.

Computer Campaign Services

Data processing.   Conducts seminars on computer use for various
                                  clients.

Harry Treleaven

Television production.   Prepared television commercials for Republican
                                  George Bush's successful campaign in the
                                  Seventh Congressional District of Texas in
                                  1966 and for Richard Nixon's campaign in
                                  1968.

Eugene Jones

Television production.   Specialized in producing eighteen television
                                  commercials from picture "stills" for Richard
                                  Nixon's 1968 campaign.

Roger Ailes

Television production.

Moved from post as executive producer of the Mike Douglas Show to produce one-hour panel shows on behalf of Richard Nixon in 1968.

Kevin Phillips

Campaign research.

Analyzed the vote potential of ethnic groups for Nixon in the 1968 presidential campaign.

APPENDIX B

Political Polls and Pollsters, 1960s

Private Pollsters

Joseph E. Bachelder
Industrial Advertising Research Institute
(New Jersey)

J. Roy Bardsley
Bardsley & Haslacher, Inc.
(Oregon)

John F. Becker
Campaign Polling Inc.
(Massachusetts)

Joe Belden
Belden Associates
(Texas)

Thomas W. Benham
Opinion Research Corp.
(New Jersey)

E. John Bucci
(Pennsylvania)

Douglas H. Carlisle
(South Carolina)

Cy Chaikin
Bennett-Chaikin Inc.
(New York)

Dorothy D. Corey
Dorothy D. Corey Research
(California)

Archibald M. Crossley
Political Surveys and Analysis Inc.
(New Jersey)

Frederick P. Currier
Market Opinion Research
(Michigan)

John W. Emery
Research Services Inc.
(Colorado)

Fran Farrell
Farrell Research Communications
(Washington, D.C.)

Mervin D. Field
Field Research Corp.
(California)

John H. Friend
John H. Friend Inc.
(Alabama)

Richard H. Funsch
Suncoast Opinion Surveys
(St. Petersburg, Fla.)

Joan Geiger
(New York)

Walter Gerson and Associates
(Washington, D.C.)

Edward L. Greenfield
The Simulmatics Corp.
(New York)

William R. Hamilton
Independent Research Associates
(North Carolina)

David Hardin
Market Facts Inc.
(Illinois)

Gerald D. Hursh
Publicom, Inc.
(Washington, D.C.)

Gordon L. Joseph
Gordon L. Joseph and Associates
(Louisiana)

John F. Kraft
John F. Kraft, Inc.
(New York)

William M. Longman
Central Surveys Inc.
(Iowa)

Alex Louis
Louis, Bowles & Grace Inc.
(Texas)

Don M. Muchmore
Opinion Research of Cal.
(California)

Joseph Napolitan Associates Inc.
(Washington, D.C.)

Eugene Newsom
Mid-South Opinion Surveys
(Arkansas)

Roy Pfautch
Civic Service Inc.
(Missouri)

Richard J. Pommrehn
Wallaces' Farmer
(Iowa)

Oliver A. Quayle III
Oliver A. Quayle and Co. Inc.
(New York)

Burns W. Roper
Roper Research Associates Inc.
(New York)

Irv Roshwalb
Audits and Surveys Co. Inc.
(New York)

Albert Sindlinger
Sindlinger & Co. Inc.
(Pennsylvania)

Richard Tobin, Jr.
First Research Corporation
(Florida)

Peter R. Vroon
National Analysts Inc.
(Pennsylvania)

Warren Waterhouse
Waterhouse Surveys
(Oregon)

Joe B. Williams
Joe B. Williams Research
(Nebraska)

Richard B. Wirthlin
Merrill/Wirthlin Inc.
(Arizona; dissolved)

Published Polls and Pollsters

Albuquerque Journal Poll

The Arizona Poll
Phoenix Gazette

The Beacon Journal Poll
(Ohio)

The Boston Globe Poll

The California Poll
Mervin D. Field

Chicago Sun Times Poll

The Cleveland Plain Dealer Poll

Columbus Evening Dispatch Poll
(Ohio)

The Denver Post Poll
Research Services Inc.

Desert News and Sunday Tribune
Bardsley & Haslacher Inc. (Utah)

The Detroit News Poll
Market Opinion Research

The Gallup Poll
American Institute of Public Opinion
(New York)

The Harris Poll
Louis Harris & Associates Inc.
(New York)

The Indianapolis News Poll

The Iowa Poll
Des Moines Register and Tribune

Lincoln Evening Journal;
Omaha World Herald
Joe B. Williams

Manchester Union-Leader Poll

The Minnesota Poll
Minneapolis Star and Tribune

New York Daily News Poll

The Oregonian Poll
Bardsley & Haslacher Inc.

The Philadelphia Evening Bulletin Poll

The Philadelphia Inquirer Poll
Albert Sindlinger

The Pinellas Poll
St. Petersburg Times
Richard H. Funsch

Portland Press Herald and Main Sunday
Telegram Poll

The South Dakota Poll
Sioux Falls Argus-Leader

The State Poll
Don M. Muchmore
(California)

The Texas Poll
The Dallas Morning News
Joe Belden

Academic Polls and Organizations

Institute for Survey Research
Temple University

National Opinion Research Center

Public Opinion Survey Unit
University of Missouri

School for Social Research
Columbia University

Survey Research Center
University of California

Survey Research Center
University of Michigan

Survey Research Center
State University of New York at Buffalo

Survey Research Laboratory
University of Wisconsin

Survey Research Unit
University of Illinois

INDEX

a